Serious Organised Crime and Police Act 2005

CHAPTER 15

CONTENTS

CHAPTER 2

SOCA: SPECIAL POWERS OF DESIGNATED STAFF

Designations

Powers exercisable

Exercise of powers

Supplementary

CHAPTER 3

SOCA: MISCELLANEOUS AND SUPPLEMENTARY

Complaints and misconduct

Application of discrimination legislation

Joint investigation teams

CHAPTER 4

PROTECTION OF WITNESSES AND OTHER PERSONS

CHAPTER 5

INTERNATIONAL OBLIGATIONS

CHAPTER 6

PROCEEDS OF CRIME

PART 3

POLICE POWERS ETC.

PART 4

PUBLIC ORDER AND CONDUCT IN PUBLIC PLACES ETC.

Harassment

Trespass on designated site

Demonstrations in vicinity of Parliament

Anti-social behaviour

Parental compensation orders

PART 5

MISCELLANEOUS

Protection of activities of certain organisations

PART 6

FINAL PROVISIONS

Serious Organised Crime and Police Act 2005

2005 CHAPTER 15

An Act to provide for the establishment and functions of the Serious Organised Crime Agency; to make provision about investigations, prosecutions, offenders and witnesses in criminal proceedings and the protection of persons involved in investigations or proceedings; to provide for the implementation of certain international obligations relating to criminal matters; to amend the Proceeds of Crime Act 2002; to make further provision for combatting crime and disorder, including new provision about powers of arrest and search warrants and about parental compensation orders; to make further provision about the police and policing and persons supporting the police; to make provision for protecting certain organisations from interference with their activities; to make provision about criminal records; to provide for the Private Security Industry Act 2001 to extend to Scotland; and for connected purposes.   [7th April 2005]

B E IT ENACTED by the Queen's most Excellent Majesty, by and with the advice and consent of the Lords Spiritual and Temporal, and Commons, in this present Parliament assembled, and by the authority of the same, as follows:—

PART 1

THE SERIOUS ORGANISED CRIME AGENCY

CHAPTER 1

SOCA: ESTABLISHMENT AND ACTIVITIES

Establishment of SOCA

1   Establishment of Serious Organised Crime Agency

(1)   There shall be a body corporate to be known as the Serious Organised Crime Agency ("SOCA").

2

Serious Organised Crime and Police Act 2005 (c. 15)
Part 1 — The Serious Organised Crime Agency
Chapter 1 — SOCA: establishment and activities

(2) Schedule 1 makes provision about the constitution, members and staff of SOCA and other matters relating to it.

(3) Each of the following bodies shall cease to exist on such date as the Secretary of State appoints by order —

    (a) the National Criminal Intelligence Service and its Service Authority, and

    (b) the National Crime Squad and its Service Authority.

Functions

2 Functions of SOCA as to serious organised crime

(1) SOCA has the functions of —

    (a) preventing and detecting serious organised crime, and

    (b) contributing to the reduction of such crime in other ways and to the mitigation of its consequences.

(2) SOCA's functions under subsection (1) are exercisable subject to subsections (3) to (5) (but subsection (3) does not apply to Scotland).

(3) If, in exercising its function under subsection (1)(a), SOCA becomes aware of conduct appearing to SOCA to involve serious or complex fraud, SOCA may thereafter exercise that function in relation to the fraud in question only —

    (a) with the agreement of the Director, or an authorised officer, of the Serious Fraud Office, or

    (b) if the Serious Fraud Office declines to act in relation to it.

(4) If, in exercising its function under subsection (1)(a), SOCA becomes aware of conduct appearing to SOCA to involve revenue fraud, SOCA may thereafter exercise that function in relation to the fraud in question only with the agreement of the Commissioners.

(5) Before exercising its function under subsection (1)(b) in any way in relation to revenue fraud, SOCA must consult the Commissioners.

(6) The issue of whether SOCA's function under subsection (1)(a) continued to be exercisable in any circumstances within subsection (3) or (4) may not be raised in any criminal proceedings.

(7) In this section "revenue fraud" includes fraud relating to taxes, duties and national insurance contributions.

(8) In this Chapter "the Commissioners" means the Commissioners for Her Majesty's Revenue and Customs.

3 Functions of SOCA as to information relating to crime

(1) SOCA has the function of gathering, storing, analysing and disseminating information relevant to —

    (a) the prevention, detection, investigation or prosecution of offences, or

    (b) the reduction of crime in other ways or the mitigation of its consequences.

(2) SOCA may disseminate such information to —

    (a) police forces within subsection (3),

Serious Organised Crime and Police Act 2005 (c. 15)
Part 1 — The Serious Organised Crime Agency
Chapter 1 — SOCA: establishment and activities

3

        (b)   special police forces,

        (c)   law enforcement agencies, or

        (d)   such other persons as it considers appropriate in connection with any of the matters mentioned in subsection (1)(a) or (b).

(3)   The police forces within this subsection are—

        (a)   police forces in the United Kingdom, and

        (b)   the States of Jersey Police Force, the salaried police force of the Island of Guernsey and the Isle of Man Constabulary.

(4)   In this section "law enforcement agency" means—

        (a)   the Commissioners or any other government department,

        (b)   the Scottish Administration,

        (c)   any other person who is charged with the duty of investigating offences or charging offenders, or

        (d)   any other person who is engaged outside the United Kingdom in the carrying on of activities similar to any carried on by SOCA or a police force.

(5)   In this Chapter "special police force" means—

        (a)   the Ministry of Defence Police,

        (b)   the British Transport Police Force,

        (c)   the Civil Nuclear Constabulary, or

        (d)   the Scottish Drug Enforcement Agency.

4   Exercise of functions: general considerations

(1)   In exercising its functions SOCA must have regard to the matters mentioned in subsection (2).

(2)   The matters are—

        (a)   SOCA's current annual plan under section 6 together with any priorities determined by SOCA under that section that are specified in the plan,

        (b)   any current strategic priorities determined by the Secretary of State under section 9, and

        (c)   any current performance targets established by SOCA.

(3)   In exercising any function to which a code of practice under section 10 relates, SOCA must have regard to the code.

General powers

5   SOCA's general powers

(1)   SOCA has the general powers conferred by this section.

(2)   SOCA may—

        (a)   institute criminal proceedings in England and Wales or Northern Ireland;

        (b)   at the request of the chief officer of a police force within section 3(3) or of a special police force, act in support of any activities of that force;

4   *Serious Organised Crime and Police Act 2005 (c. 15)*
Part 1 — The Serious Organised Crime Agency
Chapter 1 — SOCA: establishment and activities

(c)   at the request of any law enforcement agency, act in support of any activities of that agency;

(d)   enter into other arrangements for co-operating with bodies or persons (in the United Kingdom or elsewhere) which it considers appropriate in connection with the exercise of any of SOCA's functions under section 2 or 3 or any activities within subsection (3).

(3)   Despite the references to serious organised crime in section 2(1), SOCA may carry on activities in relation to other crime if they are carried on for the purposes of any of the functions conferred on SOCA by section 2 or 3.

(4)   Subsection (3) does not affect the generality of section 3(1).

(5)   SOCA may furnish such assistance as it considers appropriate in response to requests made by any government or other body exercising functions of a public nature in any country or territory outside the United Kingdom.

(6)   Subsection (5) does not apply to any request for assistance which —

(a)   could be made under section 13 of the Crime (International Co-operation) Act 2003 (c. 32) (requests by overseas authorities to obtain evidence), and

(b)   is not a request in relation to which SOCA has functions under that section by virtue of an order under section 27(2) of that Act.

(7)   In this section "law enforcement agency" has the meaning given by section 3(4).

Annual plans and reports

6   Annual plans

(1)   Before the beginning of each financial year SOCA must issue a plan setting out how SOCA intends to exercise its functions during that year ("the annual plan").

(2)   The annual plan must (in particular) set out how SOCA intends to exercise its functions in Scotland and in Northern Ireland.

(3)   The annual plan must also include a statement of —

(a)   any priorities which SOCA has determined for that year,

(b)   any current strategic priorities determined by the Secretary of State under section 9,

(c)   any current performance targets established by SOCA, and

(d)   the financial resources that are expected to be available to SOCA for that year.

(4)   Any priorities within subsection (3)(a) may relate —

(a)   to matters to which strategic priorities determined under section 9 also relate, or

(b)   to other matters,

but in any event must be so framed as to be consistent with strategic priorities determined under that section.

(5)   The annual plan must state, in relation to each priority within subsection (3)(a) or (b), how SOCA intends to give effect to that priority.

Serious Organised Crime and Police Act 2005 (c. 15)
Part 1 – The Serious Organised Crime Agency
Chapter 1 – SOCA: establishment and activities

5

(6)   SOCA must arrange for the annual plan to be published in such manner as it considers appropriate.

(7)   SOCA must send a copy of the annual plan to –
   (a)   the Secretary of State,
   (b)   the Scottish Ministers,
   (c)   the Commissioners,
   (d)   each police authority for an area in Great Britain, each joint police board and the Northern Ireland Policing Board,
   (e)   the chief officer of each police force in the United Kingdom, and
   (f)   such other persons as SOCA considers appropriate.

(8)   In subsection (7)(d) the reference to a police authority for an area in Great Britain does not include a constituent authority in an amalgamation scheme approved under section 19(1) of the Police (Scotland) Act 1967 (c. 77).

(9)   Before issuing its annual plan for any financial year, SOCA must –
   (a)   consult the Scottish Ministers and agree with them what provision the plan is to make for Scotland by virtue of subsection (2); and
   (b)   consult such other persons as it considers appropriate.

7   Annual reports

(1)   As soon as possible after the end of each financial year SOCA must issue a report on the exercise of its functions during that year (an "annual report").

(2)   The annual report must include an assessment of the extent to which the annual plan for that year under section 6 has been carried out.

(3)   SOCA must arrange for the annual report to be published in such manner as it considers appropriate.

(4)   SOCA must send a copy of the annual report to –
   (a)   the Secretary of State,
   (b)   the Scottish Ministers,
   (c)   the Commissioners,
   (d)   each police authority for an area in Great Britain, each joint police board and the Northern Ireland Policing Board,
   (e)   the chief officer of each police force in the United Kingdom, and
   (f)   such other persons as SOCA considers appropriate.

(5)   In subsection (4)(d) the reference to a police authority for an area in Great Britain does not include a constituent authority in an amalgamation scheme approved under section 19(1) of the Police (Scotland) Act 1967.

(6)   The Secretary of State must lay a copy of the annual report before Parliament.

(7)   The Scottish Ministers must lay a copy of the annual report before the Scottish Parliament.

6   *Serious Organised Crime and Police Act 2005 (c. 15)*
Part 1 — The Serious Organised Crime Agency
Chapter 1 — SOCA: establishment and activities

Central supervision and direction

8 General duty of Secretary of State and Scottish Ministers

The Secretary of State and the Scottish Ministers must exercise the powers respectively conferred on him and them under this Chapter in such manner and to such extent as appear to him and them to be best calculated to promote the efficiency and effectiveness of SOCA.

9 Strategic priorities

(1) The Secretary of State may determine strategic priorities for SOCA.

(2) Before determining any such priorities the Secretary of State must consult —
   (a) SOCA,
   (b) the Scottish Ministers, and
   (c) such other persons as he considers appropriate.

(3) The Secretary of State must arrange for any priorities determined under this section to be published in such manner as he considers appropriate.

10 Codes of practice

(1) The Secretary of State may issue codes of practice relating to the exercise by SOCA of any of its functions.

(2) The Secretary of State may from time to time revise the whole or any part of a code of practice issued under this section.

(3) Before issuing or revising a code of practice issued under this section the Secretary of State must consult —
   (a) SOCA,
   (b) the Scottish Ministers, and
   (c) such other persons as he considers appropriate.

(4) The Secretary of State must lay before Parliament —
   (a) any code of practice issued under this section, and
   (b) any revisions of such a code.

(5) The Secretary of State —
   (a) is not required by subsection (4) to lay before Parliament, or
   (b) may exclude from what he does lay before Parliament,
anything to which subsection (6) applies.

(6) This subsection applies to anything the publication of which, in the opinion of the Secretary of State —
   (a) would be against the interests of national security, or
   (b) could prejudice the prevention or detection of crime or the apprehension or prosecution of offenders, or
   (c) could jeopardise the safety of any person.

(7) The Secretary of State must provide the Scottish Ministers with a copy of —
   (a) any code of practice issued under this section, or
   (b) any revisions of such a code.

Serious Organised Crime and Police Act 2005 (c. 15)
Part 1 — The Serious Organised Crime Agency
Chapter 1 — SOCA: establishment and activities

7

11   Reports to Secretary of State

(1)   The Secretary of State may require SOCA to submit a report to him on such matters—

    (a)   connected with the exercise of SOCA's functions, or

    (b)   otherwise connected with any of SOCA's activities,

as may be specified in the requirement.

(2)   A report submitted under subsection (1) must be in such form as may be so specified.

(3)   The Secretary of State must consult the Scottish Ministers before imposing any requirement under that subsection relating to any functions or activities of SOCA—

    (a)   exercised or carried out in Scotland, or

    (b)   exercised or carried out outside, but in relation to, Scotland.

(4)   The Secretary of State may—

    (a)   arrange, or

    (b)   require SOCA to arrange,

for a report under this section to be published in such manner as he considers appropriate.

(5)   But the Secretary of State may exclude any part of a report from publication under subsection (4) if, in his opinion, publication of that part—

    (a)   would be against the interests of national security, or

    (b)   could prejudice the prevention or detection of crime or the apprehension or prosecution of offenders, or

    (c)   could jeopardise the safety of any person.

12   Power to direct submission of action plan

(1)   This section applies where an inspection report made to the Secretary of State states—

    (a)   that, in the opinion of the person making the report, the whole or any part of SOCA is (whether generally or in particular respects) not efficient or not effective; or

    (b)   that, in that person's opinion, the whole or part of SOCA will cease to be efficient or effective (whether generally or in particular respects) unless remedial measures are taken.

(2)   If the Secretary of State considers that remedial measures are required in relation to any matters identified by the report, he may direct SOCA—

    (a)   to submit an action plan to him, and

    (b)   to do so within such period as is specified in the direction (which must be a period ending not less than 4, and not more than 12, weeks after the direction is given).

(3)   An "action plan" is a plan setting out the remedial measures which SOCA proposes to take in relation to the matters in respect of which the direction is given.

(4)   The provision that a direction under this section may require to be included in an action plan includes—

8

Serious Organised Crime and Police Act 2005 (c. 15)
Part 1 – The Serious Organised Crime Agency
Chapter 1 – SOCA: establishment and activities

(a) provision setting out the steps that SOCA proposes should be taken in respect of the matters in respect of which the direction is given, and the performance targets that SOCA proposes should be met;

(b) provision setting out SOCA's proposals as to the times within which those steps are to be taken and those targets met, and the means by which the success of the plan's implementation is to be measured;

(c) provision for the making of progress reports to the Secretary of State about the plan's implementation;

(d) provision as to the times at which, and the manner in which, any progress report is to be made; and

(e) provision for the duration of the plan and for it to cease to apply in circumstances determined by the Secretary of State.

(5) But nothing in this section authorises the Secretary of State to direct the inclusion in an action plan of any requirement to do or not to do anything—

(a) in a particular case identified for the purposes of the requirement, or

(b) in relation to a particular person so identified.

(6) The Secretary of State must consult the Scottish Ministers before giving any direction under this section in connection with any functions or activities of SOCA—

(a) exercised or carried out in Scotland, or

(b) exercised or carried out outside, but in relation to, Scotland.

(7) In this section "an inspection report" means a report under section 16.

(8) If this section applies at a time when there is already an action plan in force—

(a) references in this section to the submission of an action plan to the Secretary of State include references to the submission of revisions of the existing plan, and

(b) the other provisions of this section have effect accordingly.

13 Revision of inadequate action plan

(1) This section applies where the Secretary of State is of the opinion that any remedial measures contained in an action plan submitted to him under section 12 are inadequate.

(2) The Secretary of State may notify SOCA of that opinion and of his reasons for it.

(3) The Secretary of State must consult the Scottish Ministers before forming an opinion for the purposes of subsection (1) as to any remedial measures proposed in connection with any functions or activities of SOCA –

(a) exercised or carried out in Scotland, or

(b) exercised or carried out outside, but in relation to, Scotland.

(4) If SOCA receives a notification under subsection (2) –

(a) it must consider whether to revise the plan in the light of the matters notified to it, and

(b) if it does revise the plan, it must send a copy of the revised plan to the Secretary of State.

(5) References in this section to an action plan submitted to the Secretary of State under section 12 include references to revisions submitted to him by virtue of subsection (8) of that section.

Serious Organised Crime and Police Act 2005 (c. 15)
Part 1 – The Serious Organised Crime Agency
Chapter 1 – SOCA: establishment and activities

9

14   Procedure for giving directions under section 12

(1)   The Secretary of State may not give a direction under section 12 unless the conditions in subsection (2) are satisfied.

(2)   The conditions are—
   (a)   SOCA must have been given such information about the Secretary of State's grounds for proposing to give the direction as he considers appropriate for enabling it to make representations or proposals under paragraphs (b) and (c) below;
   (b)   SOCA must have been given an opportunity of making representations about those grounds;
   (c)   SOCA must have had an opportunity of making proposals for the taking of remedial measures that would make it unnecessary to give the direction; and
   (d)   the Secretary of State must have considered any such representations and any such proposals.

15   Reports relating to directions under section 12

(1)   This section applies where the Secretary of State exercises his power to give a direction under section 12.

(2)   The Secretary of State must prepare a report on his exercise of that power.

(3)   A report under subsection (2)—
   (a)   is to be prepared at such time as the Secretary of State considers appropriate, and
   (b)   may relate to more than one exercise of the power.

(4)   The Secretary of State must—
   (a)   lay before each House of Parliament a copy of any report prepared under subsection (2), and
   (b)   send a copy of any such report to the Scottish Ministers.

(5)   The Scottish Ministers must lay before the Scottish Parliament any copy of a report sent to them under subsection (4).

16   Inspections

(1)   Her Majesty's Inspectors of Constabulary ("HMIC") must inspect SOCA from time to time.

(2)   HMIC must also inspect SOCA if requested to do so by the Secretary of State either—
   (a)   generally, or
   (b)   in respect of a particular matter.

(3)   Before requesting an inspection that would fall to be carried out wholly or partly in Scotland, the Secretary of State must consult the Scottish Ministers.

(4)   Any inspection under this section must be carried out jointly by HMIC and the Scottish inspectors—
   (a)   if it is carried out wholly in Scotland, or
   (b)   in a case where it is carried out partly in Scotland, to the extent that it is carried out there.

10   *Serious Organised Crime and Police Act 2005 (c. 15)*
Part 1 − The Serious Organised Crime Agency
Chapter 1 − SOCA: establishment and activities

(5) Following an inspection under this section, HMIC must report to the Secretary of State on the efficiency and effectiveness of SOCA either −

    (a) generally, or

    (b) in the case of an inspection under subsection (2)(b), in respect of the matter to which the inspection related.

(6) A report under subsection (5) must be in such form as the Secretary of State may direct.

(7) The Secretary of State must arrange for every report which he receives under subsection (5) to be published in such manner as he considers appropriate.

(8) The Secretary of State may exclude from publication under subsection (7) any part of a report if, in his opinion, the publication of that part −

    (a) would be against the interests of national security, or

    (b) could prejudice the prevention or detection of crime or the apprehension or prosecution of offenders, or

    (c) might jeopardise the safety of any person.

(9) The Secretary of State must send a copy of the published report −

    (a) to SOCA, and

    (b) if subsection (4) applied to the inspection, to the Scottish Ministers.

(10) SOCA must −

    (a) prepare comments on the published report, and

    (b) arrange for its comments to be published in such manner as it considers appropriate.

(11) SOCA must send a copy of any document published under subsection (10)(b) −

    (a) to the Secretary of State, and

    (b) if subsection (4) applied to the inspection, to the Scottish Ministers.

(12) The inspectors shall carry out such other duties for the purpose of furthering the efficiency and effectiveness of SOCA as the Secretary of State may from time to time direct.

(13) In this section "the Scottish inspectors" means the inspectors of constabulary appointed under section 33(1) of the Police (Scotland) Act 1967 (c. 77).

Financial provisions

17   Grants by Secretary of State

(1) The Secretary of State must make a grant to SOCA in respect of each of its financial years.

(2) The grant in respect of a financial year is to be paid −

    (a) at such time, or

    (b) in instalments of such amounts and at such times,

as the Secretary of State may determine (and any such time may fall within or after that year).

Serious Organised Crime and Police Act 2005 (c. 15)
Part 1 – *The Serious Organised Crime Agency*
Chapter 1 – *SOCA: establishment and activities*

11

18   Determinations relating to grants under section 17

(1)   The Secretary of State must determine the amount of the grant to be made under section 17 in respect of each of SOCA's financial years.

(2)   But a determination under subsection (1) may, if the Secretary of State thinks fit, specify a single amount in respect of two or more financial years.

(3)   A determination under that subsection may be varied by a subsequent determination.

(4)   Where the Secretary of State makes any determination under subsection (1), he must prepare a report—
    (a)   setting out the determination, and
    (b)   stating the considerations which he took into account in making it.

(5)   The Secretary of State must—
    (a)   send SOCA a copy of each report under subsection (4), and
    (b)   lay a copy of each such report before the House of Commons.

(6)   In connection with the exercise of his functions under this section, the Secretary of State may require SOCA—
    (a)   to provide him with such information as he may specify, and
    (b)   to do so within such period as he may specify.

19   Charges by SOCA and other receipts

(1)   SOCA may make charges in respect of—
    (a)   the provision by SOCA of any goods or services to any person, or
    (b)   an agreement for the provision by SOCA of any such goods or services.

(2)   Any charges made under subsection (1) may include amounts calculated by reference to expenditure incurred, or expected to be incurred, by SOCA otherwise than directly in connection with the provision of the goods or services concerned.

(3)   Apart from—
    (a)   grants under section 17,
    (b)   sums received under section 30(6), and
    (c)   sums borrowed by SOCA under paragraph 21 of Schedule 1,
all sums received by SOCA in the course of, or in connection with, the exercise of its functions must be paid to the Secretary of State.

(4)   Subsection (3) does not apply where the Secretary of State so directs.

(5)   Any sums received by the Secretary of State under subsection (3) must be paid into the Consolidated Fund.

20   Accounts

(1)   SOCA must—
    (a)   keep proper accounts and proper records in relation to the accounts; and
    (b)   prepare a statement of accounts in respect of each financial year.

12   *Serious Organised Crime and Police Act 2005 (c. 15)*
Part 1 – The Serious Organised Crime Agency
Chapter 1 – SOCA: establishment and activities

(2) A statement of accounts under subsection (1) must be in such form, and contain such information, as the Secretary of State may direct.

(3) SOCA must send copies of the statement of accounts for a financial year –
    (a) to the Secretary of State, and
    (b) to the Comptroller and Auditor General,
within such period following the end of the financial year as the Secretary of State may specify.

(4) The Comptroller and Auditor General must –
    (a) examine, certify and report on the statement of accounts, and
    (b) lay copies of the statement and of his report before each House of Parliament.

Operational matters

21 Operational responsibility of Director General

(1) The Director General of SOCA has the function of exercising general operational control in relation to the activities carried out in the exercise of SOCA's functions.

(2) This function includes deciding –
    (a) which particular operations are to be mounted in the exercise of any of those functions, and
    (b) how such operations are to be conducted.

22 Activities in Scotland in relation to crime

(1) SOCA may only carry out activities in Scotland in relation to an offence which it suspects has been committed (or is being committed) if it does so with the agreement of the Lord Advocate.

(2) In carrying out any such activities in Scotland SOCA must comply with such directions (whether general or special) as it may receive from the Lord Advocate or from the procurator fiscal.

(3) If it suspects that an offence has been committed (or is being committed) in Scotland, SOCA must report the matter to the procurator fiscal as soon as is practicable.

23 Mutual assistance between SOCA and law enforcement agencies: voluntary arrangements

(1) Subsection (2) applies if –
    (a) the chief officer of a police force in the British Islands or of a special police force, or
    (b) a law enforcement agency operating in the British Islands,
notifies the Director General of SOCA that that force or agency has a special need for assistance from SOCA and requests the Director General of SOCA to provide it with such assistance.

(2) In such a case the Director General of SOCA may provide that force or agency with –

Serious Organised Crime and Police Act 2005 (c. 15)
Part 1 – The Serious Organised Crime Agency
Chapter 1 – SOCA: establishment and activities

13

      (a)   such members of the staff of SOCA, or

      (b)   such other assistance,

as the Director General of SOCA considers appropriate in the circumstances.

(3)   Subsection (4) applies if the Director General of SOCA notifies –

      (a)   the chief officer of a police force in the United Kingdom or of a special police force, or

      (b)   a law enforcement agency operating in the United Kingdom,

that SOCA has a special need for assistance from that force or agency and requests it to provide SOCA with such assistance.

(4)   In such a case the chief officer of that force or the agency in question may provide SOCA with –

      (a)   such constables or members of the staff of the agency, or

      (b)   such other assistance,

as the chief officer or the agency considers appropriate in the circumstances.

(5)   But before the Scottish Drug Enforcement Agency provides any constable under subsection (4), its Director must obtain the agreement of the chief constable of the police force from which the constable is seconded to the Agency.

(6)   Where a member of the staff of SOCA is provided under this section for the assistance of a police force, a special police force or a law enforcement agency, he shall be under the direction and control of the chief officer of the force or the head of the agency (as the case may be).

(7)   Where –

      (a)   a constable,

      (b)   a member of the staff of the Scottish Drug Enforcement Agency, or

      (c)   a member of the staff of a law enforcement agency,

is provided under this section for the assistance of SOCA, he shall be under the direction and control of the Director General of SOCA (despite anything in, or in any agreement made under, any other enactment).

(8)   Where SOCA provides assistance under this section for –

      (a)   a police force in the United Kingdom or a special police force, or

      (b)   a law enforcement agency operating in the United Kingdom,

the relevant police authority or (as the case may be) that agency must pay to SOCA such contribution, if any, as may be agreed between them or, in the absence of agreement, as may be determined by the Secretary of State.

(9)   Where SOCA is provided with assistance under this section by –

      (a)   a police force in the United Kingdom or a special police force, or

      (b)   a law enforcement agency operating in the United Kingdom,

SOCA must pay to the relevant police authority or (as the case may be) that agency such contribution, if any, as may be agreed between them or, in the absence of agreement, as may be determined by the Secretary of State.

(10)   If the assistance mentioned in subsection (8) or (9) is provided for or (as the case may be) by –

      (a)   a police force in Scotland,

      (b)   the Scottish Drug Enforcement Agency, or

      (c)   the Scottish Administration,

14   *Serious Organised Crime and Police Act 2005 (c. 15)*
Part 1 – The Serious Organised Crime Agency
Chapter 1 – SOCA: establishment and activities

the Secretary of State must, before making a determination under the subsection in question, consult the Scottish Ministers.

(11) In this section—

"law enforcement agency" has the meaning given by section 3(4) (subject to any territorial restrictions contained in this section);

"police force", in relation to the British Islands, includes the States of Jersey Police Force, the salaried police force of the Island of Guernsey and the Isle of Man Constabulary;

"relevant police authority" means—

   (a) in relation to a police force in Great Britain, the police authority maintaining that force (or, in the case of a police force for a combined area, the joint police board for that area),

   (b) in relation to the Police Service of Northern Ireland or the Police Service of Northern Ireland Reserve, the Northern Ireland Policing Board,

   (c) in relation to the Ministry of Defence Police, the Secretary of State,

   (d) in relation to the British Transport Police Force, the British Transport Police Authority,

   (e) in relation to the Civil Nuclear Constabulary, the Civil Nuclear Police Authority, and

   (f) in relation to the Scottish Drug Enforcement Agency, the Agency itself.

24   Mutual assistance between SOCA and law enforcement agencies: directed arrangements

(1) This section applies where it appears to the Secretary of State—

   (a) that a body within subsection (2) has a special need for assistance from SOCA or SOCA has a special need for assistance from a body within that subsection,

   (b) that it is expedient for such assistance to be provided by SOCA or (as the case may be) the body, and

   (c) that satisfactory arrangements cannot be made, or cannot be made in time, under section 23.

(2) The bodies within this subsection are—

   (a) any police force in England and Wales or Northern Ireland,

   (b) any special police force other than the Scottish Drug Enforcement Agency, and

   (c) any law enforcement agency operating in the United Kingdom other than the Scottish Administration.

(3) In a case where this section applies the Secretary of State may (as appropriate)—

   (a) direct the chief officer of the police force to provide such constables or other assistance for the purpose of meeting the need in question as may be specified in the direction;

   (b) direct the chief officer of the special police force to provide such constables or other persons, or such other assistance, for the purpose of meeting the need in question as may be so specified;

Serious Organised Crime and Police Act 2005 (c. 15)
Part 1 — The Serious Organised Crime Agency
Chapter 1 — SOCA: establishment and activities

15

(c)   direct the head of the law enforcement agency to provide such members of the staff of that agency or other assistance for the purpose of meeting the need in question as may be so specified;

(d)   direct the Director General of SOCA to provide such members of the staff of SOCA or other assistance for the purpose of meeting the need in question as may be so specified.

(4)   A direction under subsection (3) requires the consent of the Treasury if it is to be given to the Commissioners.

(5)   Subsections (6) to (9) of section 23 apply in relation to assistance provided under this section —

(a)   by SOCA to a police force, a special police force or a law enforcement agency, or

(b)   to SOCA by a police force, a special police force or a law enforcement agency,

as they apply in relation to assistance so provided under that section.

(6)   In this section "law enforcement agency" has the meaning given by section 3(4) (subject to the territorial restriction contained in subsection (2) above).

25   Directed arrangements: Scotland

(1)   This section applies where it appears to the Scottish Ministers —

(a)   that a body within subsection (2) has a special need for assistance from SOCA or SOCA has a special need for assistance from a body within that subsection,

(b)   that it is expedient for such assistance to be provided by SOCA or (as the case may be) the body, and

(c)   that satisfactory arrangements cannot be made, or cannot be made in time, under section 23.

(2)   The bodies within this subsection are —

(a)   any police force in Scotland, and

(b)   the Scottish Drug Enforcement Agency.

(3)   In a case where this section applies the Scottish Ministers may (as appropriate) —

(a)   direct the chief officer of the police force to provide such constables or other assistance for the purpose of meeting the need in question as may be specified in the direction;

(b)   direct the Director of the Scottish Drug Enforcement Agency to provide such constables or other persons, or other assistance, for the purpose of meeting the need in question as may be so specified;

(c)   with the agreement of the Secretary of State, direct the Director General of SOCA to provide such members of the staff of SOCA or other assistance for the purpose of meeting the need in question as may be so specified.

(4)   Subsections (6) to (10) of section 23 apply in relation to assistance provided under this section —

(a)   by SOCA to a police force in Scotland or to the Scottish Drug Enforcement Agency, or

(b)   to SOCA by a police force in Scotland or by the Scottish Drug Enforcement Agency,

16

Serious Organised Crime and Police Act 2005 (c. 15)
Part 1 – The Serious Organised Crime Agency
Chapter 1 – SOCA: establishment and activities

as they apply in relation to assistance so provided under that section.

26 Use by SOCA of police premises etc.

(1) Arrangements may be made between—
  (a) SOCA, and
  (b) the relevant police authority,
under which SOCA may use such premises, equipment or other material, facilities or services made available by a police force in England and Wales or Northern Ireland as are specified or described in the arrangements.

(2) If it appears to the Secretary of State—
  (a) that it is expedient for arrangements within subsection (1) to be made between SOCA and the relevant police authority, and
  (b) that satisfactory arrangements cannot be made, or cannot be made in time, under that subsection,
he may direct SOCA and that authority to enter into such arrangements within that subsection as are specified in the direction.

(3) Before giving such a direction to SOCA or the relevant police authority the Secretary of State must—
  (a) notify that body that he is proposing to give the directions, and
  (b) consider any representations made to him by that body.

(4) Any arrangements under this section may be varied or terminated by agreement between the parties.

(5) But arrangements entered into in pursuance of a direction under subsection (2) may not be so terminated without the consent of the Secretary of State.

(6) Where any expenditure is incurred by the relevant police authority by virtue of any arrangements under this section, SOCA must pay to the authority such contribution, if any, in respect of that expenditure—
  (a) as may be agreed between them, or
  (b) in the absence of agreement, as may be determined by the Secretary of State.

(7) In this section "relevant police authority" means—
  (a) in relation to a police force in England and Wales, the police authority maintaining that force, and
  (b) in relation to the Police Service of Northern Ireland or the Police Service of Northern Ireland Reserve, the Northern Ireland Policing Board.

27 Regulations as to equipment

(1) The Secretary of State may make regulations requiring equipment used by SOCA to satisfy such requirements as to design and performance as may be prescribed by the regulations.

(2) The Secretary of State may by regulations make any of the following kinds of provision—
  (a) provision requiring SOCA, when using equipment for the purposes specified in the regulations, to use only—
    (i) the equipment which is specified in the regulations,
    (ii) equipment which is of a description so specified, or

Serious Organised Crime and Police Act 2005 (c. 15)
Part 1 – The Serious Organised Crime Agency
Chapter 1 – SOCA: establishment and activities

17

> > (iii) equipment which is of a type approved by the Secretary of State in accordance with the regulations;
>
> (b) provision prohibiting SOCA from using equipment of a type approved as mentioned in paragraph (a)(iii) except—
>
> > (i) where the conditions subject to which the approval was given are satisfied, and
> >
> > (ii) in accordance with the other terms of that approval;
>
> (c) provision requiring equipment used by SOCA to comply with such conditions as may be specified in the regulations, or as may be approved by the Secretary of State in accordance with the regulations;
>
> (d) provision prohibiting SOCA from using equipment specified in the regulations, or any equipment of a description so specified.

(3) Before making regulations under this section Secretary of State must consult—

> (a) SOCA, and
>
> (b) such other persons as he considers appropriate.

(4) In this section "equipment" includes—

> (a) vehicles, and
>
> (b) headgear and protective and other clothing.

Liability for unlawful conduct

28 Liability of SOCA for acts of seconded staff etc.

(1) SOCA is liable in respect of unlawful conduct of persons to whom this section applies in the carrying out, or the purported carrying out, of their functions as such persons in the same manner as an employer is liable in respect of any unlawful conduct of his employees in the course of their employment.

(2) In the case of any such unlawful conduct of persons to whom this section applies which is a tort, SOCA is accordingly to be treated as a joint tortfeasor. This subsection does not apply to Scotland.

(3) This section applies to—

> (a) any constable or other person who has been seconded to SOCA to serve as a member of its staff, and
>
> (b) any constable or other person who has been provided for the assistance of SOCA under section 23, 24 or 25.

29 Payment by SOCA of amounts in connection with unlawful conduct of employees etc.

(1) SOCA may, in such cases and to such extent as appear to it to be appropriate, pay—

> (a) any damages or costs awarded against a person to whom this section applies in proceedings for any unlawful conduct of that person;
>
> (b) any costs (or, in Scotland, expenses) incurred and not recovered by such a person in such proceedings, and
>
> (c) any sum required in connection with the settlement of a claim that has, or might have, given rise to such proceedings.

(2) This section applies to—

18   Serious Organised Crime and Police Act 2005 (c. 15)
                                              Part 1 – The Serious Organised Crime Agency
                                              Chapter 1 – SOCA: establishment and activities

(a) any person who is employed by SOCA,

(b) any constable or other person who has been seconded to SOCA to serve as a member of its staff, and

(c) any constable or other person who has been provided for the assistance of SOCA under section 23, 24 or 25.

30   Application of sections 28 and 29 to members of joint investigation teams

(1) Subsection (2) applies where an international joint investigation team has been formed under the leadership of a member of SOCA's staff.

(2) In such a case –

(a) section 28 has effect in relation to any member of that team who is not a member of SOCA's staff as if any unlawful conduct in the carrying out, or purported carrying out, of his functions as a member of the team were unlawful conduct of a person to whom that section applies; and

(b) section 29(1) has effect as if it applied to every member of the team to whom it would not apply apart from this subsection.

(3) Subsection (4) applies where a person ("the relevant person") is carrying out surveillance under section 76A of the Regulation of Investigatory Powers Act 2000 (c. 23) (foreign surveillance operations).

(4) In such a case –

(a) section 28 has effect as if any unlawful conduct of the relevant person in the course of carrying out the surveillance were unlawful conduct of a person to whom that section applies; and

(b) section 29(1) has effect as if it applied to the relevant person.

(5) In this section "international joint investigation team" means any investigation team formed in accordance with –

(a) any framework decision on joint investigation teams adopted under Article 34 of the Treaty on European Union;

(b) the Convention on Mutual Assistance in Criminal Matters between the Member States of the European Union and the Protocol to that Convention established in accordance with that Article of the Treaty; or

(c) any international agreement to which the United Kingdom is a party and which is specified in an order made by the Secretary of State.

(6) Where –

(a) a sum is paid by SOCA by virtue of this section, and

(b) the Secretary of State receives under any international agreement a sum by way of reimbursement (in whole or in part) of the sum paid by SOCA,

he must pay to SOCA the sum received by him by way of reimbursement.

31   Liability of special police forces and law enforcement agencies for unlawful conduct of SOCA staff

(1) The relevant authority is liable in respect of unlawful conduct of persons to whom this section applies in the carrying out, or the purported carrying out, of their functions as such persons in the same manner as an employer is liable in respect of any unlawful conduct of his employees in the course of their employment.

Serious Organised Crime and Police Act 2005 (c. 15)
Part 1 — The Serious Organised Crime Agency
Chapter 1 — SOCA: establishment and activities

19

(2)   In the case of any such unlawful conduct of persons to whom this section applies which is a tort, the relevant authority is accordingly to be treated as a joint tortfeasor.

This subsection does not apply to Scotland.

(3)   In so far as a relevant authority does not already have power to do so it may, in such cases and to such extent as appear to it to be appropriate, pay —

(a)   any damages or costs awarded against a person to whom this section applies in proceedings for any unlawful conduct of that person,

(b)   any costs (or, in Scotland, expenses) incurred and not recovered by such a person in such proceedings, and

(c)   any sum required in connection with the settlement of a claim that has, or might have, given rise to such proceedings.

(4)   This section applies to a member of the staff of SOCA who under section 23, 24 or 25 is provided for the assistance of —

(a)   a special police force, or

(b)   a law enforcement agency operating in the United Kingdom.

(5)   In this section —

"law enforcement agency" has the meaning given by section 3(4) (subject to the territorial restriction contained in subsection (4)(b) above), and

"relevant authority" —

(a)   in relation to a member of the staff of SOCA provided for the assistance of the Ministry of Defence Police, means the Secretary of State,

(b)   in relation to a member of the staff of SOCA provided for the assistance of the British Transport Police Force, means the British Transport Police Authority,

(c)   in relation to a member of the staff of SOCA provided for the assistance of the Civil Nuclear Constabulary, means the Civil Nuclear Police Authority,

(d)   in relation to a member of the staff of SOCA provided for the assistance of the Scottish Drug Enforcement Agency, means that Agency,

(e)   in relation to a member of the staff of SOCA provided for the assistance of the Commissioners, means the Commissioners,

(f)   in relation to a member of the staff of SOCA provided for the assistance of the Scottish Administration, means the Scottish Ministers, and

(g)   in relation to a member of the staff of SOCA provided for the assistance of any other law enforcement agency, means such person as is prescribed in relation to that agency by regulations made by the Secretary of State.

Use and disclosure of information

32   Use of information by SOCA

Information obtained by SOCA in connection with the exercise of any of its functions may be used by SOCA in connection with the exercise of any of its other functions.

20   *Serious Organised Crime and Police Act 2005 (c. 15)*
Part 1 – The Serious Organised Crime Agency
Chapter 1 – SOCA: establishment and activities

33 Disclosure of information by SOCA

(1) Information obtained by SOCA in connection with the exercise of any of its functions may be disclosed by SOCA if the disclosure is for any permitted purposes.

(2) "Permitted purposes" means the purposes of any of the following—

(a) the prevention, detection, investigation or prosecution of criminal offences, whether in the United Kingdom or elsewhere;

(b) the prevention, detection or investigation of conduct for which penalties other than criminal penalties are provided under the law of any part of the United Kingdom or of any country or territory outside the United Kingdom;

(c) the exercise of any function conferred on SOCA by section 2, 3 or 5 (so far as not falling within paragraph (a) or (b));

(d) the exercise of any functions of any intelligence service within the meaning of the Regulation of Investigatory Powers Act 2000 (c. 23);

(e) the exercise of any functions under Part 2 of the Football Spectators Act 1989 (c. 37);

(f) the exercise of any function which appears to the Secretary of State to be a function of a public nature and which he designates by order.

(3) A disclosure under this section does not breach—

(a) any obligation of confidence owed by the person making the disclosure, or

(b) any other restriction on the disclosure of information (however imposed).

(4) But nothing in this section authorises—

(a) a disclosure, in contravention of any provisions of the Data Protection Act 1998 (c. 29), of personal data which are not exempt from those provisions,

(b) a disclosure which is prohibited by Part 1 of the Regulation of Investigatory Powers Act 2000, or

(c) a disclosure in contravention of section 35(2).

34 Disclosure of information to SOCA

(1) Any person may disclose information to SOCA if the disclosure is made for the purposes of the exercise by SOCA of any of its functions.

(2) A disclosure under this section does not breach—

(a) any obligation of confidence owed by the person making the disclosure, or

(b) any other restriction on the disclosure of information (however imposed).

(3) But nothing in this section authorises—

(a) a disclosure, in contravention of any provisions of the Data Protection Act 1998, of personal data which are not exempt from those provisions, or

(b) a disclosure which is prohibited by Part 1 of the Regulation of Investigatory Powers Act 2000.

Serious Organised Crime and Police Act 2005 (c. 15)
Part 1 – The Serious Organised Crime Agency
Chapter 1 – SOCA: establishment and activities

21

(4) Information may not be disclosed under subsection (1) on behalf of the Commissioners unless the disclosure is authorised by the Commissioners or by an authorised officer of theirs.

35 Restrictions on further disclosure

(1) Information disclosed by SOCA under section 33 to any person or body must not be further disclosed except —

    (a) for a purpose connected with any function of that person or body for the purposes of which the information was disclosed by SOCA, or otherwise for any permitted purposes, and

    (b) with the consent of SOCA.

(2) Information disclosed to SOCA under any enactment by the Commissioners or a person acting on their behalf must not be further disclosed except —

    (a) for any permitted purposes, and

    (b) with the consent of the Commissioners or an authorised officer of Revenue and Customs.

(3) Consent under subsection (1) or (2) may be given —

    (a) in relation to a particular disclosure, or

    (b) in relation to disclosures made in circumstances specified or described in the consent.

(4) In this section "permitted purposes" has the meaning given by section 33(2).

General duties of police etc.

36 General duty of police to pass information to SOCA

(1) The chief officer of a police force in Great Britain must keep SOCA informed of any information relating to crime in his police area that appears to him to be likely to be relevant to the exercise by SOCA of any of its functions.

(2) The Chief Constable of the Police Service of Northern Ireland has a corresponding duty in relation to crime in Northern Ireland.

(3) The chief officer of a special police force must keep SOCA informed of any information relating to crime that he has become aware of in his capacity as chief officer and appears to him to be likely to be relevant to the exercise by SOCA of any of its functions.

37 General duty of police etc. to assist SOCA

(1) It is the duty of every person to whom this section applies to assist SOCA in the exercise of its functions in relation to serious organised crime.

(2) This section applies to —

    (a) any constable,

    (b) any officer of Revenue and Customs, and

    (c) any member of Her Majesty's armed forces or Her Majesty's coastguard.

22

Serious Organised Crime and Police Act 2005 (c. 15)
Part 1 — The Serious Organised Crime Agency
Chapter 1 — SOCA: establishment and activities

Prosecutions

38   Prosecution of offences investigated by SOCA

(1)   The Director of Revenue and Customs Prosecutions —

    (a)   may institute and conduct criminal proceedings in England and Wales that arise out of a criminal investigation by SOCA relating to a designated offence, and

    (b)   must take over the conduct of criminal proceedings instituted by SOCA in England and Wales in respect of a designated offence.

(2)   The Director of Revenue and Customs Prosecutions must provide such advice as he thinks appropriate, to such persons as he thinks appropriate, in relation to —

    (a)   a criminal investigation by SOCA relating to a designated offence, or

    (b)   criminal proceedings instituted in England and Wales that arise out of such an investigation.

(3)   The Director of Public Prosecutions —

    (a)   may institute and conduct criminal proceedings in England and Wales that arise out of a criminal investigation by SOCA relating to a non-designated offence, and

    (b)   must take over the conduct of criminal proceedings instituted by SOCA in England and Wales in respect of such an offence.

But paragraph (b) does not apply where the Director of the Serious Fraud Office has the conduct of the proceedings.

(4)   The Director of Public Prosecutions must provide such advice as he thinks appropriate, to such persons as he thinks appropriate, in relation to —

    (a)   a criminal investigation by SOCA relating to a non-designated offence, or

    (b)   criminal proceedings instituted in England and Wales that arise out of such an investigation.

(5)   Sections 23 and 23A of the Prosecution of Offences Act 1985 (c. 23) (power to discontinue proceedings) apply (with any necessary modifications) to proceedings conducted by the Director of Revenue and Customs Prosecutions in accordance with this section as they apply to proceedings conducted by the Director of Public Prosecutions.

(6)   In the Commissioners for Revenue and Customs Act 2005 (c. 11) —

    (a)   section 37(1) (prosecutors), and

    (b)   section 38(1) (conduct of prosecutions by appointed persons),

have effect as if the reference to section 35 of that Act included a reference to this section.

(7)   For the purposes of this section and section 39 —

    (a)   "criminal investigation" means any process —

        (i)   for considering whether an offence has been committed,

        (ii)   for discovering by whom an offence has been committed, or

        (iii)   as a result of which an offence is alleged to have been committed;

    (b)   an offence is a "designated offence" if criminal proceedings instituted by SOCA in respect of the offence fall (or, as the case may be, would

Serious Organised Crime and Police Act 2005 (c. 15) 23
Part 1 – The Serious Organised Crime Agency
Chapter 1 – SOCA: establishment and activities

fall) to be referred to the Director of Revenue and Customs Prosecutions by virtue of directions under section 39(1);

(c) "non-designated offence" means an offence which is not a designated offence;

(d) a reference to the institution of criminal proceedings is to be construed in accordance with section 15(2) of the Prosecution of Offences Act 1985 (c. 23); and

(e) a reference to the institution of proceedings by SOCA includes a reference to their institution by the Director General of SOCA or a person authorised by him.

39 Directions as to reference of cases and proceedings to appropriate prosecutor

(1) The Directors may give directions to SOCA –

(a) for enabling SOCA to determine whether cases arising out of criminal investigations by SOCA are to be referred to the Director of Revenue and Customs Prosecutions, or to the Director of Public Prosecutions, in order for him to consider whether to institute proceedings in accordance with section 38(1)(a) or (3)(a);

(b) for enabling SOCA to determine whether criminal proceedings instituted by SOCA are to be referred to the Director of Revenue and Customs Prosecutions, or to the Director of Public Prosecutions, in order for him to take over their conduct in accordance with section 38(1)(b) or (3)(b);

(c) specifying, in relation to any cases or proceedings that are to be so referred to the Director of Revenue and Customs Prosecutions or the Director of Public Prosecutions, the steps to be taken by SOCA in connection with referring them to him.

(2) Directions under subsection (1) may provide for cases or proceedings to be referred to one or other of the Directors by reference to –

(a) whether the cases or proceedings relate to an offence falling within a category of offences specified in the directions; or

(b) whether any criteria so specified are satisfied with respect to the cases or proceedings; or

(c) such other matters as the Directors think fit.

(3) The Directors may from time to time revise any directions given under this section.

(4) The Directors must publish in such manner as they think fit –

(a) any directions given under this section, and

(b) any revisions made to such directions;

and they must give a copy of any such directions or revisions to SOCA.

(5) A report to which this subsection applies must set out –

(a) any directions given under this section, and

(b) any revisions made to such directions,

in the year to which the report relates.

(6) Subsection (5) applies to –

(a) a report under section 9 of the Prosecution of Offences Act 1985 (c. 23) (report to Attorney General by Director of Public Prosecutions), and

24   *Serious Organised Crime and Police Act 2005 (c. 15)*
Part 1 — The Serious Organised Crime Agency
Chapter 1 — SOCA: establishment and activities

(b)   a report under paragraph 6 of Schedule 3 to the Commissioners for Revenue and Customs Act 2005 (c. 11) (report to Attorney General by Director of Revenue and Customs Prosecutions).

(7)   Directions under this section may make different provision for different cases, circumstances or areas.

(8)   If there is a failure to comply with directions under this section in relation to the reference of any matter to one of the Directors, neither —

     (a)   the reference, nor

     (b)   anything subsequently done in connection with the matter,

is invalid by reason of anything in the directions or in section 38.

(9)   In this section "the Directors" means the Director of Public Prosecutions and the Director of Revenue and Customs Prosecutions, acting jointly.

40   Functions of Director of Revenue and Customs Prosecutions as to persons arrested for designated offence

(1)   Sections 37 to 37B of the Police and Criminal Evidence Act 1984 (c. 60) (duties of custody officers; guidance etc.) have effect, in relation to a person arrested following a criminal investigation by SOCA relating to a designated offence, as if references to the Director of Public Prosecutions were references to the Director of Revenue and Customs Prosecutions.

(2)   In subsection (1) the reference to a designated offence is to be read in accordance with section 38(7)(b) of this Act.

Miscellaneous and supplementary

41   Directions

Any person to whom a direction is given by the Secretary of State or the Scottish Ministers under this Chapter must comply with the direction.

42   Interpretation of Chapter 1

(1)   In this Chapter —

     "chief officer" means —

         (a)   in relation to a police force in England and Wales, the chief officer of police,

         (b)   in relation to a police force in Scotland, the chief constable,

         (c)   in relation to the Police Service of Northern Ireland or the Police Service of Northern Ireland Reserve, the Chief Constable of the Police Service of Northern Ireland;

         (d)   in relation to the States of Jersey Police Force or the salaried police force of the Island of Guernsey, the chief officer of that force;

         (e)   in relation to the Isle of Man Constabulary, the chief constable;

         (f)   in relation to a special police force mentioned in section 3(5)(a), (b) or (c), the Chief Constable;

         (g)   in relation to the Scottish Drug Enforcement Agency, the Director of that Agency;

Serious Organised Crime and Police Act 2005 (c. 15)
Part 1 — The Serious Organised Crime Agency
Chapter 1 — SOCA: establishment and activities

25

"the Commissioners" has the meaning given by section 2(8);

"constable", in relation to Northern Ireland, means a member of the Police Service of Northern Ireland or the Police Service of Northern Ireland Reserve;

"financial year", in relation to SOCA, means—

    (a) the period beginning with the date on which SOCA is established and ending with the following 31st March, and

    (b) each successive period of 12 months ending with 31st March;

"functions" includes powers and duties;

"government department" includes a Northern Ireland department;

"joint police board" has the same meaning as in the Police (Scotland) Act 1967 (c. 77);

"police force" means (unless the context otherwise requires)—

    (a) a police force in England, Wales or Scotland, or

    (b) the Police Service of Northern Ireland or the Police Service of Northern Ireland Reserve;

"special police force" has the meaning given by section 3(5).

(2) In this Chapter—

    (a) "the Scottish Drug Enforcement Agency" means the organisation known by that name and established under section 36(1)(a)(ii) of the Police (Scotland) Act 1967; and

    (b) "the Director" of that Agency means the person engaged on central service (as defined by section 38(5) of that Act) and for the time being appointed by the Scottish Ministers to exercise control in relation to the activities carried out in the exercise of the Agency's functions.

(3) Section 81(5) of the Regulation of Investigatory Powers Act 2000 (c. 23) (meaning of "prevention" and "detection") applies for the purposes of this Chapter as it applies for the purposes of the provisions of that Act not contained in Chapter 1 of Part 1.

CHAPTER 2

SOCA: SPECIAL POWERS OF DESIGNATED STAFF

Designations

43 Designation of SOCA staff as persons having powers of constable etc.

(1) The Director General of SOCA may designate a member of the staff of SOCA as one or more of the following—

    (a) a person having the powers of a constable;

    (b) a person having the customs powers of an officer of Revenue and Customs;

    (c) a person having the powers of an immigration officer.

(2) A designation under this section—

    (a) may be made subject to any limitations specified in the designation (whether as to the powers exercisable by virtue of it, the purposes for which they are exercisable or otherwise); and

    (b) has effect either for a period so specified or without limit of time.

26   *Serious Organised Crime and Police Act 2005 (c. 15)*
                                    Part 1 – The Serious Organised Crime Agency
                                Chapter 2 – SOCA: special powers of designated staff

(3)   Subsection (2) applies subject to any modification or withdrawal of the designation under section 45.

(4)   A member of SOCA's staff may be designated as a person having the powers mentioned in any of paragraphs (a) to (c) of subsection (1) whether or not—

    (a)   he already has (for any reason) any powers falling within any of those paragraphs, or

    (b)   he had any such powers before becoming a member of SOCA's staff.

(5)   But a person may not be designated as a person having the powers mentioned in any of paragraphs (a) to (c) of subsection (1) unless the Director General is satisfied that that person—

    (a)   is capable of effectively exercising the powers that would be exercisable by virtue of the designation,

    (b)   has received adequate training in respect of the exercise of those powers, and

    (c)   is otherwise a suitable person to exercise those powers.

(6)   Where an employee of SOCA—

    (a)   before becoming such an employee, held an office by virtue of which he had any powers falling within subsection (1)(a), (b) or (c), and

    (b)   has not resigned that office,

that office is to be treated as suspended so long as he remains in SOCA's employment, and revives if (and only if) on ceasing to be so employed he returns to service as the holder of that office.

(7)   References in this section to the powers of a constable, the customs powers of an officer of Revenue and Customs or the powers of an immigration officer are to be read in accordance with sections 46 to 49.

44   Delegation of power to designate

(1)   The Director General of SOCA may, to such extent as he may specify, delegate his functions under section 43 to an employee of SOCA at the prescribed level.

(2)   "At the prescribed level" means employed in a grade or on a pay scale not lower than that specified in an order made by the Secretary of State.

45   Modification or withdrawal of designations

(1)   The Director General of SOCA may at any time modify or withdraw a designation made under section 43 by giving a notice to that effect to the designated person.

(2)   An employee of SOCA by whom the power to make designations under section 43 is exercisable by virtue of section 44 may at any time modify or withdraw a relevant designation by giving a notice to that effect to the designated person.

(3)   For the purposes of this section "a relevant designation", in relation to such an employee, means a designation of a kind that the employee is authorised to make by virtue of section 44.

Serious Organised Crime and Police Act 2005 (c. 15)
Part 1 — The Serious Organised Crime Agency
Chapter 2 — SOCA: special powers of designated staff

27

Powers exercisable

46   Person having powers of a constable

(1)   This section applies to a member of SOCA's staff who is for the time being designated under section 43 as a person having the powers of a constable.

(2)   The designated person has all the powers and privileges of a constable.

(3)   Those powers and privileges are exercisable by the designated person —
    (a)   throughout England and Wales and the adjacent United Kingdom waters, and
    (b)   in accordance with section 47, in Scotland or Northern Ireland and the adjacent United Kingdom waters.

(4)   If any of those powers and privileges, when exercisable by a constable, are subject to any territorial restrictions on their exercise, they are similarly subject to those restrictions when exercised by the designated person.

(5)   If any of those powers and privileges, when exercisable by a constable, are exercisable elsewhere than in the United Kingdom or the adjacent United Kingdom waters, they are similarly exercisable by the designated person.

(6)   The designated person also has any powers exercisable by virtue of subsection (7).

(7)   Any enactment under which a constable may be authorised by warrant to exercise any power in relation to any matter has effect, for the purpose of enabling the designated person to be authorised to exercise the power in relation to any such matter, as if he were a constable.

(8)   Subsections (2) to (7) have effect subject to any limitation specified in the designation under section 43(2).

(9)   In this section references to the powers and privileges of a constable are references to the powers and privileges of a constable whether under any enactment or otherwise.

47   Person having powers of constable: Scotland and Northern Ireland

(1)   This section provides for persons designated as mentioned in section 46(1) ("relevant persons") to exercise the powers and privileges mentioned in section 46(2) in Scotland or Northern Ireland and the adjacent United Kingdom waters.

(2)   If so agreed by —
    (a)   the Scottish Ministers, and
    (b)   SOCA,
    the powers and privileges are exercisable by relevant persons in Scotland and the adjacent United Kingdom waters to such extent and in such circumstances as may be specified in the agreement.

(3)   If so agreed by —
    (a)   the Director of the Scottish Drug Enforcement Agency or a person nominated by him for the purposes of this subsection, and
    (b)   SOCA,

28   Serious Organised Crime and Police Act 2005 (c. 15)
                    Part 1 – The Serious Organised Crime Agency
                  Chapter 2 – SOCA: special powers of designated staff

a relevant person may exercise the powers and privileges in Scotland in connection with a particular operation.

(4)   A person nominated for the purposes of subsection (3) must be either —

    (a)   a person for the time being appointed as Deputy Director of that Agency, or

    (b)   an appropriate officer of a police force for an area in Scotland.

(5)   If so agreed by —

    (a)   the Secretary of State, and

    (b)   SOCA,

the powers and privileges are exercisable by relevant persons in Northern Ireland and the adjacent United Kingdom waters to such extent and in such circumstances as may be specified in the agreement.

(6)   If —

    (a)   an agreement under subsection (5) ("the general authorisation") is in force, and

    (b)   an appropriate officer of the Police Service of Northern Ireland and SOCA so agree in conformity with the general authorisation,

a relevant person may exercise the powers and privileges in Northern Ireland in connection with a particular operation in accordance with the agreement mentioned in paragraph (b).

(7)   In this section —

    "appropriate officer" means an officer of or above the rank of assistant chief constable;

    "the Scottish Drug Enforcement Agency" and "the Director" of that Agency have the meanings given by section 42(2).

48   Person having customs powers

(1)   This section applies to a member of SOCA's staff who is for the time being designated under section 43 as a person having the customs powers of an officer of Revenue and Customs.

(2)   The designated person has, in relation to any customs matter, the same powers as an officer of Revenue and Customs would have.

(3)   The designated person also has any powers exercisable by virtue of subsection (4).

(4)   Any enactment under which an officer of Revenue and Customs may be authorised by warrant to exercise any power in relation to any customs matter has effect, for the purpose of enabling the designated person to be authorised to exercise the power in relation to any such matter, as if he were an officer of Revenue and Customs.

(5)   Where any power is exercisable by an officer of Revenue and Customs both —

    (a)   in relation to a customs matter, and

    (b)   in relation to any other matter,

it is exercisable by the designated person only in relation to the customs matter.

(6)   Subsections (2) to (5) have effect subject to any limitation specified in the designation under section 43(2).

Serious Organised Crime and Police Act 2005 (c. 15)
Part 1 — The Serious Organised Crime Agency
Chapter 2 — SOCA: special powers of designated staff

29

(7) In this section "customs matter" means any matter other than —

(a) a matter to which section 7 of the Commissioners for Revenue and Customs Act 2005 (c. 11) applies (former Inland Revenue matters), or

(b) any tax or duty not mentioned in Schedule 1 to that Act (which lists such matters).

49 Person having powers of an immigration officer

(1) This section applies to a member of SOCA's staff who is for the time being designated under section 43 as a person having the powers of an immigration officer.

(2) The designated person has, in relation to any matter in relation to which powers are exercisable by an immigration officer, the same powers as such an officer would have.

(3) The designated person also has any powers exercisable by virtue of subsection (4).

(4) Any enactment under which an immigration officer may be authorised by warrant to exercise any power in relation to any matter has effect, for the purpose of enabling the designated person to be authorised to exercise the power in relation to any such matter, as if he were an immigration officer.

(5) Subsections (2) to (4) have effect subject to any limitation specified in the designation under section 43(2).

(6) In this section "immigration officer" means a person who is an immigration officer within the meaning of the Immigration Act 1971 (c. 77).

Exercise of powers

50 Designations: supplementary

(1) If a designated person —

(a) exercises any power in relation to another person in reliance on his designation under section 43, or

(b) purports to do so,

he must produce evidence of his designation to the other person if requested to do so.

(2) A failure to comply with subsection (1) does not make the exercise of the power invalid.

(3) For the purpose of determining liability for the unlawful conduct of members of SOCA's staff, any conduct by a designated person in reliance, or purported reliance, on his designation is to be taken to be —

(a) if he is employed by SOCA, conduct in the course of his employment, or

(b) if he is a person to whom section 28 applies by virtue of subsection (3)(a) of that section, conduct falling within subsection (1) of that section.

(4) In the case of any unlawful conduct within subsection (3) which is a tort, SOCA is accordingly to be treated as a joint tortfeasor.

This subsection does not apply to Scotland.

30

Serious Organised Crime and Police Act 2005 (c. 15)
Part 1 – The Serious Organised Crime Agency
Chapter 2 – SOCA: special powers of designated staff

51 Assaults, obstruction or deception in connection with designations

(1) A person commits an offence if he assaults —

    (a) a designated person acting in the exercise of a relevant power, or

    (b) a person who is assisting a designated person in the exercise of such a power.

(2) A person commits an offence if he resists or wilfully obstructs —

    (a) a designated person acting in the exercise of a relevant power, or

    (b) a person who is assisting a designated person in the exercise of such a power.

(3) A person commits an offence if, with intent to deceive —

    (a) he impersonates a designated person,

    (b) he makes any statement or does any act calculated falsely to suggest that he is a designated person, or

    (c) he makes any statement or does any act calculated falsely to suggest that he has powers as a designated person that exceed the powers he actually has.

(4) A person guilty of an offence under subsection (1) or (3) is liable on summary conviction —

    (a) to imprisonment for a term not exceeding 51 weeks, or

    (b) to a fine not exceeding level 5 on the standard scale,

or to both.

(5) A person guilty of an offence under subsection (2) is liable on summary conviction —

    (a) to imprisonment for a term not exceeding 51 weeks, or

    (b) to a fine not exceeding level 3 on the standard scale,

or to both.

(6) In this section "relevant power", in relation to a designated person, means a power or privilege exercisable by that person by virtue of the designation under section 43.

(7) In the application of this section to Scotland the references to 51 weeks in subsections (4)(a) and (5)(a) are to be read as references to 12 months in each case.

(8) In the application of this section to Northern Ireland the references to 51 weeks are to be read as follows —

    (a) in subsection (4)(a) the reference is to be read as a reference to 6 months, and

    (b) in subsection (5)(a) the reference is to be read as a reference to 1 month.

Supplementary

52 Modification of enactments

(1) The Secretary of State may by order provide for any enactment (or description of enactments) to apply in relation to —

    (a) designated persons, or

    (b) the exercise of powers by such persons under this Chapter,

Serious Organised Crime and Police Act 2005 (c. 15)
Part 1 — The Serious Organised Crime Agency
Chapter 2 — SOCA: special powers of designated staff

31

with such modifications as he considers necessary or expedient.

(2) An order under this section may include provision for or in connection with—

    (a) extending to such persons any exemption or protection afforded by an enactment to any other description of persons;

    (b) providing for the disclosure of information to, or the doing of other things in relation to, such persons under any enactment;

    (c) conferring on the Director General of SOCA functions exercisable in relation to such persons.

(3) Subsection (2) does not affect the generality of subsection (1).

(4) In this section any reference to designated persons includes a reference to any description of such persons.

(5) Before exercising the power conferred by subsection (1) in relation to an enactment which (expressly or otherwise) confers any function on—

    (a) the Commissioners for Her Majesty's Revenue and Customs, or

    (b) an officer of Revenue and Customs,

the Secretary of State must consult the Commissioners.

(6) Before exercising the power conferred by subsection (1) in relation to an enactment which extends to Scotland, the Secretary of State must consult the Scottish Ministers.

(7) The power conferred by subsection (1) is exercisable by the Scottish Ministers (rather than by the Secretary of State) where the provision to be made is within the legislative competence of the Scottish Parliament.

53 Employment provisions

(1) A member of SOCA's staff who is for the time being designated under section 43 as a person having the powers of a constable is not, by virtue of section 46(2), to be treated as being in police service for the purposes of the enactments mentioned in subsection (2).

(2) The enactments are—

    (a) section 280 of the Trade Union and Labour Relations (Consolidation) Act 1992 (c. 52) (person in police service excluded from definitions of "worker" and "employee");

    (b) section 200 of the Employment Rights Act 1996 (c. 18) (certain provisions of the Act not to apply to persons in police service);

    (c) Article 145 of the Trade Union and Labour Relations (Northern Ireland) Order 1995 (S.I. 1995/1980 (N.I. 12)); and

    (d) Article 243 of the Employment Rights (Northern Ireland) Order 1996 (S.I. 1996/1919 (N.I. 16)).

54 Interpretation of Chapter 2

(1) In this Chapter—

    "designated person" means a person for the time being designated under section 43;

    "United Kingdom waters" means the sea and other waters within the seaward limits of the United Kingdom's territorial sea.

32   Serious Organised Crime and Police Act 2005 (c. 15)
                                              Part 1 – The Serious Organised Crime Agency
                                        Chapter 2 – SOCA: special powers of designated staff

(2) Any reference in this Chapter to the exercise of powers by virtue of a designation under section 43 is, in a case where any limitations were imposed under subsection (2) of that section, a reference to their exercise in conformity with those limitations.

CHAPTER 3

SOCA: MISCELLANEOUS AND SUPPLEMENTARY

Complaints and misconduct

55   Complaints and misconduct

(1) Schedule 2 makes provision for, and in connection with, the operation in relation to SOCA of Part 2 of the Police Reform Act 2002 (c. 30) (which relates to complaints and misconduct).

(2) In the Police (Northern Ireland) Act 1998 (c. 32) –
    (a) after section 60 insert –

"60ZA Serious Organised Crime Agency

    (1) An agreement for the establishment in relation to members of the staff of the Serious Organised Crime Agency of procedures corresponding or similar to any of those established by virtue of this Part may, with the approval of the Secretary of State, be made between the Ombudsman and the Agency.

    (2) Where no such procedures are in force in relation to the Agency, the Secretary of State may by order establish such procedures.

    (3) An agreement under this section may at any time be varied or terminated with the approval of the Secretary of State.

    (4) Before making an order under this section the Secretary of State shall consult –
        (a) the Ombudsman; and
        (b) the Agency.

    (5) Nothing in any other statutory provision shall prevent the Agency from carrying into effect procedures established by virtue of this section.

    (6) No such procedures shall have effect in relation to anything done by a member of the staff of the Agency outside Northern Ireland."; and
    (b) in section 61(5) (reports), at the end of paragraph (b) insert "; and
        (c) if the report concerns the Serious Organised Crime Agency, to the Agency."

Serious Organised Crime and Police Act 2005 (c. 15)
Part 1 — The Serious Organised Crime Agency
Chapter 3 — SOCA: Miscellaneous and supplementary

33

Application of discrimination legislation

56   Application of discrimination legislation to SOCA seconded staff

(1)   For the purposes of the provisions to which this subsection applies any constable or other person who has been seconded to SOCA to serve as a member of its staff shall be treated as being employed by SOCA as respects any act done by it in relation to that person.

(2)   Subsection (1) applies to —
  (a)   Part 2 of the Sex Discrimination Act 1975 (c. 65);
  (b)   Part 2 of the Race Relations Act 1976 (c. 74);
  (c)   Part II of the Sex Discrimination (Northern Ireland) Order 1976 (S.I. 1976/1042 (N.I. 15));
  (d)   Part 2 of the Disability Discrimination Act 1995 (c. 50);
  (e)   Part II of the Race Relations (Northern Ireland) Order 1997 (S.I. 1997/869 (N.I. 6)); and
  (f)   the Fair Employment and Treatment (Northern Ireland) Order 1998 (S.I. 1998/3162 (N.I. 21)), except Part VII.

(3)   For the purposes of the provisions to which this subsection applies —
  (a)   any constable or other person who has been seconded to SOCA to serve as a member of its staff shall be treated as being employed by SOCA (and as not being employed by any other person); and
  (b)   anything done by such a person in the performance, or purported performance, of his functions as such a person shall be treated as done in the course of that employment.

(4)   Subsection (3) applies to —
  (a)   section 41 of the Sex Discrimination Act 1975;
  (b)   section 32 of the Race Relations Act 1976;
  (c)   Article 42 of the Sex Discrimination (Northern Ireland) Order 1976;
  (d)   section 58 of the Disability Discrimination Act 1995;
  (e)   Article 32 of the Race Relations (Northern Ireland) Order 1997; and
  (f)   Article 36 of the Fair Employment and Treatment (Northern Ireland) Order 1998.

Joint investigation teams

57   Assaults or obstruction in connection with joint investigation teams

(1)   This section applies where an international joint investigation team has been formed under the leadership of a member of SOCA's staff.

(2)   A person commits an offence if he assaults a member of the team who is carrying out his functions as a member of the team.

(3)   A person commits an offence if he resists or wilfully obstructs a member of the team who is carrying out his functions as a member of that team.

(4)   A person guilty of an offence under subsection (2) is liable on summary conviction —
  (a)   to imprisonment for a term not exceeding 51 weeks, or
  (b)   to a fine not exceeding level 5 on the standard scale,

34

Serious Organised Crime and Police Act 2005 (c. 15)
Part 1 — The Serious Organised Crime Agency
Chapter 3 — SOCA: Miscellaneous and supplementary

or to both.

(5) A person guilty of an offence under subsection (3) is liable on summary conviction —

    (a) to imprisonment for a term not exceeding 51 weeks, or

    (b) to a fine not exceeding level 3 on the standard scale,

or to both.

(6) In this section "international joint investigation team" means any investigation team formed in accordance with —

    (a) any framework decision on joint investigation teams adopted under Article 34 of the Treaty on European Union,

    (b) the Convention on Mutual Assistance in Criminal Matters between the Member States of the European Union and the Protocol to that Convention established in accordance with that Article of the Treaty, or

    (c) any international agreement to which the United Kingdom is a party and which is specified in an order made by the Secretary of State.

(7) In the application of this section to Scotland the references to 51 weeks in subsections (4)(a) and (5)(a) are to be read as references to 12 months in each case.

(8) In the application of this section to Northern Ireland the references to 51 weeks are to be read as follows —

    (a) in subsection (4)(a) the reference is to be read as a reference to 6 months, and

    (b) in subsection (5)(a) the reference is to be read as a reference to 1 month.

Transfers

58 Transfers to SOCA

Schedule 3 makes provision about the transfer of staff, property, rights and liabilities to SOCA.

Amendments

59 Minor and consequential amendments relating to SOCA

Schedule 4 contains minor and consequential amendments relating to SOCA.

Serious Organised Crime and Police Act 2005 (c. 15)   35
Part 2 — Investigations, prosecutions, proceedings and proceeds of crime
Chapter 1 — Investigatory powers of DPP, etc.

PART 2

INVESTIGATIONS, PROSECUTIONS, PROCEEDINGS AND PROCEEDS OF CRIME

CHAPTER 1

INVESTIGATORY POWERS OF DPP, ETC.

Introductory

60   Investigatory powers of DPP etc.

(1)   This Chapter confers powers on —
   (a)   the Director of Public Prosecutions,
   (b)   the Director of Revenue and Customs Prosecutions, and
   (c)   the Lord Advocate,
in relation to the giving of disclosure notices in connection with the investigation of offences to which this Chapter applies.

(2)   The Director of Public Prosecutions may, to such extent as he may determine, delegate the exercise of his powers under this Chapter to a Crown prosecutor.

(3)   The Director of Revenue and Customs Prosecutions may, to such extent as he may determine, delegate the exercise of his powers under this Chapter to a Revenue and Customs Prosecutor.

(4)   The Lord Advocate may, to such extent as he may determine, delegate the exercise of his powers under this Chapter to a procurator fiscal.

(5)   In this Chapter "the Investigating Authority" means —
   (a)   the Director of Public Prosecutions,
   (b)   the Director of Revenue and Customs Prosecutions, or
   (c)   the Lord Advocate.

(6)   But, in circumstances where the powers of any of those persons are exercisable by any other person by virtue of subsection (2), (3) or (4), references to "the Investigating Authority" accordingly include any such other person.

61   Offences to which this Chapter applies

(1)   This Chapter applies to the following offences —
   (a)   any offence listed in Schedule 2 to the Proceeds of Crime Act 2002 (c. 29) (lifestyle offences: England and Wales);
   (b)   any offence listed in Schedule 4 to that Act (lifestyle offences: Scotland);
   (c)   any offence under sections 15 to 18 of the Terrorism Act 2000 (c. 11) (offences relating to fund-raising, money laundering etc.);
   (d)   any offence under section 170 of the Customs and Excise Management Act 1979 (c. 2) (fraudulent evasion of duty) or section 72 of the Value Added Tax Act 1994 (c. 23) (offences relating to VAT) which is a qualifying offence;
   (e)   any offence under section 17 of the Theft Act 1968 (c. 60) (false accounting), or any offence at common law of cheating in relation to the public revenue, which is a qualifying offence;

36   *Serious Organised Crime and Police Act 2005 (c. 15)*
Part 2 – Investigations, prosecutions, proceedings and proceeds of crime
Chapter 1 – Investigatory powers of DPP, etc.

    (f)   any offence under section 1 of the Criminal Attempts Act 1981 (c. 47), or in Scotland at common law, of attempting to commit any offence in paragraph (c) or any offence in paragraph (d) or (e) which is a qualifying offence;

    (g)   any offence under section 1 of the Criminal Law Act 1977 (c. 45), or in Scotland at common law, of conspiracy to commit any offence in paragraph (c) or any offence in paragraph (d) or (e) which is a qualifying offence.

(2)   For the purposes of subsection (1) an offence in paragraph (d) or (e) of that subsection is a qualifying offence if the Investigating Authority certifies that in his opinion —

    (a)   in the case of an offence in paragraph (d) or an offence of cheating the public revenue, the offence involved or would have involved a loss, or potential loss, to the public revenue of an amount not less than £5,000;

    (b)   in the case of an offence under section 17 of the Theft Act 1968 (c. 60), the offence involved or would have involved a loss or gain, or potential loss or gain, of an amount not less than £5,000.

(3)   A document purporting to be a certificate under subsection (2) is to be received in evidence and treated as such a certificate unless the contrary is proved.

(4)   The Secretary of State may by order —

    (a)   amend subsection (1), in its application to England and Wales, so as to remove an offence from it or add an offence to it;

    (b)   amend subsection (2), in its application to England and Wales, so as to —

        (i)   take account of any amendment made by virtue of paragraph (a) above, or

        (ii)   vary the sums for the time being specified in subsection (2)(a) and (b).

(5)   The Scottish Ministers may by order —

    (a)   amend subsection (1), in its application to Scotland, so as to remove an offence from it or add an offence to it;

    (b)   amend subsection (2), in its application to Scotland, so as to —

        (i)   take account of any amendment made by virtue of paragraph (a) above, or

        (ii)   vary the sums for the time being specified in subsection (2)(a) and (b).

Disclosure notices

62   Disclosure notices

(1)   If it appears to the Investigating Authority —

    (a)   that there are reasonable grounds for suspecting that an offence to which this Chapter applies has been committed,

    (b)   that any person has information (whether or not contained in a document) which relates to a matter relevant to the investigation of that offence, and

    (c)   that there are reasonable grounds for believing that information which may be provided by that person in compliance with a disclosure notice

Serious Organised Crime and Police Act 2005 (c. 15)
Part 2 — Investigations, prosecutions, proceedings and proceeds of crime
Chapter 1 — Investigatory powers of DPP, etc.

37

is likely to be of substantial value (whether or not by itself) to that investigation,

he may give, or authorise an appropriate person to give, a disclosure notice to that person.

(2) In this Chapter "appropriate person" means —

    (a) a constable,

    (b) a member of the staff of SOCA who is for the time being designated under section 43, or

    (c) an officer of Revenue and Customs.

(3) In this Chapter "disclosure notice" means a notice in writing requiring the person to whom it is given to do all or any of the following things in accordance with the specified requirements, namely —

    (a) answer questions with respect to any matter relevant to the investigation;

    (b) provide information with respect to any such matter as is specified in the notice;

    (c) produce such documents, or documents of such descriptions, relevant to the investigation as are specified in the notice.

(4) In subsection (3) "the specified requirements" means such requirements specified in the disclosure notice as relate to —

    (a) the time at or by which,

    (b) the place at which, or

    (c) the manner in which,

the person to whom the notice is given is to do any of the things mentioned in paragraphs (a) to (c) of that subsection; and those requirements may include a requirement to do any of those things at once.

(5) A disclosure notice must be signed or counter-signed by the Investigating Authority.

(6) This section has effect subject to section 64 (restrictions on requiring information etc.).

63 Production of documents

(1) This section applies where a disclosure notice has been given under section 62.

(2) An authorised person may —

    (a) take copies of or extracts from any documents produced in compliance with the notice, and

    (b) require the person producing them to provide an explanation of any of them.

(3) Documents so produced may be retained for so long as the Investigating Authority considers that it is necessary to retain them (rather than copies of them) in connection with the investigation for the purposes of which the disclosure notice was given.

(4) If the Investigating Authority has reasonable grounds for believing —

    (a) that any such documents may have to be produced for the purposes of any legal proceedings, and

    (b) that they might otherwise be unavailable for those purposes,

38

Serious Organised Crime and Police Act 2005 (c. 15)
Part 2 – Investigations, prosecutions, proceedings and proceeds of crime
Chapter 1 – Investigatory powers of DPP, etc.

they may be retained until the proceedings are concluded.

(5)   If a person who is required by a disclosure notice to produce any documents does not produce the documents in compliance with the notice, an authorised person may require that person to state, to the best of his knowledge and belief, where they are.

(6)   In this section "authorised person" means any appropriate person who either—

    (a)   is the person by whom the notice was given, or

    (b)   is authorised by the Investigating Authority for the purposes of this section.

(7)   This section has effect subject to section 64 (restrictions on requiring information etc.).

64   Restrictions on requiring information etc.

(1)   A person may not be required under section 62 or 63—

    (a)   to answer any privileged question,

    (b)   to provide any privileged information, or

    (c)   to produce any privileged document,

except that a lawyer may be required to provide the name and address of a client of his.

(2)   A "privileged question" is a question which the person would be entitled to refuse to answer on grounds of legal professional privilege in proceedings in the High Court.

(3)   "Privileged information" is information which the person would be entitled to refuse to provide on grounds of legal professional privilege in such proceedings.

(4)   A "privileged document" is a document which the person would be entitled to refuse to produce on grounds of legal professional privilege in such proceedings.

(5)   A person may not be required under section 62 to produce any excluded material (as defined by section 11 of the Police and Criminal Evidence Act 1984 (c. 60)).

(6)   In the application of this section to Scotland—

    (a)   subsections (1) to (5) do not have effect, but

    (b)   a person may not be required under section 62 or 63 to answer any question, provide any information or produce any document which he would be entitled, on grounds of legal privilege, to refuse to answer or (as the case may be) provide or produce.

(7)   In subsection (6)(b), "legal privilege" has the meaning given by section 412 of the Proceeds of Crime Act 2002 (c. 29).

(8)   A person may not be required under section 62 or 63 to disclose any information or produce any document in respect of which he owes an obligation of confidence by virtue of carrying on any banking business, unless—

    (a)   the person to whom the obligation of confidence is owed consents to the disclosure or production, or

Serious Organised Crime and Police Act 2005 (c. 15) 39
Part 2 – Investigations, prosecutions, proceedings and proceeds of crime
Chapter 1 – Investigatory powers of DPP, etc.

(b)   the requirement is made by, or in accordance with a specific authorisation given by, the Investigating Authority.

(9)   Subject to the preceding provisions, any requirement under section 62 or 63 has effect despite any restriction on disclosure (however imposed).

65   Restrictions on use of statements

(1)   A statement made by a person in response to a requirement imposed under section 62 or 63 ("the relevant statement") may not be used in evidence against him in any criminal proceedings unless subsection (2) or (3) applies.

(2)   This subsection applies where the person is being prosecuted –

   (a)   for an offence under section 67 of this Act, or

   (b)   for an offence under section 5 of the Perjury Act 1911 (c. 6) (false statements made on oath otherwise than in judicial proceedings or made otherwise than on oath), or

   (c)   for an offence under section 2 of the False Oaths (Scotland) Act 1933 (c. 20) (false statutory declarations and other false statements without oath) or at common law for an offence of attempting to pervert the course, or defeat the ends, of justice.

(3)   This subsection applies where the person is being prosecuted for some other offence and –

   (a)   the person, when giving evidence in the proceedings, makes a statement inconsistent with the relevant statement, and

   (b)   in the proceedings evidence relating to the relevant statement is adduced, or a question about it is asked, by or on behalf of the person.

Enforcement

66   Power to enter and seize documents

(1)   A justice of the peace may issue a warrant under this section if, on an information on oath laid by the Investigating Authority, he is satisfied –

   (a)   that any of the conditions mentioned in subsection (2) is met in relation to any documents of a description specified in the information, and

   (b)   that the documents are on premises so specified.

(2)   The conditions are –

   (a)   that a person has been required by a disclosure notice to produce the documents but has not done so;

   (b)   that it is not practicable to give a disclosure notice requiring their production;

   (c)   that giving such a notice might seriously prejudice the investigation of an offence to which this Chapter applies.

(3)   A warrant under this section is a warrant authorising an appropriate person named in it –

   (a)   to enter and search the premises, using such force as is reasonably necessary;

   (b)   to take possession of any documents appearing to be documents of a description specified in the information, or to take any other steps

40   *Serious Organised Crime and Police Act 2005 (c. 15)*
Part 2 — Investigations, prosecutions, proceedings and proceeds of crime
Chapter 1 — Investigatory powers of DPP, etc.

which appear to be necessary for preserving, or preventing interference with, any such documents;

(c)   in the case of any such documents consisting of information recorded otherwise than in legible form, to take possession of any computer disk or other electronic storage device which appears to contain the information in question, or to take any other steps which appear to be necessary for preserving, or preventing interference with, that information;

(d)   to take copies of or extracts from any documents or information falling within paragraph (b) or (c);

(e)   to require any person on the premises to provide an explanation of any such documents or information or to state where any such documents or information may be found;

(f)   to require any such person to give the appropriate person such assistance as he may reasonably require for the taking of copies or extracts as mentioned in paragraph (d).

(4)   A person executing a warrant under this section may take other persons with him, if it appears to him to be necessary to do so.

(5)   A warrant under this section must, if so required, be produced for inspection by the owner or occupier of the premises or anyone acting on his behalf.

(6)   If the premises are unoccupied or the occupier is temporarily absent, a person entering the premises under the authority of a warrant under this section must leave the premises as effectively secured against trespassers as he found them.

(7)   Where possession of any document or device is taken under this section —

(a)   the document may be retained for so long as the Investigating Authority considers that it is necessary to retain it (rather than a copy of it) in connection with the investigation for the purposes of which the warrant was sought, or

(b)   the device may be retained for so long as he considers that it is necessary to retain it in connection with that investigation,

as the case may be.

(8)   If the Investigating Authority has reasonable grounds for believing —

(a)   that any such document or device may have to be produced for the purposes of any legal proceedings, and

(b)   that it might otherwise be unavailable for those purposes,

it may be retained until the proceedings are concluded.

(9)   Nothing in this section authorises a person to take possession of, or make copies of or take extracts from, any document or information which, by virtue of section 64, could not be required to be produced or disclosed under section 62 or 63.

(10)   In the application of this section to Scotland —

(a)   subsection (1) has effect as if, for the words from the beginning to "satisfied —", there were substituted "A sheriff may issue a warrant under this section, on the application of a procurator fiscal, if he is satisfied —";

(b)   subsections (1)(a) and (3)(b) have effect as if, for "in the information", there were substituted "in the application"; and

(c)   subsections (4) to (6) do not have effect.

Serious Organised Crime and Police Act 2005 (c. 15)
Part 2 — Investigations, prosecutions, proceedings and proceeds of crime
Chapter 1 — Investigatory powers of DPP, etc.

41

67   Offences in connection with disclosure notices or search warrants

(1)   A person commits an offence if, without reasonable excuse, he fails to comply with any requirement imposed on him under section 62 or 63.

(2)   A person commits an offence if, in purported compliance with any requirement imposed on him under section 62 or 63 —
   (a)   he makes a statement which is false or misleading, and
   (b)   he either knows that it is false or misleading or is reckless as to whether it is false or misleading.
"False or misleading" means false or misleading in a material particular.

(3)   A person commits an offence if he wilfully obstructs any person in the exercise of any rights conferred by a warrant under section 66.

(4)   A person guilty of an offence under subsection (1) or (3) is liable on summary conviction —
   (a)   to imprisonment for a term not exceeding 51 weeks, or
   (b)   to a fine not exceeding level 5 on the standard scale,
or to both.

(5)   A person guilty of an offence under subsection (2) is liable —
   (a)   on conviction on indictment, to imprisonment for a term not exceeding two years or to a fine, or to both;
   (b)   on summary conviction, to imprisonment for a term not exceeding 12 months or to a fine not exceeding the statutory maximum, or to both.

(6)   In the application of this section to Scotland, the reference to 51 weeks in subsection (4)(a) is to be read as a reference to 12 months.

Supplementary

68   Procedure applicable to search warrants

In Part 1 of Schedule 1 to the Criminal Justice and Police Act 2001 (c. 16) (powers of seizure to which section 50 applies) after paragraph 73E (inserted by the Human Tissue Act 2004 (c. 30)) insert —

"Serious Organised Crime and Police Act 2005

73F   The power of seizure conferred by section 66 of the Serious Organised Crime and Police Act 2005 (seizure of documents for purposes of investigation by DPP or other Investigating Authority)."

69   Manner in which disclosure notice may be given

(1)   This section provides for the manner in which a disclosure notice may be given under section 62.

(2)   The notice may be given to a person by —
   (a)   delivering it to him,
   (b)   leaving it at his proper address,
   (c)   sending it by post to him at that address.

(3)   The notice may be given —

42   *Serious Organised Crime and Police Act 2005 (c. 15)*
Part 2 — *Investigations, prosecutions, proceedings and proceeds of crime*
Chapter 1 — *Investigatory powers of DPP, etc.*

> (a) in the case of a body corporate, to the secretary or clerk of that body;
>
> (b) in the case of a partnership, to a partner or a person having the control or management of the partnership business;
>
> (c) in the case of an unincorporated association (other than a partnership), to an officer of the association.

(4) For the purposes of this section and section 7 of the Interpretation Act 1978 (c. 30) (service of documents by post) in its application to this section, the proper address of a person is his usual or last-known address (whether residential or otherwise), except that—

> (a) in the case of a body corporate or its secretary or clerk, it is the address of the registered office of that body or its principal office in the United Kingdom,
>
> (b) in the case of a partnership, a partner or a person having the control or management of the partnership business, it is that of the principal office of the partnership in the United Kingdom, and
>
> (c) in the case of an unincorporated association (other than a partnership) or an officer of the association, it is that of the principal office of the association in the United Kingdom.

(5) This section does not apply to Scotland.

70   Interpretation of Chapter 1

(1) In this Chapter—

> "appropriate person" has the meaning given by section 62(2);
>
> "the Investigating Authority" is to be construed in accordance with section 60(5) and (6);
>
> "disclosure notice" has the meaning given by section 62(3);
>
> "document" includes information recorded otherwise than in legible form.

(2) In relation to information recorded otherwise than in legible form, any reference in this Chapter to the production of documents is a reference to the production of a copy of the information in legible form.

CHAPTER 2

OFFENDERS ASSISTING INVESTIGATIONS AND PROSECUTIONS

71   Assistance by offender: immunity from prosecution

(1) If a specified prosecutor thinks that for the purposes of the investigation or prosecution of any offence it is appropriate to offer any person immunity from prosecution he may give the person a written notice under this subsection (an "immunity notice").

(2) If a person is given an immunity notice, no proceedings for an offence of a description specified in the notice may be brought against that person in England and Wales or Northern Ireland except in circumstances specified in the notice.

(3) An immunity notice ceases to have effect in relation to the person to whom it is given if the person fails to comply with any conditions specified in the notice.

Serious Organised Crime and Police Act 2005 (c. 15)
Part 2 — Investigations, prosecutions, proceedings and proceeds of crime
Chapter 2 — Offenders assisting investigations and prosecutions

43

(4) Each of the following is a specified prosecutor—
   (a) the Director of Public Prosecutions;
   (b) the Director of Revenue and Customs Prosecutions;
   (c) the Director of the Serious Fraud Office;
   (d) the Director of Public Prosecutions for Northern Ireland;
   (e) a prosecutor designated for the purposes of this section by a prosecutor mentioned in paragraphs (a) to (d).

(5) The Director of Public Prosecutions or a person designated by him under subsection (4)(e) may not give an immunity notice in relation to proceedings in Northern Ireland.

(6) The Director of Public Prosecutions for Northern Ireland or a person designated by him under subsection (4)(e) may not give an immunity notice in relation to proceedings in England and Wales.

(7) An immunity notice must not be given in relation to an offence under section 188 of the Enterprise Act 2002 (c. 40) (cartel offences).

72 Assistance by offender: undertakings as to use of evidence

(1) If a specified prosecutor thinks that for the purposes of the investigation or prosecution of any offence it is appropriate to offer any person an undertaking that information of any description will not be used against the person in any proceedings to which this section applies he may give the person a written notice under this subsection (a "restricted use undertaking").

(2) This section applies to—
   (a) criminal proceedings;
   (b) proceedings under Part 5 of the Proceeds of Crime Act 2002 (c. 29).

(3) If a person is given a restricted use undertaking the information described in the undertaking must not be used against that person in any proceedings to which this section applies brought in England and Wales or Northern Ireland except in the circumstances specified in the undertaking.

(4) A restricted use undertaking ceases to have effect in relation to the person to whom it is given if the person fails to comply with any conditions specified in the undertaking.

(5) The Director of Public Prosecutions for Northern Ireland or a person designated by him under section 71(4)(e) may not give a restricted use undertaking in relation to proceedings in England and Wales.

(6) The Director of Public Prosecutions or a person designated by him under section 71(4)(e) may not give a restricted use undertaking in relation to proceedings in Northern Ireland.

(7) Specified prosecutor must be construed in accordance with section 71(4).

73 Assistance by defendant: reduction in sentence

(1) This section applies if a defendant—
   (a) following a plea of guilty is either convicted of an offence in proceedings in the Crown Court or is committed to the Crown Court for sentence, and

44

Serious Organised Crime and Police Act 2005 (c. 15)
Part 2 — Investigations, prosecutions, proceedings and proceeds of crime
Chapter 2 — Offenders assisting investigations and prosecutions

      (b)   has, pursuant to a written agreement made with a specified prosecutor, assisted or offered to assist the investigator or prosecutor in relation to that or any other offence.

(2)   In determining what sentence to pass on the defendant the court may take into account the extent and nature of the assistance given or offered.

(3)   If the court passes a sentence which is less than it would have passed but for the assistance given or offered, it must state in open court—

      (a)   that it has passed a lesser sentence than it would otherwise have passed, and

      (b)   what the greater sentence would have been.

(4)   Subsection (3) does not apply if the court thinks that it would not be in the public interest to disclose that the sentence has been discounted; but in such a case the court must give written notice of the matters specified in paragraphs (a) and (b) of subsection (3) to both the prosecutor and the defendant.

(5)   Nothing in any enactment which—

      (a)   requires that a minimum sentence is passed in respect of any offence or an offence of any description or by reference to the circumstances of any offender (whether or not the enactment also permits the court to pass a lesser sentence in particular circumstances), or

      (b)   in the case of a sentence which is fixed by law, requires the court to take into account certain matters for the purposes of making an order which determines or has the effect of determining the minimum period of imprisonment which the offender must serve (whether or not the enactment also permits the court to fix a lesser period in particular circumstances),

affects the power of a court to act under subsection (2).

(6)   If, in determining what sentence to pass on the defendant, the court takes into account the extent and nature of the assistance given or offered as mentioned in subsection (2), that does not prevent the court from also taking account of any other matter which it is entitled by virtue of any other enactment to take account of for the purposes of determining—

      (a)   the sentence, or

      (b)   in the case of a sentence which is fixed by law, any minimum period of imprisonment which an offender must serve.

(7)   If subsection (3) above does not apply by virtue of subsection (4) above, sections 174(1)(a) and 270 of the Criminal Justice Act 2003 (c. 44) (requirement to explain reasons for sentence or other order) do not apply to the extent that the explanation will disclose that a sentence has been discounted in pursuance of this section.

(8)   In this section—

      (a)   a reference to a sentence includes, in the case of a sentence which is fixed by law, a reference to the minimum period an offender is required to serve, and a reference to a lesser sentence must be construed accordingly;

      (b)   a reference to imprisonment includes a reference to any other custodial sentence within the meaning of section 76 of the Powers of Criminal Courts (Sentencing) Act 2000 (c. 6) or Article 2 of the Criminal Justice (Northern Ireland) Order 1996 (S.I. 1996/3160).

Serious Organised Crime and Police Act 2005 (c. 15)
Part 2 – Investigations, prosecutions, proceedings and proceeds of crime
Chapter 2 – Offenders assisting investigations and prosecutions

45

(9) An agreement with a specified prosecutor may provide for assistance to be given to that prosecutor or to any other prosecutor.

(10) References to a specified prosecutor must be construed in accordance with section 71.

74 Assistance by defendant: review of sentence

(1) This section applies if —
   (a) the Crown Court has passed a sentence on a person in respect of an offence, and
   (b) the person falls within subsection (2).

(2) A person falls within this subsection if —
   (a) he receives a discounted sentence in consequence of his having offered in pursuance of a written agreement to give assistance to the prosecutor or investigator of an offence but he knowingly fails to any extent to give assistance in accordance with the agreement;
   (b) he receives a discounted sentence in consequence of his having offered in pursuance of a written agreement to give assistance to the prosecutor or investigator of an offence and, having given the assistance in accordance with the agreement, in pursuance of another written agreement gives or offers to give further assistance;
   (c) he receives a sentence which is not discounted but in pursuance of a written agreement he subsequently gives or offers to give assistance to the prosecutor or investigator of an offence.

(3) A specified prosecutor may at any time refer the case back to the court by which the sentence was passed if —
   (a) the person is still serving his sentence, and
   (b) the specified prosecutor thinks it is in the interests of justice to do so.

(4) A case so referred must, if possible, be heard by the judge who passed the sentence to which the referral relates.

(5) If the court is satisfied that a person who falls within subsection (2)(a) knowingly failed to give the assistance it may substitute for the sentence to which the referral relates such greater sentence (not exceeding that which it would have passed but for the agreement to give assistance) as it thinks appropriate.

(6) In a case of a person who falls within subsection (2)(b) or (c) the court may —
   (a) take into account the extent and nature of the assistance given or offered;
   (b) substitute for the sentence to which the referral relates such lesser sentence as it thinks appropriate.

(7) Any part of the sentence to which the referral relates which the person has already served must be taken into account in determining when a greater or lesser sentence imposed by subsection (5) or (6) has been served.

(8) A person in respect of whom a reference is made under this section and the specified prosecutor may with the leave of the Court of Appeal appeal to the Court of Appeal against the decision of the Crown Court.

46   *Serious Organised Crime and Police Act 2005 (c. 15)*
                          Part 2 — Investigations, prosecutions, proceedings and proceeds of crime
                                Chapter 2 — Offenders assisting investigations and prosecutions

(9)   Section 33(3) of the Criminal Appeal Act 1968 (c. 19) (limitation on appeal from the criminal division of the Court of Appeal) does not prevent an appeal to the Supreme Court under this section.

(10) A discounted sentence is a sentence passed in pursuance of section 73 or subsection (6) above.

(11) References —
      (a)   to a written agreement are to an agreement made in writing with a specified prosecutor;
      (b)   to a specified prosecutor must be construed in accordance with section 71.

(12) In relation to any proceedings under this section, the Secretary of State may make an order containing provision corresponding to any provision in —
      (a)   the Criminal Appeal Act 1968 (subject to any specified modifications), or
      (b)   the Criminal Appeal (Northern Ireland) Act 1980 (c. 47) (subject to any specified modifications).

(13) A person does not fall within subsection (2) if —
      (a)   he was convicted of an offence for which the sentence is fixed by law, and
      (b)   he did not plead guilty to the offence for which he was sentenced.

(14) Section 174(1)(a) or 270 of the Criminal Justice Act 2003 (c. 44) (as the case may be) applies to a sentence substituted under subsection (5) above unless the court thinks that it is not in the public interest to disclose that the person falls within subsection (2)(a) above.

(15) Subsections (3) to (9) of section 73 apply for the purposes of this section as they apply for the purposes of that section and any reference in those subsections to subsection (2) of that section must be construed as a reference to subsection (6) of this section.

75   Proceedings under section 74: exclusion of public

(1)   This section applies to —
      (a)   any proceedings relating to a reference made under section 74(3), and
      (b)   any other proceedings arising in consequence of such proceedings.

(2)   The court in which the proceedings will be or are being heard may make such order as it thinks appropriate —
      (a)   to exclude from the proceedings any person who does not fall within subsection (4);
      (b)   to give such directions as it thinks appropriate prohibiting the publication of any matter relating to the proceedings (including the fact that the reference has been made).

(3)   An order under subsection (2) may be made only to the extent that the court thinks —
      (a)   that it is necessary to do so to protect the safety of any person, and
      (b)   that it is in the interests of justice.

(4)   The following persons fall within this subsection —
      (a)   a member or officer of the court;

Serious Organised Crime and Police Act 2005 (c. 15)
Part 2 – Investigations, prosecutions, proceedings and proceeds of crime
Chapter 2 – Offenders assisting investigations and prosecutions

47

    (b)   a party to the proceedings;

    (c)   counsel or a solicitor for a party to the proceedings;

    (d)   a person otherwise directly concerned with the proceedings.

(5)   This section does not affect any other power which the court has by virtue of any rule of law or other enactment—

    (a)   to exclude any person from proceedings, or

    (b)   to restrict the publication of any matter relating to proceedings.

CHAPTER 3

FINANCIAL REPORTING ORDERS

76   Financial reporting orders: making

(1)   A court sentencing or otherwise dealing with a person convicted of an offence mentioned in subsection (3) may also make a financial reporting order in respect of him.

(2)   But it may do so only if it is satisfied that the risk of the person's committing another offence mentioned in subsection (3) is sufficiently high to justify the making of a financial reporting order.

(3)   The offences are—

    (a)   an offence under any of the following provisions of the Theft Act 1968 (c. 60)—

        section 15 (obtaining property by deception),

        section 15A (obtaining a money transfer by deception),

        section 16 (obtaining a pecuniary advantage by deception),

        section 20(2) (procuring execution of valuable security, etc.),

    (b)   an offence under either of the following provisions of the Theft Act 1978 (c. 31)—

        section 1 (obtaining services by deception),

        section 2 (evasion of liability by deception),

    (c)   any offence specified in Schedule 2 to the Proceeds of Crime Act 2002 (c. 29) ("lifestyle offences").

(4)   The Secretary of State may by order amend subsection (3) so as to remove an offence from it or add an offence to it.

(5)   A financial reporting order—

    (a)   comes into force when it is made, and

    (b)   has effect for the period specified in the order, beginning with the date on which it is made.

(6)   If the order is made by a magistrates' court, the period referred to in subsection (5)(b) must not exceed 5 years.

(7)   Otherwise, that period must not exceed—

    (a)   if the person is sentenced to imprisonment for life, 20 years,

    (b)   otherwise, 15 years.

48   *Serious Organised Crime and Police Act 2005 (c. 15)*
Part 2 — Investigations, prosecutions, proceedings and proceeds of crime
Chapter 3 — Financial reporting orders

77   Financial reporting orders: making in Scotland

(1)   A court sentencing or otherwise dealing with a person convicted of an offence mentioned in subsection (3) may also make a financial reporting order in respect of him.

(2)   But he or it may do so only if satisfied that the risk of the person's committing another offence mentioned in subsection (3) is sufficiently high to justify the making of a financial reporting order.

(3)   The offences are —

    (a)   at common law, the offence of fraud,

    (b)   any offence specified in Schedule 4 to the Proceeds of Crime Act 2002 (c. 29) ("lifestyle offences": Scotland).

(4)   The Scottish Ministers may by order amend subsection (3) so as to remove an offence from it or add an offence to it.

(5)   A financial reporting order —

    (a)   comes into force when it is made, and

    (b)   has effect for the period specified in the order, beginning with the date on which it is made.

(6)   If the order is made by the sheriff, the period referred to in subsection (5)(b) must not exceed 5 years.

(7)   If the order is made by the High Court of Justiciary, that period must not exceed —

    (a)   if the person is sentenced to imprisonment for life, 20 years,

    (b)   otherwise, 15 years.

78   Financial reporting orders: making in Northern Ireland

(1)   A court sentencing or otherwise dealing with a person convicted of an offence mentioned in subsection (3) may also make a financial reporting order in respect of him.

(2)   But the court may do so only if it is satisfied that the risk of the person's committing another offence mentioned in subsection (3) is sufficiently high to justify the making of a financial reporting order.

(3)   The offences are —

    (a)   an offence under any of the following provisions of the Theft Act (Northern Ireland) 1969 (c. 16 (N.I.)) —

        section 15 (obtaining property by deception),

        section 15A (obtaining a money transfer by deception),

        section 16 (obtaining a pecuniary advantage by deception),

        section 19(2) (procuring execution of valuable security, etc.),

    (b)   an offence under either of the following provisions of the Theft (Northern Ireland) Order 1978 (S.I. 1978/1407 (N.I. 23)) —

        Article 3 (obtaining services by deception),

        Article 4 (evasion of liability by deception),

    (c)   any offence specified in Schedule 5 to the Proceeds of Crime Act 2002 ("lifestyle offences": Northern Ireland).

(4)   A financial reporting order —

Serious Organised Crime and Police Act 2005 (c. 15)
Part 2 – Investigations, prosecutions, proceedings and proceeds of crime
Chapter 3 – Financial reporting orders

49

(a) comes into force when it is made, and

(b) has effect for the period specified in the order, beginning with the date on which it is made.

(5) If the order is made by a magistrates' court, or by the county court on appeal, the period referred to in subsection (4)(b) must not exceed 5 years.

(6) Otherwise, that period must not exceed –

(a) if the person is sentenced to imprisonment for life, 20 years,

(b) otherwise, 15 years.

79 Financial reporting orders: effect

(1) A person in relation to whom a financial reporting order has effect must do the following.

(2) He must make a report, in respect of –

(a) the period of a specified length beginning with the date on which the order comes into force, and

(b) subsequent periods of specified lengths, each period beginning immediately after the end of the previous one.

(3) He must set out in each report, in the specified manner, such particulars of his financial affairs relating to the period in question as may be specified.

(4) He must include any specified documents with each report.

(5) He must make each report within the specified number of days after the end of the period in question.

(6) He must make each report to the specified person.

(7) Rules of court may provide for the maximum length of the periods which may be specified under subsection (2).

(8) In this section, "specified" means specified by the court in the order.

(9) In Scotland the specified person must be selected by the court from a list set out in an order made for the purposes of this section by the Scottish Ministers.

(10) A person who without reasonable excuse includes false or misleading information in a report, or otherwise fails to comply with any requirement of this section, is guilty of an offence and is liable on summary conviction to –

(a) imprisonment for a term not exceeding –

(i) in England and Wales, 51 weeks,

(ii) in Scotland, 12 months,

(iii) in Northern Ireland, 6 months, or

(b) a fine not exceeding level 5 on the standard scale,

or to both.

80 Financial reporting orders: variation and revocation

(1) An application for variation or revocation of a financial reporting order may be made by –

(a) the person in respect of whom it has been made,

(b) the person to whom reports are to be made under it (see section 79(6)).

50

Serious Organised Crime and Police Act 2005 (c. 15)
Part 2 – Investigations, prosecutions, proceedings and proceeds of crime
Chapter 3 – Financial reporting orders

(2) The application must be made to the court which made the order.

(3) But if the order was made on appeal, the application must be made to the court which originally sentenced the person in respect of whom the order was made.

(4) If (in either case) that court was a magistrates' court, the application may be made to any magistrates' court acting in the same local justice area (or in Northern Ireland for the same county court division) as that court.

(5) Subsections (3) and (4) do not apply to Scotland.

81   Financial reporting orders: verification and disclosure

(1) In this section, "the specified person" means the person to whom reports under a financial reporting order are to be made.

(2) The specified person may, for the purpose of doing either of the things mentioned in subsection (4), disclose a report to any person who he reasonably believes may be able to contribute to doing either of those things.

(3) Any other person may disclose information to —
   (a) the specified person, or
   (b) a person to whom the specified person has disclosed a report,
   for the purpose of contributing to doing either of the things mentioned in subsection (4).

(4) The things mentioned in subsections (2) and (3) are —
   (a) checking the accuracy of the report or of any other report made pursuant to the same order,
   (b) discovering the true position.

(5) The specified person may also disclose a report for the purposes of —
   (a) the prevention, detection, investigation or prosecution of criminal offences, whether in the United Kingdom or elsewhere,
   (b) the prevention, detection or investigation of conduct for which penalties other than criminal penalties are provided under the law of any part of the United Kingdom or of any country or territory outside the United Kingdom.

(6) A disclosure under this section does not breach —
   (a) any obligation of confidence owed by the person making the disclosure, or
   (b) any other restriction on the disclosure of information (however imposed).

(7) But nothing in this section authorises a disclosure, in contravention of any provisions of the Data Protection Act 1998 (c. 29), of personal data which are not exempt from those provisions.

(8) In this section, references to a report include any of its contents, any document included with the report, or any of the contents of such a document.

Serious Organised Crime and Police Act 2005 (c. 15)
Part 2 – Investigations, prosecutions, proceedings and proceeds of crime
Chapter 4 – Protection of witnesses and other persons

51

CHAPTER 4

PROTECTION OF WITNESSES AND OTHER PERSONS

82   Protection of persons involved in investigations or proceedings

(1)   A protection provider may make such arrangements as he considers appropriate for the purpose of protecting a person of a description specified in Schedule 5 if—

    (a)   the protection provider considers that the person's safety is at risk by virtue of his being a person of a description so specified, and

    (b)   the person is ordinarily resident in the United Kingdom.

(2)   A protection provider may vary or cancel any arrangements made by him under subsection (1) if he considers it appropriate to do so.

(3)   If a protection provider makes arrangements under subsection (1) or cancels arrangements made under that subsection, he must record that he has done so.

(4)   In determining whether to make arrangements under subsection (1), or to vary or cancel arrangements made under that subsection, a protection provider must, in particular, have regard to—

    (a)   the nature and extent of the risk to the person's safety,

    (b)   the cost of the arrangements,

    (c)   the likelihood that the person, and any person associated with him, will be able to adjust to any change in their circumstances which may arise from the making of the arrangements or from their variation or cancellation (as the case may be), and

    (d)   if the person is or might be a witness in legal proceedings (whether or not in the United Kingdom), the nature of the proceedings and the importance of his being a witness in those proceedings.

(5)   A protection provider is—

    (a)   a chief officer of a police force in England and Wales;

    (b)   a chief constable of a police force in Scotland;

    (c)   the Chief Constable of the Police Service of Northern Ireland;

    (d)   the Director General of SOCA;

    (e)   any of the Commissioners for Her Majesty's Revenue and Customs;

    (f)   the Director of the Scottish Drug Enforcement Agency;

    (g)   a person designated by a person mentioned in any of the preceding paragraphs to exercise his functions under this section.

(6)   The Secretary of State may, after consulting the Scottish Ministers, by order amend Schedule 5 so as to add, modify or omit any entry.

(7)   Nothing in this section affects any power which a person has (otherwise than by virtue of this section) to make arrangements for the protection of another person.

83   Joint arrangements

(1)   Arrangements may be made under section 82(1) by two or more protection providers acting jointly.

52   *Serious Organised Crime and Police Act 2005 (c. 15)*
            Part 2 – Investigations, prosecutions, proceedings and proceeds of crime
            Chapter 4 – Protection of witnesses and other persons

(2)   If arrangements are made jointly by virtue of subsection (1), any powers conferred on a protection provider by this Chapter are exercisable in relation to the arrangements by –

    (a)   all of the protection providers acting together, or

    (b)   one of the protection providers, or some of the protection providers acting together, with the agreement of the others.

(3)   Nothing in this section or in section 84 affects any power which a protection provider has to request or obtain assistance from another protection provider.

84   Transfer of responsibility to other protection provider

(1)   A protection provider who makes arrangements under section 82(1) may agree with another protection provider that, as from a date specified in the agreement –

    (a)   the protection provider will cease to discharge any responsibilities which he has in relation to the arrangements, and

    (b)   the other protection provider will discharge those responsibilities instead.

(2)   Any such agreement may include provision for the making of payments in respect of any costs incurred or likely to be incurred in consequence of the agreement.

(3)   If an agreement is made under subsection (1), any powers conferred on a protection provider by this Chapter (including the power conferred by subsection (1)) are, as from the date specified in the agreement, exercisable by the other protection provider as if he had made the arrangements under section 82(1).

(4)   Each protection provider who makes an agreement under subsection (1) must record that he has done so.

85   Duty to assist protection providers

(1)   This section applies if a protection provider requests assistance from a public authority in connection with the making of arrangements under section 82(1) or the implementation, variation or cancellation of such arrangements.

(2)   The public authority must take reasonable steps to provide the assistance requested.

(3)   "Public authority" includes any person certain of whose functions are of a public nature but does not include –

    (a)   a court or tribunal,

    (b)   either House of Parliament or a person exercising functions in connection with proceedings in Parliament, or

    (c)   the Scottish Parliament or a person exercising functions in connection with proceedings in the Scottish Parliament.

86   Offence of disclosing information about protection arrangements

(1)   A person commits an offence if –

Serious Organised Crime and Police Act 2005 (c. 15)
Part 2 − Investigations, prosecutions, proceedings and proceeds of crime
Chapter 4 − Protection of witnesses and other persons

53

> (a) he discloses information which relates to the making of arrangements under section 82(1) or to the implementation, variation or cancellation of such arrangements, and
>
> (b) he knows or suspects that the information relates to the making of such arrangements or to their implementation, variation or cancellation.

(2) A person who commits an offence under this section is liable —

> (a) on conviction on indictment, to imprisonment for a term not exceeding two years, to a fine or to both;
>
> (b) on summary conviction, to imprisonment for a term not exceeding 12 months, to a fine not exceeding the statutory maximum or to both.

(3) In the application of this section to Scotland or Northern Ireland, the reference in subsection (2)(b) to 12 months is to be read as a reference to 6 months.

87 Defences to liability under section 86

(1) A person (P) is not guilty of an offence under section 86 if —

> (a) at the time when P disclosed the information, he was or had been a protected person,
>
> (b) the information related only to arrangements made for the protection of P or for the protection of P and a person associated with him, and
>
> (c) at the time when P disclosed the information, it was not likely that its disclosure would endanger the safety of any person.

(2) A person (D) is not guilty of an offence under section 86 if —

> (a) D disclosed the information with the agreement of a person (P) who, at the time the information was disclosed, was or had been a protected person,
>
> (b) the information related only to arrangements made for the protection of P or for the protection of P and a person associated with him, and
>
> (c) at the time when D disclosed the information, it was not likely that its disclosure would endanger the safety of any person.

(3) A person is not guilty of an offence under section 86 if he disclosed the information for the purposes of safeguarding national security or for the purposes of the prevention, detection or investigation of crime.

(4) A person is not guilty of an offence under section 86 if —

> (a) at the time when he disclosed the information, he was a protection provider or involved in the making of arrangements under section 82(1) or in the implementation, variation or cancellation of such arrangements, and
>
> (b) he disclosed the information for the purposes of the making, implementation, variation or cancellation of such arrangements.

(5) The Secretary of State may by order make provision prescribing circumstances in which a person who discloses information as mentioned in section 86(1) is not guilty in England and Wales or in Northern Ireland of an offence under that section.

(6) The Scottish Ministers may by order make provision prescribing circumstances in which a person who discloses information as mentioned in section 86(1) is not guilty in Scotland of an offence under that section.

54

Serious Organised Crime and Police Act 2005 (c. 15)
Part 2 − Investigations, prosecutions, proceedings and proceeds of crime
Chapter 4 − Protection of witnesses and other persons

(7) If sufficient evidence is adduced to raise an issue with respect to a defence under or by virtue of this section, the court or jury must assume that the defence is satisfied unless the prosecution proves beyond reasonable doubt that it is not.

88 Offences of disclosing information relating to persons assuming new identity

(1) A person (P) commits an offence if −

    (a) P is or has been a protected person,

    (b) P assumed a new identity in pursuance of arrangements made under section 82(1),

    (c) P discloses information which indicates that he assumed, or might have assumed, a new identity, and

    (d) P knows or suspects that the information disclosed by him indicates that he assumed, or might have assumed, a new identity.

(2) A person (D) commits an offence if −

    (a) D discloses information which relates to a person (P) who is or has been a protected person,

    (b) P assumed a new identity in pursuance of arrangements made under section 82(1),

    (c) the information disclosed by D indicates that P assumed, or might have assumed, a new identity, and

    (d) D knows or suspects −

        (i) that P is or has been a protected person, and

        (ii) that the information disclosed by D indicates that P assumed, or might have assumed, a new identity.

(3) A person who commits an offence under this section is liable −

    (a) on conviction on indictment, to imprisonment for a term not exceeding two years, to a fine or to both;

    (b) on summary conviction, to imprisonment for a term not exceeding 12 months, to a fine not exceeding the statutory maximum or to both.

(4) In the application of this section to Scotland or Northern Ireland, the reference in subsection (3)(b) to 12 months is to be read as a reference to 6 months.

89 Defences to liability under section 88

(1) P is not guilty of an offence under section 88(1) if, at the time when he disclosed the information, it was not likely that its disclosure would endanger the safety of any person.

(2) D is not guilty of an offence under section 88(2) if −

    (a) D disclosed the information with the agreement of P, and

    (b) at the time when D disclosed the information, it was not likely that its disclosure would endanger the safety of any person.

(3) D is not guilty of an offence under section 88(2) if he disclosed the information for the purposes of safeguarding national security or for the purposes of the prevention, detection or investigation of crime.

(4) D is not guilty of an offence under section 88(2) if −

Serious Organised Crime and Police Act 2005 (c. 15)
Part 2 — Investigations, prosecutions, proceedings and proceeds of crime
Chapter 4 — Protection of witnesses and other persons

55

    (a)   at the time when he disclosed the information, he was a protection provider or involved in the making of arrangements under section 82(1) or in the implementation, variation or cancellation of such arrangements, and

    (b)   he disclosed the information for the purposes of the making, implementation, variation or cancellation of such arrangements.

(5)   The Secretary of State may by order make provision prescribing circumstances in which a person who discloses information as mentioned in subsection (1) or (2) of section 88 is not guilty in England and Wales or in Northern Ireland of an offence under that subsection.

(6)   The Scottish Ministers may by order make provision prescribing circumstances in which a person who discloses information as mentioned in subsection (1) or (2) of section 88 is not guilty in Scotland of an offence under that subsection.

(7)   If sufficient evidence is adduced to raise an issue with respect to a defence under or by virtue of this section, the court or jury must assume that the defence is satisfied unless the prosecution proves beyond reasonable doubt that it is not.

90   Protection from liability

(1)   This section applies if—

    (a)   arrangements are made for the protection of a person under section 82(1), and

    (b)   the protected person assumes a new identity in pursuance of the arrangements.

(2)   No proceedings (whether civil or criminal) may be brought against a person to whom this section applies in respect of the making by him of a false or misleading representation if the representation—

    (a)   relates to the protected person, and

    (b)   is made solely for the purpose of ensuring that the arrangements made for him to assume a new identity are, or continue to be, effective.

(3)   The persons to whom this section applies are—

    (a)   the protected person;

    (b)   a person who is associated with the protected person;

    (c)   a protection provider;

    (d)   a person involved in the making of arrangements under section 82(1) or in the implementation, variation or cancellation of such arrangements.

91   Transitional provision

(1)   This section applies to arrangements which were, at any time before the commencement of section 82, made by a protection provider, or any person acting with his authority, for the purpose of protecting a person of a description specified in Schedule 5.

(2)   If the following three conditions are satisfied, the arrangements are to be treated as having been made by the protection provider under section 82(1).

(3)   The first condition is that the protection provider could have made the arrangements under section 82(1) had it been in force at the time when the arrangements were made.

56
Serious Organised Crime and Police Act 2005 (c. 15)
Part 2 — Investigations, prosecutions, proceedings and proceeds of crime
Chapter 4 — Protection of witnesses and other persons

(4) The second condition is that the arrangements were in operation immediately before the commencement of section 82.

(5) The third condition is that the protection provider determines that it is appropriate to treat the arrangements as having been made under section 82(1).

(6) A determination under subsection (5) may be made at any time before the end of the period of six months beginning with the day on which section 82 comes into force.

(7) A protection provider must make a record of a determination under subsection (5).

(8) Subsection (9) applies if—
   (a) at any time before the commencement of section 82, arrangements were made by a person specified in subsection (11), or any person acting with the authority of such a person, for the purpose of protecting a person of a description specified in Schedule 5, and
   (b) functions in relation to the arrangements are, at any time before the end of the period of six months mentioned in subsection (6), exercisable by a protection provider.

(9) The provision made by subsections (1) to (7) applies in relation to the arrangements as if they had been made by the protection provider.

(10) Accordingly, if the three conditions mentioned in subsections (3) to (5) are satisfied in relation to the arrangements, they are to be treated, by virtue of subsection (2), as having been made by the protection provider under section 82(1).

(11) The persons specified in this subsection are—
   (a) the Director General of the National Criminal Intelligence Service;
   (b) the Director General of the National Crime Squad;
   (c) any of the Commissioners of Her Majesty's Customs and Excise.

92 Transitional provision: supplemental

(1) In this section—
   (a) "the arrangements" are arrangements which are treated as having been made by a protection provider by virtue of section 91(2), and
   (b) "the relevant date" is the date of the record made by the protection provider, in relation to the arrangements, in pursuance of section 91(7).

(2) A person does not commit an offence under section 86(1) by disclosing information relating to the arrangements unless the information is disclosed on or after the relevant date.

(3) But it is immaterial whether the information relates to something done in connection with the arrangements before or on or after the relevant date.

(4) A person does not commit an offence under section 88(1) or (2) by disclosing information relating to a person who assumed a new identity in pursuance of the arrangements unless the information is disclosed on or after the relevant date.

Serious Organised Crime and Police Act 2005 (c. 15)
Part 2 — Investigations, prosecutions, proceedings and proceeds of crime
Chapter 4 — Protection of witnesses and other persons

57

(5) But it is immaterial whether the person assumed a new identity before or on or after the relevant date.

(6) Section 90 applies in relation to a false or misleading representation relating to a person who assumed a new identity in pursuance of the arrangements only if the false or misleading representation is made on or after the relevant date.

(7) But it is immaterial whether the person assumed a new identity before or on or after the relevant date.

93 Provision of information

(1) This section applies if —
  (a) a protection provider makes arrangements under section 82(1), or
  (b) a protection provider determines under section 91(5) that it is appropriate to treat arrangements to which that section applies as having been made under section 82(1).

(2) The protection provider must inform the person to whom the arrangements relate of the provisions of this Chapter as they apply in relation to the arrangements.

(3) If the protection provider considers that the person would be unable to understand the information, by reason of his age or of any incapacity, the information must instead be given to a person who appears to the protection provider —
  (a) to be interested in the welfare of the person to whom the arrangements relate, and
  (b) to be the appropriate person to whom to give the information.

(4) If arrangements are made jointly under section 82(1) (by virtue of section 83), the protection providers involved in the arrangements must nominate one of those protection providers to perform the duties imposed by this section.

94 Interpretation of Chapter 4

(1) This section applies for the purposes of this Chapter.

(2) "Protection provider" is to be construed in accordance with section 82.

(3) A person is a protected person if —
  (a) arrangements have been made for his protection under subsection (1) of section 82, and
  (b) the arrangements have not been cancelled under subsection (2) of that section.

(4) A person is associated with another person if any of the following apply —
  (a) they are members of the same family;
  (b) they live in the same household;
  (c) they have lived in the same household.

(5) A person assumes a new identity if either or both of the following apply —
  (a) he becomes known by a different name;
  (b) he makes representations about his personal history or circumstances which are false or misleading.

58   Serious Organised Crime and Police Act 2005 (c. 15)
                    Part 2 — Investigations, prosecutions, proceedings and proceeds of crime
                                    Chapter 4 — Protection of witnesses and other persons

(6) A reference to a person who is a witness in legal proceedings includes a reference to a person who provides any information or any document or other thing which might be used in evidence in those proceedings or which (whether or not admissible as evidence in those proceedings) —

(a) might tend to confirm evidence which will or might be admitted in those proceedings,

(b) might be referred to in evidence given in those proceedings by another witness, or

(c) might be used as the basis for any cross examination in the course of those proceedings,

and a reference to a person who might be, or to a person who has been, a witness in legal proceedings is to be construed accordingly.

(7) A reference to a person who is a witness in legal proceedings does not include a reference to a person who is an accused person in criminal proceedings unless he is a witness for the prosecution and a reference to a person who might be, or to a person who has been, a witness in legal proceedings is to be construed accordingly.

(8) A reference to a person who is or has been a member of staff of an organisation includes a reference to a person who is or has been seconded to the organisation to serve as a member of its staff.

(9) "The Scottish Drug Enforcement Agency" and "the Director" of that Agency have the meanings given by section 42(2).

CHAPTER 5

INTERNATIONAL OBLIGATIONS

95   Enforcement of overseas forfeiture orders

In section 9 of the Criminal Justice (International Co-operation) Act 1990 (c. 5) (enforcement of overseas forfeiture orders), for subsection (6) (offences to which section applies) substitute —

"(6) This section applies to any offence that corresponds to or is similar to —

(a) an offence under the law of England and Wales;

(b) an offence under the law of Scotland; or

(c) an offence under the law of Northern Ireland."

96   Mutual assistance in freezing property or evidence

(1) The Secretary of State or the Scottish Ministers may by order make provision —

(a) for the purpose of implementing any obligation of the United Kingdom created or arising by or under the Decision or enabling any such obligation to be implemented,

(b) for the purpose of enabling any rights enjoyed or to be enjoyed by the United Kingdom under or by virtue of the Decision to be exercised, or

(c) for the purpose of dealing with matters arising out of or related to any such obligation or rights.

Serious Organised Crime and Police Act 2005 (c. 15)   59
Part 2 — Investigations, prosecutions, proceedings and proceeds of crime
Chapter 5 — International obligations

(2) In subsection (1) "the Decision" means Council Framework Decision 2003/577/JHA of 22 July 2003 on the execution in the European Union of orders freezing property or evidence.

(3) The provision that may be made under subsection (1) by the Secretary of State includes, subject to subsections (5) and (7), any provision (of any extent) that might be made by Act of Parliament.

(4) The provision that may be made under subsection (1) by the Scottish Ministers includes, subject to subsections (6) and (7), any provision that might be made by Act of the Scottish Parliament.

(5) The power conferred by subsection (1) on the Secretary of State does not include power to make provision that would be within the legislative competence of the Scottish Parliament if it were included in an Act of that Parliament.

(6) The power conferred by subsection (1) on the Scottish Ministers is limited to the making of provision that would be within the legislative competence of the Scottish Parliament if it were included in an Act of that Parliament.

(7) The powers conferred by subsection (1) do not include power —
   (a) to make any provision imposing or increasing taxation,
   (b) to make any provision taking effect from a date earlier than that of the making of the instrument containing the provision,
   (c) to confer any power to legislate by means of orders, rules, regulations or other subordinate instrument, other than rules of procedure for a court or tribunal, or
   (d) to create criminal offences.

(8) Subsection (7)(c) does not preclude —
   (a) the modification of a power to legislate conferred otherwise than under subsection (1), or
   (b) the extension of any such power to purposes of the like nature as those for which it was conferred,
   and a power to give directions as to matters of administration is not to be regarded as a power to legislate within the meaning of subsection (7)(c).

CHAPTER 6

PROCEEDS OF CRIME

97 Confiscation orders by magistrates' courts

(1) The Secretary of State may by order make such provision as he considers appropriate for or in connection with enabling confiscation orders under —
   (a) Part 2 of the Proceeds of Crime Act 2002 (c. 29) (confiscation: England and Wales), or
   (b) Part 4 of that Act (confiscation: Northern Ireland),
   to be made by magistrates' courts in England and Wales or Northern Ireland (as the case may be).

(2) But an order under subsection (1) may not enable such a confiscation order to be made by any magistrates' court in respect of an amount exceeding £10,000.

60   *Serious Organised Crime and Police Act 2005 (c. 15)*
Part 2 — Investigations, prosecutions, proceedings and proceeds of crime
Chapter 6 — Proceeds of crime

(3) An order under subsection (1) may amend, repeal, revoke or otherwise modify any provision of Part 2 or 4 of the 2002 Act or any other enactment relating to, or to things done under or for the purposes of, either (or any provision) of those Parts.

98   Civil recovery: freezing orders

(1) In the Proceeds of Crime Act 2002 (c. 29), after section 245 insert—

"Property freezing orders (England and Wales and Northern Ireland)

245A Application for property freezing order

(1) Where the enforcement authority may take proceedings for a recovery order in the High Court, the authority may apply to the court for a property freezing order (whether before or after starting the proceedings).

(2) A property freezing order is an order that—

    (a) specifies or describes the property to which it applies, and

    (b) subject to any exclusions (see section 245C(1)(b) and (2)), prohibits any person to whose property the order applies from in any way dealing with the property.

(3) An application for a property freezing order may be made without notice if the circumstances are such that notice of the application would prejudice any right of the enforcement authority to obtain a recovery order in respect of any property.

(4) The court may make a property freezing order on an application if it is satisfied that the condition in subsection (5) is met and, where applicable, that the condition in subsection (6) is met.

(5) The first condition is that there is a good arguable case—

    (a) that the property to which the application for the order relates is or includes recoverable property, and

    (b) that, if any of it is not recoverable property, it is associated property.

(6) The second condition is that, if—

    (a) the property to which the application for the order relates includes property alleged to be associated property, and

    (b) the enforcement authority has not established the identity of the person who holds it,

the authority has taken all reasonable steps to do so.

245B Variation and setting aside of order

(1) The court may at any time vary or set aside a property freezing order.

(2) If the court makes an interim receiving order that applies to all of the property to which a property freezing order applies, it must set aside the property freezing order.

(3) If the court makes an interim receiving order that applies to some but not all of the property to which a property freezing order applies, it

Serious Organised Crime and Police Act 2005 (c. 15)
Part 2 — Investigations, prosecutions, proceedings and proceeds of crime
Chapter 6 — Proceeds of crime

61

must vary the property freezing order so as to exclude any property to which the interim receiving order applies.

(4) If the court decides that any property to which a property freezing order applies is neither recoverable property nor associated property, it must vary the order so as to exclude the property.

(5) Before exercising power under this Chapter to vary or set aside a property freezing order, the court must (as well as giving the parties to the proceedings an opportunity to be heard) give such an opportunity to any person who may be affected by its decision.

(6) Subsection (5) does not apply where the court is acting as required by subsection (2) or (3).

245C Exclusions

(1) The power to vary a property freezing order includes (in particular) power to make exclusions as follows —
  (a) power to exclude property from the order, and
  (b) power, otherwise than by excluding property from the order, to make exclusions from the prohibition on dealing with the property to which the order applies.

(2) Exclusions from the prohibition on dealing with the property to which the order applies (other than exclusions of property from the order) may also be made when the order is made.

(3) An exclusion may, in particular, make provision for the purpose of enabling any person —
  (a) to meet his reasonable living expenses, or
  (b) to carry on any trade, business, profession or occupation.

(4) An exclusion may be made subject to conditions.

(5) Where the court exercises the power to make an exclusion for the purpose of enabling a person to meet legal expenses that he has incurred, or may incur, in respect of proceedings under this Part, it must ensure that the exclusion —
  (a) is limited to reasonable legal expenses that the person has reasonably incurred or that he reasonably incurs,
  (b) specifies the total amount that may be released for legal expenses in pursuance of the exclusion, and
  (c) is made subject to the required conditions (see section 286A) in addition to any conditions imposed under subsection (4).

(6) The court, in deciding whether to make an exclusion for the purpose of enabling a person to meet legal expenses of his in respect of proceedings under this Part —
  (a) must have regard (in particular) to the desirability of the person being represented in any proceedings under this Part in which he is a participant, and
  (b) must, where the person is the respondent, disregard the possibility that legal representation of the person in any such proceedings might, were an exclusion not made, be funded by the Legal Services Commission or the Northern Ireland Legal Services Commission.

62   *Serious Organised Crime and Police Act 2005 (c. 15)*
Part 2 — Investigations, prosecutions, proceedings and proceeds of crime
Chapter 6 — Proceeds of crime

(7)   If excluded property is not specified in the order it must be described in the order in general terms.

(8)   The power to make exclusions must, subject to subsection (6), be exercised with a view to ensuring, so far as practicable, that the satisfaction of any right of the enforcement authority to recover the property obtained through unlawful conduct is not unduly prejudiced.

(9)   Subsection (8) does not apply where the court is acting as required by section 245B(3) or (4).

245D Restriction on proceedings and remedies

(1)   While a property freezing order has effect —
   (a)   the court may stay any action, execution or other legal process in respect of the property to which the order applies, and
   (b)   no distress may be levied against the property to which the order applies except with the leave of the court and subject to any terms the court may impose.

(2)   If a court (whether the High Court or any other court) in which proceedings are pending in respect of any property is satisfied that a property freezing order has been applied for or made in respect of the property, it may either stay the proceedings or allow them to continue on any terms it thinks fit.

(3)   If a property freezing order applies to a tenancy of any premises, no landlord or other person to whom rent is payable may exercise the right of forfeiture by peaceable re-entry in relation to the premises in respect of any failure by the tenant to comply with any term or condition of the tenancy, except with the leave of the court and subject to any terms the court may impose.

(4)   Before exercising any power conferred by this section, the court must (as well as giving the parties to any of the proceedings concerned an opportunity to be heard) give such an opportunity to any person who may be affected by the court's decision."

(2) In the Proceeds of Crime Act 2002 (c. 29), after section 255 insert —

"Prohibitory property orders (Scotland)

255A Application for prohibitory property order

(1)   Where the enforcement authority may take proceedings for a recovery order in the Court of Session, the authority may apply to the court for a prohibitory property order (whether before or after starting the proceedings).

(2)   A prohibitory property order is an order that —
   (a)   specifies or describes the property to which it applies, and
   (b)   subject to any exclusions (see section 255C(1)(b) and (2)), prohibits any person to whose property the order applies from in any way dealing with the property.

(3)   An application for a prohibitory property order may be made without notice if the circumstances are such that notice of the application would

Serious Organised Crime and Police Act 2005 (c. 15)
Part 2 – Investigations, prosecutions, proceedings and proceeds of crime
Chapter 6 – Proceeds of crime

63

prejudice any right of the enforcement authority to obtain a recovery order in respect of any property.

(4) The court may make a prohibitory property order on an application if it is satisfied that the condition in subsection (5) is met and, where applicable, that the condition in subsection (6) is met.

(5) The first condition is that there is a good arguable case—

    (a) that the property to which the application for the order relates is or includes recoverable property, and

    (b) that, if any of it is not recoverable property, it is associated property.

(6) The second condition is that, if—

    (a) the property to which the application for the order relates includes property alleged to be associated property, and

    (b) the enforcement authority has not established the identity of the person who holds it,

the authority has taken all reasonable steps to do so.

255B Variation and recall of prohibitory property order

(1) The court may at any time vary or recall a prohibitory property order.

(2) If the court makes an interim administration order that applies to all of the property to which a prohibitory property order applies, it must recall the prohibitory property order.

(3) If the court makes an interim administration order that applies to some but not all of the property to which a prohibitory property order applies, it must vary the prohibitory property order so as to exclude any property to which the interim administration order applies.

(4) If the court decides that any property to which a prohibitory property order applies is neither recoverable property nor associated property, it must vary the order so as to exclude the property.

(5) Before exercising power under this Chapter to vary or recall a prohibitory property order, the court must (as well as giving the parties to the proceedings an opportunity to be heard) give such an opportunity to any person who may be affected by its decision.

(6) Subsection (5) does not apply where the court is acting as required by subsection (2) or (3).

255C Exclusions

(1) The power to vary a prohibitory property order includes (in particular) power to make exclusions as follows—

    (a) power to exclude property from the order, and

    (b) power, otherwise than by excluding property from the order, to make exclusions from the prohibition on dealing with the property to which the order applies.

(2) Exclusions from the prohibition on dealing with the property to which the order applies (other than exclusions of property from the order) may also be made when the order is made.

64

Serious Organised Crime and Police Act 2005 (c. 15)
Part 2 — Investigations, prosecutions, proceedings and proceeds of crime
Chapter 6 — Proceeds of crime

(3) An exclusion may, in particular, make provision for the purpose of enabling any person—
   (a) to meet his reasonable living expenses, or
   (b) to carry on any trade, business, profession or occupation.

(4) An exclusion may be made subject to conditions.

(5) An exclusion may not be made for the purpose of enabling any person to meet any legal expenses in respect of proceedings under this Part.

(6) If excluded property is not specified in the order it must be described in the order in general terms.

(7) The power to make exclusions must be exercised with a view to ensuring, so far as practicable, that the satisfaction of any right of the enforcement authority to recover the property obtained through unlawful conduct is not unduly prejudiced.

(8) Subsection (7) does not apply where the court is acting as required by section 255B(3) or (4).

255D Restriction on proceedings and remedies

(1) While a prohibitory property order has effect the court may sist any action, execution or other legal process in respect of the property to which the order applies.

(2) If a court (whether the Court of Session or any other court) in which proceedings are pending in respect of any property is satisfied that a prohibitory property order has been applied for or made in respect of the property, it may either sist the proceedings or allow them to continue on any terms it thinks fit.

(3) Before exercising any power conferred by this section, the court must (as well as giving the parties to any of the proceedings concerned an opportunity to be heard) give such an opportunity to any person who may be affected by the court's decision.

255E Arrestment of property affected by prohibitory property order

(1) On the application of the enforcement authority the Court of Session may, in relation to moveable recoverable property to which a prohibitory property order applies (whether generally or to such of it as is specified in the application), grant warrant for arrestment.

(2) An application under subsection (1) may be made at the same time as the application for the prohibitory property order or at any time thereafter.

(3) Such a warrant for arrestment may be granted only if the property would be arrestable if the person entitled to it were a debtor.

(4) A warrant under subsection (1) has effect as if granted on the dependence of an action for debt at the instance of the enforcement authority against the person and may be executed, recalled, loosed or restricted accordingly.

(5) An arrestment executed under this section ceases to have effect when, or in so far as, the prohibitory property order ceases to apply in respect

Serious Organised Crime and Police Act 2005 (c. 15)
Part 2 — Investigations, prosecutions, proceedings and proceeds of crime
Chapter 6 — Proceeds of crime

65

of the property in relation to which the warrant for arrestment was granted.

(6) If an arrestment ceases to have effect to any extent by virtue of subsection (5) the enforcement authority must apply to the Court of Session for an order recalling or, as the case may be, restricting the arrestment.

255F Inhibition of property affected by prohibitory property order

(1) On the application of the enforcement authority, the Court of Session may, in relation to the property mentioned in subsection (2), grant warrant for inhibition against any person specified in a prohibitory property order.

(2) That property is heritable property situated in Scotland to which the prohibitory property order applies (whether generally or to such of it as is specified in the application).

(3) The warrant for inhibition—

  (a) has effect as if granted on the dependence of an action for debt by the enforcement authority against the person and may be executed, recalled, loosed or restricted accordingly, and

  (b) has the effect of letters of inhibition and must forthwith be registered by the enforcement authority in the register of inhibitions and adjudications.

(4) Section 155 of the Titles to Land Consolidation (Scotland) Act 1868 (c. 101) (effective date of inhibition) applies in relation to an inhibition for which warrant is granted under subsection (1) as it applies to an inhibition by separate letters or contained in a summons.

(5) An inhibition executed under this section ceases to have effect when, or in so far as, the prohibitory property order ceases to apply in respect of the property in relation to which the warrant for inhibition was granted.

(6) If an inhibition ceases to have effect to any extent by virtue of subsection (5) the enforcement authority must—

  (a) apply for the recall or, as the case may be, the restriction of the inhibition, and

  (b) ensure that the recall or restriction is reflected in the register of inhibitions and adjudications."

99 Civil recovery: interim receivers' expenses etc.

(1) The Proceeds of Crime Act 2002 (c. 29) is amended as follows.

(2) In section 280 (civil recovery orders: applying realised proceeds), after subsection (2) insert—

  "(3) The Director may apply a sum received by him under subsection (2) in making payment of the remuneration and expenses of—

    (a) the trustee, or

    (b) any interim receiver appointed in, or in anticipation of, the proceedings for the recovery order.

66   *Serious Organised Crime and Police Act 2005 (c. 15)*
                  Part 2 − Investigations, prosecutions, proceedings and proceeds of crime
                                              Chapter 6 − Proceeds of crime

(4)   Subsection (3)(a) does not apply in relation to the remuneration of the trustee if the trustee is a member of the staff of the Agency."

(3)   In section 284 (payment of interim administrator or trustee (Scotland)) −

   (a)   the existing words become subsection (1), and

   (b)   after that subsection insert −

      "(2)   The Scottish Ministers may apply a sum received by them under section 280(2) in making payment of such fees or expenses.

      (3)   Subsection (2) does not apply in relation to the fees of a trustee for civil recovery if the trustee is a member of their staff."

(4)   In paragraph 5 of Schedule 1 (finances of the Assets Recovery Agency), after sub-paragraph (1) (paragraph (b) of which provides for the expenses of the Director and staff of the Agency to be paid out of money provided by Parliament) insert −

      "(1A)   Sub-paragraph (1)(b) has effect subject to anything in this Act."

100   Detention of seized cash: meaning of "48 hours"

(1)   In the Proceeds of Crime Act 2002 (c. 29), Chapter 3 of Part 5 (civil recovery of cash in summary proceedings) is amended as follows.

(2)   In section 295 (detention of seized cash, initially for 48 hours), after subsection (1) insert −

   "(1A)   The period of 48 hours mentioned in subsection (1) is to be calculated in accordance with subsection (1B).

   (1B)   In calculating a period of 48 hours in accordance with this subsection, no account shall be taken of −
      (a)   any Saturday or Sunday,
      (b)   Christmas Day,
      (c)   Good Friday,
      (d)   any day that is a bank holiday under the Banking and Financial Dealings Act 1971 in the part of the United Kingdom within which the cash is seized, or
      (e)   any day prescribed under section 8(2) of the Criminal Procedure (Scotland) Act 1995 as a court holiday in a sheriff court in the sheriff court district within which the cash is seized."

(3)   In sections 290(6), 296(1) and 302(2), after "48 hours" insert "(calculated in accordance with section 295(1B))".

101   Appeal in proceedings for forfeiture of cash

(1)   For section 299 of the Proceeds of Crime Act 2002 (appeal against forfeiture of

Serious Organised Crime and Police Act 2005 (c. 15)
Part 2 – Investigations, prosecutions, proceedings and proceeds of crime
Chapter 6 – Proceeds of crime

67

cash) substitute—

"299 Appeal against decision under section 298

(1) Any party to proceedings for an order for the forfeiture of cash under section 298 who is aggrieved by an order under that section or by the decision of the court not to make such an order may appeal—

    (a) in relation to England and Wales, to the Crown Court;

    (b) in relation to Scotland, to the Sheriff Principal;

    (c) in relation to Northern Ireland, to a county court.

(2) An appeal under subsection (1) must be made before the end of the period of 30 days starting with the day on which the court makes the order or decision.

(3) The court hearing the appeal may make any order it thinks appropriate.

(4) If the court upholds an appeal against an order forfeiting the cash, it may order the release of the cash."

(2) This section does not apply to a decision of a court not to order the forfeiture of cash under section 298 of that Act taken before this section comes into force.

102 Money laundering: defence where overseas conduct is legal under local law

(1) In the Proceeds of Crime Act 2002 (c. 29), Part 7 (money laundering) is amended as follows.

(2) In section 327 (concealing etc.), after subsection (2) insert—

    "(2A) Nor does a person commit an offence under subsection (1) if—

        (a) he knows, or believes on reasonable grounds, that the relevant criminal conduct occurred in a particular country or territory outside the United Kingdom, and

        (b) the relevant criminal conduct—

            (i) was not, at the time it occurred, unlawful under the criminal law then applying in that country or territory, and

            (ii) is not of a description prescribed by an order made by the Secretary of State.

    (2B) In subsection (2A) "the relevant criminal conduct" is the criminal conduct by reference to which the property concerned is criminal property."

(3) In section 328 (arrangements), after subsection (2) insert—

    "(3) Nor does a person commit an offence under subsection (1) if—

        (a) he knows, or believes on reasonable grounds, that the relevant criminal conduct occurred in a particular country or territory outside the United Kingdom, and

        (b) the relevant criminal conduct—

            (i) was not, at the time it occurred, unlawful under the criminal law then applying in that country or territory, and

            (ii) is not of a description prescribed by an order made by the Secretary of State.

68

Serious Organised Crime and Police Act 2005 (c. 15)
Part 2 – Investigations, prosecutions, proceedings and proceeds of crime
Chapter 6 – Proceeds of crime

(4)   In subsection (3) "the relevant criminal conduct" is the criminal conduct by reference to which the property concerned is criminal property."

(4)   In section 329 (acquisition, use and possession), after subsection (2) insert—

"(2A)   Nor does a person commit an offence under subsection (1) if—
  (a)   he knows, or believes on reasonable grounds, that the relevant criminal conduct occurred in a particular country or territory outside the United Kingdom, and
  (b)   the relevant criminal conduct—
      (i)   was not, at the time it occurred, unlawful under the criminal law then applying in that country or territory, and
      (ii)   is not of a description prescribed by an order made by the Secretary of State.

(2B)   In subsection (2A) "the relevant criminal conduct" is the criminal conduct by reference to which the property concerned is criminal property."

(5)   In section 330 (failure to disclose: regulated sector), after subsection (7) insert—

"(7A)   Nor does a person commit an offence under this section if—
  (a)   he knows, or believes on reasonable grounds, that the money laundering is occurring in a particular country or territory outside the United Kingdom, and
  (b)   the money laundering—
      (i)   is not unlawful under the criminal law applying in that country or territory, and
      (ii)   is not of a description prescribed in an order made by the Secretary of State."

(6)   In section 331 (failure to disclose: nominated officers in the regulated sector), after subsection (6) insert—

"(6A)   Nor does a person commit an offence under this section if—
  (a)   he knows, or believes on reasonable grounds, that the money laundering is occurring in a particular country or territory outside the United Kingdom, and
  (b)   the money laundering—
      (i)   is not unlawful under the criminal law applying in that country or territory, and
      (ii)   is not of a description prescribed in an order made by the Secretary of State."

(7)   In section 332 (failure to disclose: other nominated officers), after subsection (6) insert—

"(7)   Nor does a person commit an offence under this section if—
  (a)   he knows, or believes on reasonable grounds, that the money laundering is occurring in a particular country or territory outside the United Kingdom, and
  (b)   the money laundering—
      (i)   is not unlawful under the criminal law applying in that country or territory, and

Serious Organised Crime and Police Act 2005 (c. 15)
Part 2 – Investigations, prosecutions, proceedings and proceeds of crime
Chapter 6 – Proceeds of crime

69

       (ii) is not of a description prescribed in an order made by the Secretary of State."

103 Money laundering: threshold amounts

(1) The Proceeds of Crime Act 2002 (c. 29) is amended as follows.

(2) In section 327 (concealing etc.), after subsection (2B) (which is inserted by section 102 of this Act) insert —

"(2C) A deposit-taking body that does an act mentioned in paragraph (c) or (d) of subsection (1) does not commit an offence under that subsection if —

    (a) it does the act in operating an account maintained with it, and

    (b) the value of the criminal property concerned is less than the threshold amount determined under section 339A for the act."

(3) In section 328 (arrangements), after subsection (4) (which is inserted by section 102 of this Act) insert —

"(5) A deposit-taking body that does an act mentioned in subsection (1) does not commit an offence under that subsection if —

    (a) it does the act in operating an account maintained with it, and

    (b) the arrangement facilitates the acquisition, retention, use or control of criminal property of a value that is less than the threshold amount determined under section 339A for the act."

(4) In section 329 (acquisition, use and possession), after subsection (2B) (which is inserted by section 102 of this Act) insert —

"(2C) A deposit-taking body that does an act mentioned in subsection (1) does not commit an offence under that subsection if —

    (a) it does the act in operating an account maintained with it, and

    (b) the value of the criminal property concerned is less than the threshold amount determined under section 339A for the act."

(5) In Part 7 (money laundering), after section 339 insert —

"Threshold amounts

339A Threshold amounts

(1) This section applies for the purposes of sections 327(2C), 328(5) and 329(2C).

(2) The threshold amount for acts done by a deposit-taking body in operating an account is £250 unless a higher amount is specified under the following provisions of this section (in which event it is that higher amount).

(3) An officer of Revenue and Customs, or a constable, may specify the threshold amount for acts done by a deposit-taking body in operating an account —

    (a) when he gives consent, or gives notice refusing consent, to the deposit-taking body's doing of an act mentioned in section 327(1), 328(1) or 329(1) in opening, or operating, the account or a related account, or

70   *Serious Organised Crime and Police Act 2005 (c. 15)*
Part 2 − Investigations, prosecutions, proceedings and proceeds of crime
Chapter 6 − Proceeds of crime

(b)   on a request from the deposit-taking body.

(4)   Where the threshold amount for acts done in operating an account is specified under subsection (3) or this subsection, an officer of Revenue and Customs, or a constable, may vary the amount (whether on a request from the deposit-taking body or otherwise) by specifying a different amount.

(5)   Different threshold amounts may be specified under subsections (3) and (4) for different acts done in operating the same account.

(6)   The amount specified under subsection (3) or (4) as the threshold amount for acts done in operating an account must, when specified, not be less than the amount specified in subsection (2).

(7)   The Secretary of State may by order vary the amount for the time being specified in subsection (2).

(8)   For the purposes of this section, an account is related to another if each is maintained with the same deposit-taking body and there is a person who, in relation to each account, is the person or one of the persons entitled to instruct the body as respects the operation of the account."

(6)   In section 340 (interpretation of Part 7), after subsection (13) insert—

"(14)   "Deposit-taking body" means—
     (a)   a business which engages in the activity of accepting deposits, or
     (b)   the National Savings Bank."

(7)   In section 459(4)(a) and (6)(a) (provision for certain orders to be subject to affirmative procedure), after "309," insert "339A(7),".

104   Money laundering: disclosures to identify persons and property

(1)   In the Proceeds of Crime Act 2002 (c. 29), Part 7 (money laundering) is amended as follows.

(2)   In section 330(1) (regulated sector: failure to disclose: offence committed if three conditions satisfied), for "each of the following three conditions is satisfied" substitute "the conditions in subsections (2) to (4) are satisfied".

(3)   For section 330(4) to (6) (the required disclosure) substitute—

"(3A)   The third condition is—
     (a)   that he can identify the other person mentioned in subsection (2) or the whereabouts of any of the laundered property, or
     (b)   that he believes, or it is reasonable to expect him to believe, that the information or other matter mentioned in subsection (3) will or may assist in identifying that other person or the whereabouts of any of the laundered property.

(4)   The fourth condition is that he does not make the required disclosure to—
     (a)   a nominated officer, or
     (b)   a person authorised for the purposes of this Part by the Director General of the Serious Organised Crime Agency,

Serious Organised Crime and Police Act 2005 (c. 15)
Part 2 — Investigations, prosecutions, proceedings and proceeds of crime
Chapter 6 — Proceeds of crime

71

as soon as is practicable after the information or other matter mentioned in subsection (3) comes to him.

(5) The required disclosure is a disclosure of —

    (a) the identity of the other person mentioned in subsection (2), if he knows it,

    (b) the whereabouts of the laundered property, so far as he knows it, and

    (c) the information or other matter mentioned in subsection (3).

(5A) The laundered property is the property forming the subject-matter of the money laundering that he knows or suspects, or has reasonable grounds for knowing or suspecting, that other person to be engaged in.

(6) But he does not commit an offence under this section if —

    (a) he has a reasonable excuse for not making the required disclosure,

    (b) he is a professional legal adviser and —

        (i) if he knows either of the things mentioned in subsection (5)(a) and (b), he knows the thing because of information or other matter that came to him in privileged circumstances, or

        (ii) the information or other matter mentioned in subsection (3) came to him in privileged circumstances, or

    (c) subsection (7) applies to him."

(4) For section 331(4) to (6) (failure to disclose: nominated officers in the regulated sector: the required disclosure) substitute —

"(3A) The third condition is —

    (a) that he knows the identity of the other person mentioned in subsection (2), or the whereabouts of any of the laundered property, in consequence of a disclosure made under section 330,

    (b) that that other person, or the whereabouts of any of the laundered property, can be identified from the information or other matter mentioned in subsection (3), or

    (c) that he believes, or it is reasonable to expect him to believe, that the information or other matter will or may assist in identifying that other person or the whereabouts of any of the laundered property.

(4) The fourth condition is that he does not make the required disclosure to a person authorised for the purposes of this Part by the Director General of the Serious Organised Crime Agency as soon as is practicable after the information or other matter mentioned in subsection (3) comes to him.

(5) The required disclosure is a disclosure of —

    (a) the identity of the other person mentioned in subsection (2), if disclosed to him under section 330,

    (b) the whereabouts of the laundered property, so far as disclosed to him under section 330, and

    (c) the information or other matter mentioned in subsection (3).

72

Serious Organised Crime and Police Act 2005 (c. 15)
Part 2 — Investigations, prosecutions, proceedings and proceeds of crime
Chapter 6 — Proceeds of crime

(5A) The laundered property is the property forming the subject-matter of the money laundering that he knows or suspects, or has reasonable grounds for knowing or suspecting, that other person to be engaged in.

(6) But he does not commit an offence under this section if he has a reasonable excuse for not making the required disclosure."

(5) In section 332(3) (failure to disclose: other nominated officers: the second condition), for "section 337 or 338" substitute "the applicable section".

(6) For section 332(4) to (6) (the required disclosure) substitute—

"(3A) The third condition is—

  (a) that he knows the identity of the other person mentioned in subsection (2), or the whereabouts of any of the laundered property, in consequence of a disclosure made under the applicable section,

  (b) that that other person, or the whereabouts of any of the laundered property, can be identified from the information or other matter mentioned in subsection (3), or

  (c) that he believes, or it is reasonable to expect him to believe, that the information or other matter will or may assist in identifying that other person or the whereabouts of any of the laundered property.

(4) The fourth condition is that he does not make the required disclosure to a person authorised for the purposes of this Part by the Director General of the Serious Organised Crime Agency as soon as is practicable after the information or other matter mentioned in subsection (3) comes to him.

(5) The required disclosure is a disclosure of—

  (a) the identity of the other person mentioned in subsection (2), if disclosed to him under the applicable section,

  (b) the whereabouts of the laundered property, so far as disclosed to him under the applicable section, and

  (c) the information or other matter mentioned in subsection (3).

(5A) The laundered property is the property forming the subject-matter of the money laundering that he knows or suspects that other person to be engaged in.

(5B) The applicable section is section 337 or, as the case may be, section 338.

(6) But he does not commit an offence under this section if he has a reasonable excuse for not making the required disclosure."

(7) In section 337 (protected disclosures), after subsection (4) insert—

"(4A) Where a disclosure consists of a disclosure protected under subsection (1) and a disclosure of either or both of—

  (a) the identity of the other person mentioned in subsection (3), and

  (b) the whereabouts of property forming the subject-matter of the money laundering that the discloser knows or suspects, or has reasonable grounds for knowing or suspecting, that other person to be engaged in,

Serious Organised Crime and Police Act 2005 (c. 15)
Part 2 – Investigations, prosecutions, proceedings and proceeds of crime
Chapter 6 – Proceeds of crime

73

the disclosure of the thing mentioned in paragraph (a) or (b) (as well as the disclosure protected under subsection (1)) is not to be taken to breach any restriction on the disclosure of information (however imposed)."

105 Money laundering: form and manner of disclosures

(1) In the Proceeds of Crime Act 2002 (c. 29), Part 7 (money laundering) is amended as follows.

(2) In each of sections 330(9)(b), 337(5)(b) and 338(5)(b) (disclosure to nominated officer is ineffective if employer's procedures not followed), omit "and in accordance with the procedure established by the employer for the purpose".

(3) In section 334 (penalties), after subsection (2) insert—

"(3) A person guilty of an offence under section 339(1A) is liable on summary conviction to a fine not exceeding level 5 on the standard scale."

(4) In section 338(1) (authorised disclosures), omit paragraph (b) (disclosure must be made in prescribed form and manner) but not the "and" at the end.

(5) In section 339 (form and manner of disclosures), for subsections (2) and (3) substitute—

"(1A) A person commits an offence if he makes a disclosure under section 330, 331, 332 or 338 otherwise than in the form prescribed under subsection (1) or otherwise than in the manner so prescribed.

(1B) But a person does not commit an offence under subsection (1A) if he has a reasonable excuse for making the disclosure otherwise than in the form prescribed under subsection (1) or (as the case may be) otherwise than in the manner so prescribed.

(2) The power under subsection (1) to prescribe the form in which a disclosure must be made includes power to provide for the form to include a request to a person making a disclosure that the person provide information specified or described in the form if he has not provided it in making the disclosure.

(3) Where under subsection (2) a request is included in a form prescribed under subsection (1), the form must—
   (a) state that there is no obligation to comply with the request, and
   (b) explain the protection conferred by subsection (4) on a person who complies with the request."

106 Money laundering: miscellaneous amendments

(1) In the Proceeds of Crime Act 2002, Part 7 (money laundering) is amended as follows.

(2) In section 330 (regulated sector: failure to disclose), after subsection (9) insert—

"(9A) But a disclosure which satisfies paragraphs (a) and (b) of subsection (9) is not to be taken as a disclosure to a nominated officer if the person making the disclosure—
   (a) is a professional legal adviser,

74   *Serious Organised Crime and Police Act 2005 (c. 15)*
Part 2 — Investigations, prosecutions, proceedings and proceeds of crime
Chapter 6 — Proceeds of crime

   (b) makes it for the purpose of obtaining advice about making a disclosure under this section, and

   (c) does not intend it to be a disclosure under this section."

(3) In section 337(5)(a) (disclosure to person nominated to receive disclosures under section 337), after "disclosures under" insert "section 330 or".

(4) In section 338(1)(c) (first or second condition must be satisfied for disclosure to be authorised), for "or second" substitute ", second or third".

(5) In section 338 (authorised disclosures), after subsection (2) insert —

  "(2A) The second condition is that —

   (a) the disclosure is made while the alleged offender is doing the prohibited act,

   (b) he began to do the act at a time when, because he did not then know or suspect that the property constituted or represented a person's benefit from criminal conduct, the act was not a prohibited act, and

   (c) the disclosure is made on his own initiative and as soon as is practicable after he first knows or suspects that the property constitutes or represents a person's benefit from criminal conduct."

(6) In section 338(3) (the second condition), for "second" substitute "third".

107 Money laundering offences

(1) The Proceeds of Crime Act 2002 (c. 29) is amended as follows.

(2) In section 364 (meaning of customer information) in subsection (5) —
  (a) after paragraph (a) insert —
    "(aa) constitutes an offence specified in section 415(1A) of this Act,";
  (b) in paragraph (b) after "paragraph (a)" insert "or (aa)".

(3) In section 398 (meaning of customer information: Scotland) in subsection (5) —
  (a) after paragraph (a) insert —
    "(aa) constitutes an offence specified in section 415(1A) of this Act,";
  (b) in paragraph (b) after "paragraph (a)" insert "or (aa)".

(4) In section 415 (money laundering offences) after subsection (1) insert —

  "(1A) Each of the following is a money laundering offence —
   (a) an offence under section 93A, 93B or 93C of the Criminal Justice Act 1988;
   (b) an offence under section 49, 50 or 51 of the Drug Trafficking Act 1994;
   (c) an offence under section 37 or 38 of the Criminal Law (Consolidation) (Scotland) Act 1995;
   (d) an offence under article 45, 46 or 47 of the Proceeds of Crime (Northern Ireland) Order 1996."

Serious Organised Crime and Police Act 2005 (c. 15)
Part 2 – Investigations, prosecutions, proceedings and proceeds of crime
Chapter 6 – Proceeds of crime

75

108 **International co-operation**

(1) Part 11 of the Proceeds of Crime Act 2002 (c. 29) (co-operation) is amended as follows.

(2) In section 444 (external requests and orders), for subsection (3)(a) (Order under the section may include provision about the functions of the Secretary of State, the Lord Advocate, the Scottish Ministers and the Director of the Assets Recovery Agency) substitute —

"(a) provision about the functions of any of the listed persons in relation to external requests and orders;".

(3) In that section, after subsection (3) insert —

"(4) For the purposes of subsection (3)(a) "the listed persons" are —
 (a) the Secretary of State;
 (b) the Lord Advocate;
 (c) the Scottish Ministers;
 (d) the Director;
 (e) the Director of Public Prosecutions;
 (f) the Director of Public Prosecutions for Northern Ireland;
 (g) the Director of the Serious Fraud Office; and
 (h) the Director of Revenue and Customs Prosecutions."

(4) In section 447(3) (meaning of "external investigation"), after paragraph (a) insert —

"(aa) the extent or whereabouts of property obtained as a result of or in connection with criminal conduct, or".

109 **Minor and consequential amendments relating to Chapter 6**

Schedule 6, which contains minor and consequential amendments relating to provisions of this Chapter, has effect.

PART 3

POLICE POWERS ETC.

Powers of arrest

110 **Powers of arrest**

(1) For section 24 of PACE (arrest without warrant for arrestable offences) substitute —

"24 **Arrest without warrant: constables**

(1) A constable may arrest without a warrant —
 (a) anyone who is about to commit an offence;
 (b) anyone who is in the act of committing an offence;
 (c) anyone whom he has reasonable grounds for suspecting to be about to commit an offence;
 (d) anyone whom he has reasonable grounds for suspecting to be committing an offence.

(2)   If a constable has reasonable grounds for suspecting that an offence has been committed, he may arrest without a warrant anyone whom he has reasonable grounds to suspect of being guilty of it.

(3)   If an offence has been committed, a constable may arrest without a warrant—

    (a)   anyone who is guilty of the offence;

    (b)   anyone whom he has reasonable grounds for suspecting to be guilty of it.

(4)   But the power of summary arrest conferred by subsection (1), (2) or (3) is exercisable only if the constable has reasonable grounds for believing that for any of the reasons mentioned in subsection (5) it is necessary to arrest the person in question.

(5)   The reasons are—

    (a)   to enable the name of the person in question to be ascertained (in the case where the constable does not know, and cannot readily ascertain, the person's name, or has reasonable grounds for doubting whether a name given by the person as his name is his real name);

    (b)   correspondingly as regards the person's address;

    (c)   to prevent the person in question—

        (i)   causing physical injury to himself or any other person;

        (ii)   suffering physical injury;

        (iii)   causing loss of or damage to property;

        (iv)   committing an offence against public decency (subject to subsection (6)); or

        (v)   causing an unlawful obstruction of the highway;

    (d)   to protect a child or other vulnerable person from the person in question;

    (e)   to allow the prompt and effective investigation of the offence or of the conduct of the person in question;

    (f)   to prevent any prosecution for the offence from being hindered by the disappearance of the person in question.

(6)   Subsection (5)(c)(iv) applies only where members of the public going about their normal business cannot reasonably be expected to avoid the person in question.

24A   Arrest without warrant: other persons

(1)   A person other than a constable may arrest without a warrant—

    (a)   anyone who is in the act of committing an indictable offence;

    (b)   anyone whom he has reasonable grounds for suspecting to be committing an indictable offence.

(2)   Where an indictable offence has been committed, a person other than a constable may arrest without a warrant—

    (a)   anyone who is guilty of the offence;

    (b)   anyone whom he has reasonable grounds for suspecting to be guilty of it.

(3)   But the power of summary arrest conferred by subsection (1) or (2) is exercisable only if—

(a) the person making the arrest has reasonable grounds for believing that for any of the reasons mentioned in subsection (4) it is necessary to arrest the person in question; and

(b) it appears to the person making the arrest that it is not reasonably practicable for a constable to make it instead.

(4) The reasons are to prevent the person in question —

    (a) causing physical injury to himself or any other person;

    (b) suffering physical injury;

    (c) causing loss of or damage to property; or

    (d) making off before a constable can assume responsibility for him."

(2) Section 25 of PACE (general arrest conditions) shall cease to have effect.

(3) In section 66 of PACE (codes of practice), in subsection (1)(a) —

    (a) omit "or" at the end of sub-paragraph (i),

    (b) at the end of sub-paragraph (ii) insert "or

        (iii) to arrest a person;"

(4) The sections 24 and 24A of PACE substituted by subsection (1) are to have effect in relation to any offence whenever committed.

111 Powers of arrest: supplementary

Schedule 7, which supplements section 110 by providing for the repeal of certain enactments (including some which are spent) and by making further supplementary provision, has effect.

Exclusion zones

112 Power to direct a person to leave a place

(1) A constable may direct a person to leave a place if he believes, on reasonable grounds, that the person is in the place at a time when he would be prohibited from entering it by virtue of —

    (a) an order to which subsection (2) applies, or

    (b) a condition to which subsection (3) applies.

(2) This subsection applies to an order which —

    (a) was made, by virtue of any enactment, following the person's conviction of an offence, and

    (b) prohibits the person from entering the place or from doing so during a period specified in the order.

(3) This subsection applies to a condition which —

    (a) was imposed, by virtue of any enactment, as a condition of the person's release from a prison in which he was serving a sentence of imprisonment following his conviction of an offence, and

    (b) prohibits the person from entering the place or from doing so during a period specified in the condition.

(4) A direction under this section may be given orally.

(5)   Any person who knowingly contravenes a direction given to him under this section is guilty of an offence and liable on summary conviction to imprisonment for a term not exceeding 51 weeks or to a fine not exceeding level 4 on the standard scale, or to both.

(6)   A constable in uniform may arrest without warrant any person he reasonably suspects is committing or has committed an offence under subsection (5).

(7)   Subsection (6) ceases to have effect on the commencement of section 110.

(8)   In subsection (3)(a) —

  (a)   "sentence of imprisonment" and "prison" are to be construed in accordance with section 62(5) of the Criminal Justice and Court Services Act 2000 (c. 43);

  (b)   the reference to a release from prison includes a reference to a temporary release.

(9)   In this section, "place" includes an area.

(10) This section applies whether or not the order or condition mentioned in subsection (1) was made or imposed before or after the commencement of this section.

Search warrants

113   Search warrants: premises

(1)   PACE is amended as follows.

(2)   Section 8 (power to authorise entry and search of premises) is amended as provided in subsections (3) and (4).

(3)   In subsection (1) —

  (a)   in paragraph (b), for "specified in the application" substitute "mentioned in subsection (1A) below",

  (b)   in paragraph (e), at the end add "in relation to each set of premises specified in the application".

(4)   After subsection (1) insert —

  "(1A)   The premises referred to in subsection (1)(b) above are —

    (a)   one or more sets of premises specified in the application (in which case the application is for a "specific premises warrant"); or

    (b)   any premises occupied or controlled by a person specified in the application, including such sets of premises as are so specified (in which case the application is for an "all premises warrant").

  (1B)   If the application is for an all premises warrant, the justice of the peace must also be satisfied —

    (a)   that because of the particulars of the offence referred to in paragraph (a) of subsection (1) above, there are reasonable grounds for believing that it is necessary to search premises occupied or controlled by the person in question which are not specified in the application in order to find the material referred to in paragraph (b) of that subsection; and

(b)   that it is not reasonably practicable to specify in the application all the premises which he occupies or controls and which might need to be searched."

(5)   Section 15 (search warrants—safeguards) is amended as provided in subsections (6) to (8).

(6)   For subsection (2)(b) substitute—
      "(b)   to specify the matters set out in subsection (2A) below; and".

(7)   After subsection (2) insert—

      "(2A)   The matters which must be specified pursuant to subsection (2)(b) above are—
         (a)   if the application is for a specific premises warrant made by virtue of section 8(1A)(a) above or paragraph 12 of Schedule 1 below, each set of premises which it is desired to enter and search;
         (b)   if the application is for an all premises warrant made by virtue of section 8(1A)(b) above or paragraph 12 of Schedule 1 below—
            (i)   as many sets of premises which it is desired to enter and search as it is reasonably practicable to specify;
            (ii)   the person who is in occupation or control of those premises and any others which it is desired to enter and search;
            (iii)   why it is necessary to search more premises than those specified under sub-paragraph (i); and
            (iv)   why it is not reasonably practicable to specify all the premises which it is desired to enter and search."

(8)   For subsection (6)(a)(iv) substitute—
      "(iv)   each set of premises to be searched, or (in the case of an all premises warrant) the person who is in occupation or control of premises to be searched, together with any premises under his occupation or control which can be specified and which are to be searched; and".

(9)   In section 16 (execution of warrants)—
      (a)   after subsection (3) insert—
         "(3A)   If the warrant is an all premises warrant, no premises which are not specified in it may be entered or searched unless a police officer of at least the rank of inspector has in writing authorised them to be entered.",
      (b)   in subsection (9), after paragraph (b) add—
         "and, unless the warrant is a specific premises warrant specifying one set of premises only, he shall do so separately in respect of each set of premises entered and searched, which he shall in each case state in the endorsement.",
      (c)   in subsection (12), for "the premises" substitute "premises".

(10)   Schedule 1 (special procedure) is amended as follows.

(11)   In each of paragraphs 2(a)(ii) and 3(a), at the end add ", or on premises occupied or controlled by a person specified in the application (including all

such premises on which there are reasonable grounds for believing that there is such material as it is reasonably practicable so to specify);".

(12)   In paragraph 3(b), for "the premises" substitute "such premises".

(13)   In paragraph 12 −

(a)   in sub-paragraph (a)(ii), after "fulfilled" insert "in relation to each set of premises specified in the application",

(b)   at the end add "or (as the case may be) all premises occupied or controlled by the person referred to in paragraph 2(a)(ii) or 3(a), including such sets of premises as are specified in the application (an "all premises warrant")".

(14)   After paragraph 12 insert −

"12A   The judge may not issue an all premises warrant unless he is satisfied −

(a)   that there are reasonable grounds for believing that it is necessary to search premises occupied or controlled by the person in question which are not specified in the application, as well as those which are, in order to find the material in question; and

(b)   that it is not reasonably practicable to specify all the premises which he occupies or controls which might need to be searched."

(15)   In paragraph 14(a), omit "to which the application relates".

114   Search warrants: other amendments

(1)   PACE is amended as follows.

(2)   In section 8 (power to authorise entry and search of premises), after the subsection (1B) inserted by section 113(4) of this Act insert −

"(1C)   The warrant may authorise entry to and search of premises on more than one occasion if, on the application, the justice of the peace is satisfied that it is necessary to authorise multiple entries in order to achieve the purpose for which he issues the warrant.

(1D)   If it authorises multiple entries, the number of entries authorised may be unlimited, or limited to a maximum."

(3)   Section 15 (search warrants − safeguards) is amended as provided in subsections (4) to (7).

(4)   In subsection (2)(a) −

(a)   omit "and" at the end of sub-paragraph (i),

(b)   at the end of sub-paragraph (ii) insert "and",

(c)   after that sub-paragraph insert −

"(iii)   if the application is for a warrant authorising entry and search on more than one occasion, the ground on which he applies for such a warrant, and whether he seeks a warrant authorising an unlimited number of entries, or (if not) the maximum number of entries desired;".

(5) In subsection (5), at the end add "unless it specifies that it authorises multiple entries".

(6) After subsection (5) insert—

"(5A) If it specifies that it authorises multiple entries, it must also specify whether the number of entries authorised is unlimited, or limited to a specified maximum."

(7) For subsection (7) substitute—

"(7) Two copies shall be made of a specific premises warrant (see section 8(1A)(a) above) which specifies only one set of premises and does not authorise multiple entries; and as many copies as are reasonably required may be made of any other kind of warrant."

(8) In section 16 (execution of warrants)—
    (a) in subsection (3), for "one month" substitute "three months",
    (b) after the subsection (3A) inserted by section 113(9)(a) of this Act, insert—

"(3B) No premises may be entered or searched for the second or any subsequent time under a warrant which authorises multiple entries unless a police officer of at least the rank of inspector has in writing authorised that entry to those premises.",
    (c) for subsection (10) substitute—

"(10) A warrant shall be returned to the appropriate person mentioned in subsection (10A) below—
        (a) when it has been executed; or
        (b) in the case of a specific premises warrant which has not been executed, or an all premises warrant, or any warrant authorising multiple entries, upon the expiry of the period of three months referred to in subsection (3) above or sooner.

(10A) The appropriate person is—
        (a) if the warrant was issued by a justice of the peace, the designated officer for the local justice area in which the justice was acting when he issued the warrant;
        (b) if it was issued by a judge, the appropriate officer of the court from which he issued it."

(9) In Schedule 1 (special procedure), in paragraph 17, for "a Circuit judge" substitute "a judge of the High Court, a Circuit judge, a Recorder".

Fireworks

115 Power to stop and search for prohibited fireworks

(1) Section 1 of PACE (powers of constables to stop and search) is amended as follows.

(2) In subsection (2), for "or any article to which subsection (8A) below applies" substitute ", any article to which subsection (8A) below applies or any firework to which subsection (8B) below applies".

(3)   In subsection (3), for "or any article to which subsection (8A) below applies" substitute ", any article to which subsection (8A) below applies or any firework to which subsection (8B) below applies".

(4)   In subsection (6), for "or an article to which subsection (8A) below applies" substitute ", an article to which subsection (8A) below applies or a firework to which subsection (8B) below applies".

(5)   After subsection (8A) insert—

    "(8B)   This subsection applies to any firework which a person possesses in contravention of a prohibition imposed by fireworks regulations.

    (8C)   In this section—
        (a)   "firework" shall be construed in accordance with the definition of "fireworks" in section 1(1) of the Fireworks Act 2003; and
        (b)   "fireworks regulations" has the same meaning as in that Act."

Photographing of suspects etc.

116   Photographing of suspects etc.

(1)   Section 64A of PACE (photographing of suspects etc.) is amended as follows.

(2)   After subsection (1) insert—

    "(1A)   A person falling within subsection (1B) below may, on the occasion of the relevant event referred to in subsection (1B), be photographed elsewhere than at a police station—
        (a)   with the appropriate consent; or
        (b)   if the appropriate consent is withheld or it is not practicable to obtain it, without it.

    (1B)   A person falls within this subsection if he has been—
        (a)   arrested by a constable for an offence;
        (b)   taken into custody by a constable after being arrested for an offence by a person other than a constable;
        (c)   made subject to a requirement to wait with a community support officer under paragraph 2(3) or (3B) of Schedule 4 to the Police Reform Act 2002 ("the 2002 Act");
        (d)   given a penalty notice by a constable in uniform under Chapter 1 of Part 1 of the Criminal Justice and Police Act 2001, a penalty notice by a constable under section 444A of the Education Act 1996, or a fixed penalty notice by a constable in uniform under section 54 of the Road Traffic Offenders Act 1988;
        (e)   given a notice in relation to a relevant fixed penalty offence (within the meaning of paragraph 1 of Schedule 4 to the 2002 Act) by a community support officer by virtue of a designation applying that paragraph to him; or
        (f)   given a notice in relation to a relevant fixed penalty offence (within the meaning of paragraph 1 of Schedule 5 to the 2002 Act) by an accredited person by virtue of accreditation specifying that that paragraph applies to him."

(3)   In subsection (4)(a), after "prosecution" insert "or to the enforcement of a sentence".

(4)   In subsection (5), after paragraph (b) insert "; and

      (c)   "sentence" includes any order made by a court in England and Wales when dealing with an offender in respect of his offence.""

(5)   After subsection (6) insert—

"(6A)   In this section, a "photograph" includes a moving image, and corresponding expressions shall be construed accordingly."

Fingerprints and footwear impressions

117   Fingerprints

(1)   Section 61 of PACE (fingerprinting) is amended as provided in subsections (2) to (4).

(2)   After subsection (6) insert—

"(6A)   A constable may take a person's fingerprints without the appropriate consent if—

      (a)   the constable reasonably suspects that the person is committing or attempting to commit an offence, or has committed or attempted to commit an offence; and

      (b)   either of the two conditions mentioned in subsection (6B) is met.

(6B)   The conditions are that—

      (a)   the name of the person is unknown to, and cannot be readily ascertained by, the constable;

      (b)   the constable has reasonable grounds for doubting whether a name furnished by the person as his name is his real name.

(6C)   The taking of fingerprints by virtue of subsection (6A) does not count for any of the purposes of this Act as taking them in the course of the investigation of an offence by the police."

(3)   In subsection (7), for "or (6)" substitute ", (6) or (6A)".

(4)   In subsection (7A)—

      (a)   after "police station," insert "or by virtue of subsection (6A) at a place other than a police station,",

      (b)   in paragraph (a), after "an officer" insert "(or, in a subsection (6A) case, the constable)".

(5)   In section 63A of PACE (fingerprints and samples: supplementary provisions)—

      (a)   after subsection (1) insert—

"(1ZA)   Fingerprints taken by virtue of section 61(6A) above may be checked against other fingerprints to which the person seeking to check has access and which are held by or on behalf of any one or more relevant law-enforcement authorities or which are held in connection with or as a result of an investigation of an offence.",

      (b)   in subsection (1A), after "subsection (1)" insert "and (1ZA)".

(6)   Section 64 of PACE (destruction of fingerprints and samples) is amended as follows.

(7)   In subsection (1A), for "or the conduct of a prosecution" substitute ", the conduct of a prosecution or the identification of a deceased person or of the person from whom a body part came".

(8)   After subsection (1B) insert—

"(1BA)   Fingerprints taken from a person by virtue of section 61(6A) above must be destroyed as soon as they have fulfilled the purpose for which they were taken."

(9)   In subsection (3AB), for "subsection (3)" substitute "subsection (1BA) or (3)".

(10)   in subsection (3AC)—

(a)   in paragraph (a), after "that" insert "fingerprint or",

(b)   at the end add the following new sentence—

"This subsection does not apply to fingerprints taken from a person by virtue of section 61(6A) above."

118   Impressions of footwear

(1)   PACE is amended as provided in subsections (2) to (4).

(2)   After section 61 insert—

"61A   Impressions of footwear

(1)   Except as provided by this section, no impression of a person's footwear may be taken without the appropriate consent.

(2)   Consent to the taking of an impression of a person's footwear must be in writing if it is given at a time when he is at a police station.

(3)   Where a person is detained at a police station, an impression of his footwear may be taken without the appropriate consent if—

(a)   he is detained in consequence of his arrest for a recordable offence, or has been charged with a recordable offence, or informed that he will be reported for a recordable offence; and

(b)   he has not had an impression taken of his footwear in the course of the investigation of the offence by the police.

(4)   Where a person mentioned in paragraph (a) of subsection (3) above has already had an impression taken of his footwear in the course of the investigation of the offence by the police, that fact shall be disregarded for the purposes of that subsection if the impression of his footwear taken previously is—

(a)   incomplete; or

(b)   is not of sufficient quality to allow satisfactory analysis, comparison or matching (whether in the case in question or generally).

(5)   If an impression of a person's footwear is taken at a police station, whether with or without the appropriate consent—

(a)   before it is taken, an officer shall inform him that it may be the subject of a speculative search; and

(b) the fact that the person has been informed of this possibility shall be recorded as soon as is practicable after the impression has been taken, and if he is detained at a police station, the record shall be made on his custody record.

(6) In a case where, by virtue of subsection (3) above, an impression of a person's footwear is taken without the appropriate consent —
  (a) he shall be told the reason before it is taken; and
  (b) the reason shall be recorded on his custody record as soon as is practicable after the impression is taken.

(7) The power to take an impression of the footwear of a person detained at a police station without the appropriate consent shall be exercisable by any constable.

(8) Nothing in this section applies to any person —
  (a) arrested or detained under the terrorism provisions;
  (b) arrested under an extradition arrest power."

(3) Section 63A (fingerprints and samples: supplementary provisions) is amended as follows —
  (a) in subsection (1), after "fingerprints", in both places, insert ", impressions of footwear",
  (b) in subsection (1C) —
    (i) in paragraph (a), after "fingerprints" insert ", impressions of footwear",
    (ii) in paragraph (b), after "fingerprints" insert ", of the impressions of footwear",
    (iii) after the third "fingerprints" insert "or impressions of footwear",
    (iv) after the fourth "fingerprints" insert ", impressions of footwear".

(4) Section 64 (destruction of fingerprints and samples) is amended as follows —
  (a) in subsection (1A), after "fingerprints" in both places where it occurs insert ", impressions of footwear",
  (b) in subsection (1B)(a), after "fingerprint" insert "or an impression of footwear",
  (c) in subsection (3), after "fingerprints" insert ", impressions of footwear",
  (d) in subsection (3AA) —
    (i) for "and fingerprints" substitute ", fingerprints and impressions of footwear",
    (ii) in paragraph (b), for "or, as the case may be, fingerprint" substitute ", fingerprint, (or as the case may be) an impression of footwear",
  (e) in subsection (3AB) —
    (i) after each of the first and third places "fingerprint" occurs insert ", impression of footwear",
    (ii) after the second place "fingerprint" occurs, insert ", nor the impression of footwear,",
  (f) in subsection (3AC), after "fingerprint" in each place where it occurs (including the "fingerprint" in paragraph (a) inserted by section 117(10)(a) of this Act), insert ", impression of footwear",

(g)   in subsection (3AD), after "fingerprint" insert ", impression of footwear",

(h)   in subsection (5), after "fingerprints" in each place where it occurs insert "or impressions of footwear",

(i)   in subsection (6), after "fingerprints" insert "or impressions of footwear",

(j)   in subsection (6A), after "fingerprints" insert "or impressions of footwear".

Intimate samples

119   Intimate samples

(1)   Section 65 of PACE (which defines certain terms for the purposes of Part 5 of that Act) is amended as follows.

(2)   In the definition of "intimate sample", for paragraph (c) substitute—

> "(c)   a swab taken from any part of a person's genitals (including pubic hair) or from a person's body orifice other than the mouth;".

(3)   In the definition of "non-intimate sample", for paragraph (c) substitute—

> "(c)   a swab taken from any part of a person's body other than a part from which a swab taken would be an intimate sample;".

Custody officers

120   Staff custody officers: designation

(1)   Section 38 of the Police Reform Act 2002 (c. 30) (police powers for police authority employees) is amended as provided in subsections (2) to (4).

(2)   In subsection (2), after paragraph (d) add—

> "(e)   staff custody officer."

(3)   In subsection (6), after paragraph (d) add—

> "(e)   in the case of a person designated as a staff custody officer, Part 4A."

(4)   After subsection (9) add—

> "(10)   References in this section, section 42 or section 46(4) to powers and duties conferred or imposed on a designated person, or to a designated person's being authorised or required to do anything by virtue of a designation under this section, or to a power or duty exercisable by a designated person in reliance on or by virtue of a designation under this section are, in the case of a staff custody officer at a police station designated under section 35(1) of the 1984 Act, references to those things in relation to him after his appointment as a custody officer for that police station under section 36(2) of that Act."

(5)   After Part 4 of Schedule 4 to the Police Reform Act 2002 (powers exercisable by

police civilians) insert—

"Part 4A

Staff custody officers

Exercise of functions of custody officers

35A (1) Where a designation applies this paragraph to any person, he may (subject to sub-paragraph (2)) perform all the functions of a custody officer under the 1984 Act (except those under section 45A(4) of that Act) and under any other enactment which confers functions on such a custody officer.

(2) But in relation to a police station designated under section 35(1) of the 1984 Act, the person must first also be appointed a custody officer for that police station under section 36(2) of that Act.

(3) A person performing the functions of a custody officer by virtue of a designation under this paragraph (together with, if appropriate, an appointment as such) shall have all the powers and duties of a custody officer.

(4) Except in sections 36 and 45A(4) of the 1984 Act, references in any enactment to a custody officer within the meaning of that Act include references to a person performing the functions of a custody officer by virtue of a designation under this paragraph."

121 Custody officers: amendments to PACE

(1) Section 36 of PACE (custody officers at police stations) is amended as provided in subsections (2) to (6).

(2) For subsection (3) substitute—

"(3) No person may be appointed a custody officer unless—
    (a) he is a police officer of at least the rank of sergeant; or
    (b) he is a staff custody officer."

(3) In subsection (5), for "an officer" substitute "an individual".

(4) In subsection (7)—
    (a) in paragraph (a)—
        (i) after "by an officer" insert "or a staff custody officer",
        (ii) for "such an officer" substitute "such a person",
    (b) in paragraph (b), for "such officer" substitute "such person".

(5) In subsection (8)—
    (a) after "in" insert "section 34 above or in",
    (b) for "an officer" substitute "a person".

(6) After subsection (10) add—

"(11) In this section, "staff custody officer" means a person who has been designated as such under section 38 of the Police Reform Act 2002."

(7) In section 39 of PACE (responsibilities in relation to persons detained)—

    (a)   in subsection (6)(a), after "custody officer" insert "(or, if the custody officer is a staff custody officer, any police officer or any police employee)",

    (b)   after subsection (6) add —

        "(7)   In subsection (6) above —

            "police employee" means a person employed under section 15 of the Police Act 1996;

            "staff custody officer" has the same meaning as in the Police Reform Act 2002."

Designated and accredited persons

122 Powers of designated and accredited persons

(1)   The Police Reform Act 2002 (c. 30) is amended as follows.

(2)   In section 42 (supplementary provisions relating to designations) —

    (a)   in subsection (2), after "section 41 shall" insert ", subject to subsection (2A),",

    (b)   after subsection (2) insert—

        "(2A)   A police officer of or above the rank of inspector may direct a particular investigating officer not to wear a uniform for the purposes of a particular operation; and if he so directs, subsection (2) shall not apply in relation to that investigating officer for the purposes of that operation.

        (2B)   In subsection (2A), "investigating officer" means a person designated as an investigating officer under section 38 by the chief officer of police of the same force as the officer giving the direction."

(3)   Schedule 4 (powers exercisable by police civilians) is amended as follows —

    (a)   in paragraph 1, after sub-paragraph (2) insert—

        "(2A)   The reference to the powers mentioned in sub-paragraph (2)(a) does not include those powers so far as they relate to an offence under the provisions in the following list—

            section 1 of the Theft Act 1968,

            section 87 of the Environmental Protection Act 1990.",

    (b)   in paragraph 15A (power to modify paragraph 1(2)(a)), for sub-paragraph (1) substitute—

        "(1)   The Secretary of State may by order amend paragraph 1(2A) so as to remove a provision from the list or add a provision to the list; but the list must contain only provisions mentioned in the first column of the Table in section 1(1) of the Criminal Justice and Police Act 2001.",

    and in the heading to paragraph 15A, for "1(2)(a)" substitute "1(2A)".

(4)   Schedule 5 (powers exercisable by accredited persons) is amended as provided in subsections (5) and (6).

(5)   In paragraph 1 (power to issue fixed penalty notices) —

(a)   in sub-paragraph (2)(aa), omit "except in respect of an offence under section 12 of the Licensing Act 1872 or section 91 of the Criminal Justice Act 1967",

(b)   after sub-paragraph (2) insert —

"(2A)   The reference to the powers mentioned in sub-paragraph (2)(aa) does not include those powers so far as they relate to an offence under the provisions in the following list —

section 12 of the Licensing Act 1872,

section 91 of the Criminal Justice Act 1967,

section 1 of the Theft Act 1968,

section 1(1) of the Criminal Damage Act 1971,

section 87 of the Environmental Protection Act 1990."

(6)   In paragraph 9A (power to modify paragraph 1(2)(aa)), for sub-paragraph (1) substitute —

"(1)   The Secretary of State may by order amend paragraph 1(2A) so as to remove a provision from the list or add a provision to the list; but the list must contain only provisions mentioned in the first column of the Table in section 1(1) of the Criminal Justice and Police Act 2001.",

and in the heading to paragraph 9A, for "1(2)(aa)" substitute "1(2A)".

(7)   Schedules 8 and 9 to this Act, which provide for additional powers and duties for designated and accredited persons under the Police Reform Act 2002 (c. 30), have effect.

Provision of information for use by police staff

123   Provision of information for use by police staff

(1)   In section 71 of the Criminal Justice and Court Services Act 2000 (c. 43) (access to driver licensing records), in subsection (4), after "In this section" insert " —

"constables" includes —

(a)   persons employed by a police authority under section 15(1) of the Police Act 1996 who are under the direction and control of the chief officer of police of the police force maintained by that authority,

(b)   persons employed by a police authority under section 9(1) of the Police (Scotland) Act 1967 who are under the direction and control of the chief constable of the police force maintained for the authority's area,

(c)   police support staff (within the meaning of the Police (Northern Ireland) Act 2000), and

(d)   persons employed by the British Transport Police Authority under section 27(1) of the Railways and Transport Safety Act 2003 who are under the direction and control of the Chief Constable of the British Transport Police Force".

(2)   In section 18 of the Vehicles (Crime) Act 2001 (c. 3) (register of registration plate suppliers), after subsection (8) insert —

"(9)   In this section, "constables" includes —

(a) persons employed by a police authority under section 15(1) of the Police Act 1996 who are under the direction and control of the chief officer of police of the police force maintained by that authority,

(b) persons employed by a police authority under section 9(1) of the Police (Scotland) Act 1967 who are under the direction and control of the chief constable of the police force maintained for the authority's area, and

(c) persons employed by the British Transport Police Authority under section 27(1) of the Railways and Transport Safety Act 2003 who are under the direction and control of the Chief Constable of the British Transport Police Force.".

(3) In section 36 of the Vehicles (Crime) Act 2001 (c. 3) (access to certain motor insurance information), in subsection (3), after "In this section—" insert—

" "constables" includes—

(a) persons employed by a police authority under section 15(1) of the Police Act 1996 who are under the direction and control of the chief officer of police of the police force maintained by that authority,

(b) persons employed by a police authority under section 9(1) of the Police (Scotland) Act 1967 who are under the direction and control of the chief constable of the police force maintained for the authority's area, and

(c) persons employed by the British Transport Police Authority under section 27(1) of the Railways and Transport Safety Act 2003 who are under the direction and control of the Chief Constable of the British Transport Police Force;".

Interpretation of Part 3

124 Interpretation of Part 3

In this Part, "PACE" means the Police and Criminal Evidence Act 1984 (c. 60).

PART 4

PUBLIC ORDER AND CONDUCT IN PUBLIC PLACES ETC.

Harassment

125 Harassment intended to deter lawful activities

(1) The Protection from Harassment Act 1997 (c. 40) is amended as follows.

(2) In section 1 (prohibition of harassment)—
   (a) after subsection (1) insert—

   "(1A) A person must not pursue a course of conduct —
      (a) which involves harassment of two or more persons, and
      (b) which he knows or ought to know involves harassment of those persons, and

        (c)   by which he intends to persuade any person (whether or not one of those mentioned above) –

               (i)   not to do something that he is entitled or required to do, or

              (ii)   to do something that he is not under any obligation to do.";

  (b)   in subsection (2), after "amounts to" insert "or involves" and after "amounted to" insert "or involved";

  (c)   in subsection (3), after "Subsection (1)" insert "or (1A)".

(3)   In section 2(1) (offence of harassment) for "section 1" substitute "section 1(1) or (1A)".

(4)   In section 3(1) (civil remedy) for "section 1" substitute "section 1(1)".

(5)   After section 3 insert –

"3A   Injunctions to protect persons from harassment within section 1(1A)

(1)   This section applies where there is an actual or apprehended breach of section 1(1A) by any person ("the relevant person").

(2)   In such a case –

    (a)   any person who is or may be a victim of the course of conduct in question, or

    (b)   any person who is or may be a person falling within section 1(1A)(c),

may apply to the High Court or a county court for an injunction restraining the relevant person from pursuing any conduct which amounts to harassment in relation to any person or persons mentioned or described in the injunction.

(3)   Section 3(3) to (9) apply in relation to an injunction granted under subsection (2) above as they apply in relation to an injunction granted as mentioned in section 3(3)(a)."

(6)   In section 5(2) (restraining orders) after "victim" insert "or victims".

(7)   In section 7 (interpretation of sections 1 to 5) –

  (a)   for subsection (3) substitute –

    "(3)   A "course of conduct" must involve –

        (a)   in the case of conduct in relation to a single person (see section 1(1)), conduct on at least two occasions in relation to that person, or

        (b)   in the case of conduct in relation to two or more persons (see section 1(1A)), conduct on at least one occasion in relation to each of those persons."; and

  (b)   after subsection (4) add –

    "(5)   References to a person, in the context of the harassment of a person, are references to a person who is an individual."

126   Harassment etc. of a person in his home

(1)   After section 42 of the Criminal Justice and Police Act 2001 (c. 16) insert—

"42A Offence of harassment etc. of a person in his home

(1)   A person commits an offence if—

    (a)   that person is present outside or in the vicinity of any premises that are used by any individual ("the resident") as his dwelling;

    (b)   that person is present there for the purpose (by his presence or otherwise) of representing to the resident or another individual (whether or not one who uses the premises as his dwelling), or of persuading the resident or such another individual—

        (i)   that he should not do something that he is entitled or required to do; or

        (ii)   that he should do something that he is not under any obligation to do;

    (c)   that person—

        (i)   intends his presence to amount to the harassment of, or to cause alarm or distress to, the resident; or

        (ii)   knows or ought to know that his presence is likely to result in the harassment of, or to cause alarm or distress to, the resident; and

    (d)   the presence of that person—

        (i)   amounts to the harassment of, or causes alarm or distress to, any person falling within subsection (2); or

        (ii)   is likely to result in the harassment of, or to cause alarm or distress to, any such person.

(2)   A person falls within this subsection if he is—

    (a)   the resident,

    (b)   a person in the resident's dwelling, or

    (c)   a person in another dwelling in the vicinity of the resident's dwelling.

(3)   The references in subsection (1)(c) and (d) to a person's presence are references to his presence either alone or together with that of any other persons who are also present.

(4)   For the purposes of this section a person (A) ought to know that his presence is likely to result in the harassment of, or to cause alarm or distress to, a resident if a reasonable person in possession of the same information would think that A's presence was likely to have that effect.

(5)   A person guilty of an offence under this section shall be liable, on summary conviction, to imprisonment for a term not exceeding 51 weeks or to a fine not exceeding level 4 on the standard scale, or to both.

(6)   In relation to an offence committed before the commencement of section 281(5) of the Criminal Justice Act 2003 (alteration of penalties for summary offences), the reference in subsection (5) to 51 weeks is to be read as a reference to 6 months.

(7)   In this section "dwelling" has the same meaning as in Part 1 of the Public Order Act 1986."

(2)   A constable in uniform may arrest without warrant any person he reasonably suspects is committing or has committed an offence under section 42A (as inserted by subsection (1)).

(3)   Subsection (2) ceases to have effect on the commencement of section 110 of this Act.

127   Harassment etc: police direction to stay away from person's home

(1)   Section 42 of the Criminal Justice and Police Act 2001 (c. 16) (police directions stopping harassment of a person in his home) is amended as follows.

(2)   For subsection (4) substitute —

> "(4)   The requirements that may be imposed by a direction under this section include —
>
> > (a)   a requirement to leave the vicinity of the premises in question, and
> >
> > (b)   a requirement to leave that vicinity and not to return to it within such period as the constable may specify, not being longer than 3 months;
>
> and (in either case) the requirement to leave the vicinity may be to do so immediately or after a specified period of time."

(3)   In subsection (7), for "contravenes a direction given to him under this section" substitute "fails to comply with a requirement in a direction given to him under this section (other than a requirement under subsection (4)(b))".

(4)   After subsection (7) insert —

> "(7A)   Any person to whom a constable has given a direction including a requirement under subsection (4)(b) commits an offence if he —
>
> > (a)   returns to the vicinity of the premises in question within the period specified in the direction beginning with the date on which the direction is given; and
> >
> > (b)   does so for the purpose described in subsection (1)(b).
>
> (7B)   A person guilty of an offence under subsection (7A) shall be liable, on summary conviction, to imprisonment for a term not exceeding 51 weeks or to a fine not exceeding level 4 on the standard scale, or to both.
>
> (7C)   In relation to an offence committed before the commencement of section 281(5) of the Criminal Justice Act 2003 (alteration of penalties for summary offences), the reference in subsection (7B) to 51 weeks is to be read as a reference to 6 months."

Trespass on designated site

128   Offence of trespassing on designated site

(1)   A person commits an offence if he enters, or is on, any designated site in England and Wales or Northern Ireland as a trespasser.

(2)   A "designated site" means a site —

> (a)   specified or described (in any way) in an order made by the Secretary of State, and

     (b)   designated for the purposes of this section by the order.

(3)   The Secretary of State may only designate a site for the purposes of this section if —

     (a)   it is comprised in Crown land; or

     (b)   it is comprised in land belonging to Her Majesty in Her private capacity or to the immediate heir to the Throne in his private capacity; or

     (c)   it appears to the Secretary of State that it is appropriate to designate the site in the interests of national security.

(4)   It is a defence for a person charged with an offence under this section to prove that he did not know, and had no reasonable cause to suspect, that the site in relation to which the offence is alleged to have been committed was a designated site.

(5)   A person guilty of an offence under this section is liable on summary conviction —

     (a)   to imprisonment for a term not exceeding 51 weeks, or

     (b)   to a fine not exceeding level 5 on the standard scale,

or to both.

(6)   No proceedings for an offence under this section may be instituted against any person —

     (a)   in England and Wales, except by or with the consent of the Attorney General, or

     (b)   in Northern Ireland, except by or with the consent of the Attorney General for Northern Ireland.

(7)   For the purposes of this section a person who is on any designated site as a trespasser does not cease to be a trespasser by virtue of being allowed time to leave the site.

(8)   In this section —

     (a)   "site" means the whole or part of any building or buildings, or any land, or both;

     (b)   "Crown land" means land in which there is a Crown interest or a Duchy interest.

(9)   For this purpose —

       "Crown interest" means an interest belonging to Her Majesty in right of the Crown, and

       "Duchy interest" means an interest belonging to Her Majesty in right of the Duchy of Lancaster or belonging to the Duchy of Cornwall.

(10)   In the application of this section to Northern Ireland, the reference to 51 weeks in subsection (5)(a) is to be read as a reference to 6 months.

129   Corresponding Scottish offence

(1)   A person commits an offence if he enters, or is on, any designated Scottish site without lawful authority.

(2)   A "designated Scottish site" means a site in Scotland —

     (a)   specified or described (in any way) in an order made by the Secretary of State, and

     (b)   designated for the purposes of this section by the order.

(3) The Secretary of State may only designate a site for the purposes of this section if it appears to him that it is appropriate to designate the site in the interests of national security.

(4) It is a defence for a person charged with an offence under this section to prove that he did not know, and had no reasonable cause to suspect, that the site in relation to which the offence is alleged to have been committed was a designated Scottish site.

(5) A person guilty of an offence under this section is liable on summary conviction —

    (a) to imprisonment for a term not exceeding 12 months, or

    (b) to a fine not exceeding level 5 on the standard scale,

or to both.

(6) For the purposes of subsection (1), a person who is on any designated Scottish site without lawful authority does not acquire lawful authority by virtue of being allowed time to leave the site.

(7) In this section "site" means the whole or part of any building or buildings, or any land, or both.

130 Designated sites: powers of arrest

(1) A constable in uniform may, in England or Wales, arrest without warrant any person he reasonably suspects is committing or has committed an offence under section 128.

This subsection ceases to have effect on the commencement of section 110.

(2) An offence under section 128 is to be treated as an arrestable offence for the purposes of the Police and Criminal Evidence (Northern Ireland) Order 1989 (S.I. 1989/1341 (N.I. 12)).

(3) A constable in uniform may, in Scotland, arrest without warrant any person he reasonably suspects is committing or has committed an offence under section 129.

131 Designated sites: access

(1) The following provisions do not apply to land in respect of which a designation order is in force —

    (a) section 2(1) of the Countryside and Rights of Way Act 2000 (c. 37) (rights of public in relation to access land),

    (b) Part III of the Countryside (Northern Ireland) Order 1983 (S.I. 1983/ 1895 (N.I. 18)) (access to open country), and

    (c) section 1 of the Land Reform (Scotland) Act 2003 (asp 2) (access rights).

(2) The Secretary of State may take such steps as he considers appropriate to inform the public of the effect of any designation order, including, in particular, displaying notices on or near the site to which the order relates.

(3) But the Secretary of State may only —

    (a) display any such notice, or

    (b) take any other steps under subsection (2),

in or on any building or land, if the appropriate person consents.

(4)   The "appropriate person" is —

(a)   a person appearing to the Secretary of State to have a sufficient interest in the building or land to consent to the notice being displayed or the steps being taken, or

(b)   a person acting on behalf of such a person.

(5)   In this section a "designation order" means —

(a)   in relation to England and Wales or Northern Ireland, an order under section 128, or

(b)   in relation to Scotland, an order under section 129.

Demonstrations in vicinity of Parliament

132   Demonstrating without authorisation in designated area

(1)   Any person who —

(a)   organises a demonstration in a public place in the designated area, or

(b)   takes part in a demonstration in a public place in the designated area, or

(c)   carries on a demonstration by himself in a public place in the designated area,

is guilty of an offence if, when the demonstration starts, authorisation for the demonstration has not been given under section 134(2).

(2)   It is a defence for a person accused of an offence under subsection (1) to show that he reasonably believed that authorisation had been given.

(3)   Subsection (1) does not apply if the demonstration is —

(a)   a public procession of which notice is required to be given under subsection (1) of section 11 of the Public Order Act 1986 (c. 64), or of which (by virtue of subsection (2) of that section) notice is not required to be given, or

(b)   a public procession for the purposes of section 12 or 13 of that Act.

(4)   Subsection (1) also does not apply in relation to any conduct which is lawful under section 220 of the Trade Union and Labour Relations (Consolidation) Act 1992 (c. 52).

(5)   If subsection (1) does not apply by virtue of subsection (3) or (4), nothing in sections 133 to 136 applies either.

(6)   Section 14 of the Public Order Act 1986 (imposition of conditions on public assemblies) does not apply in relation to a public assembly which is also a demonstration in a public place in the designated area.

(7)   In this section and in sections 133 to 136 —

(a)   "the designated area" means the area specified in an order under section 138,

(b)   "public place" means any highway or any place to which at the material time the public or any section of the public has access, on payment or otherwise, as of right or by virtue of express or implied permission,

(c)   references to any person organising a demonstration include a person participating in its organisation,

(d)   references to any person organising a demonstration do not include a person carrying on a demonstration by himself,

    (e)   references to any person or persons taking part in a demonstration (except in subsection (1) of this section) include a person carrying on a demonstration by himself.

133 Notice of demonstrations in designated area

(1)   A person seeking authorisation for a demonstration in the designated area must give written notice to that effect to the Commissioner of Police of the Metropolis (referred to in this section and section 134 as "the Commissioner").

(2)   The notice must be given —
    (a)   if reasonably practicable, not less than 6 clear days before the day on which the demonstration is to start, or
    (b)   if that is not reasonably practicable, then as soon as it is, and in any event not less than 24 hours before the time the demonstration is to start.

(3)   The notice must be given —
    (a)   if the demonstration is to be carried on by more than one person, by any of the persons organising it,
    (b)   if it is to be carried on by a person by himself, by that person.

(4)   The notice must state —
    (a)   the date and time when the demonstration is to start,
    (b)   the place where it is to be carried on,
    (c)   how long it is to last,
    (d)   whether it is to be carried on by a person by himself or not,
    (e)   the name and address of the person giving the notice.

(5)   A notice under this section must be given by —
    (a)   delivering it to a police station in the metropolitan police district, or
    (b)   sending it by post by recorded delivery to such a police station.

(6)   Section 7 of the Interpretation Act 1978 (c. 30) (under which service of a document is deemed to have been effected at the time it would be delivered in the ordinary course of post) does not apply to a notice under this section.

134 Authorisation of demonstrations in designated area

(1)   This section applies if a notice complying with the requirements of section 133 is received at a police station in the metropolitan police district by the time specified in section 133(2).

(2)   The Commissioner must give authorisation for the demonstration to which the notice relates.

(3)   In giving authorisation, the Commissioner may impose on the persons organising or taking part in the demonstration such conditions specified in the authorisation and relating to the demonstration as in the Commissioner's reasonable opinion are necessary for the purpose of preventing any of the following —
    (a)   hindrance to any person wishing to enter or leave the Palace of Westminster,
    (b)   hindrance to the proper operation of Parliament,
    (c)   serious public disorder,

    (d)   serious damage to property,

    (e)   disruption to the life of the community,

    (f)   a security risk in any part of the designated area,

    (g)   risk to the safety of members of the public (including any taking part in the demonstration).

(4)   The conditions may, in particular, impose requirements as to —

    (a)   the place where the demonstration may, or may not, be carried on,

    (b)   the times at which it may be carried on,

    (c)   the period during which it may be carried on,

    (d)   the number of persons who may take part in it,

    (e)   the number and size of banners or placards used,

    (f)   maximum permissible noise levels.

(5)   The authorisation must specify the particulars of the demonstration given in the notice under section 133 pursuant to subsection (4) of that section, with any modifications made necessary by any condition imposed under subsection (3) of this section.

(6)   The Commissioner must give notice in writing of —

    (a)   the authorisation,

    (b)   any conditions imposed under subsection (3), and

    (c)   the particulars mentioned in subsection (5),

to the person who gave the notice under section 133.

(7)   Each person who takes part in or organises a demonstration in the designated area is guilty of an offence if —

    (a)   he knowingly fails to comply with a condition imposed under subsection (3) which is applicable to him (except where it is varied under section 135), or

    (b)   he knows or should have known that the demonstration is carried on otherwise than in accordance with the particulars set out in the authorisation by virtue of subsection (5).

(8)   It is a defence for a person accused of an offence under subsection (7) to show —

    (a)   (in a paragraph (a) case) that the failure to comply, or

    (b)   (in a paragraph (b) case) that the divergence from the particulars,

arose from circumstances beyond his control, or from something done with the agreement, or by the direction, of a police officer.

(9)   The notice required by subsection (6) may be sent by post to the person who gave the notice under section 133 at the address stated in that notice pursuant to subsection (4)(e) of that section.

(10)   If the person to whom the notice required by subsection (6) is to be given has agreed, it may be sent to him by email or by facsimile transmission at the address or number notified by him for the purpose to the Commissioner (and a notice so sent is "in writing" for the purposes of that subsection).

135   Supplementary directions

(1)   This section applies if the senior police officer reasonably believes that it is necessary, in order to prevent any of the things mentioned in paragraphs (a) to (g) of subsection (3) of section 134 —

(a)   to impose additional conditions on those taking part in or organising a demonstration authorised under that section, or

(b)   to vary any condition imposed under that subsection or under paragraph (a) (including such a condition as varied under subsection (2)).

(2)   The senior police office may give directions to those taking part in or organising the demonstration imposing such additional conditions or varying any such condition already imposed.

(3)   A person taking part in or organising the demonstration who knowingly fails to comply with a condition which is applicable to him and which is imposed or varied by a direction under this section is guilty of an offence.

(4)   It is a defence for him to show that the failure to comply arose from circumstances beyond his control.

(5)   In this section, "the senior police officer" means the most senior in rank of the police officers present at the scene (or any one of them if there are more than one of the same rank).

136   Offences under sections 132 to 135: penalties

(1)   A person guilty of an offence under section 132(1)(a) is liable on summary conviction to imprisonment for a term not exceeding 51 weeks, to a fine not exceeding level 4 on the standard scale, or to both.

(2)   A person guilty of an offence under section 132(1)(b) or (c) is liable on summary conviction to a fine not exceeding level 3 on the standard scale.

(3)   A person guilty of an offence under section 134(7) or 135(3) is liable on summary conviction—

(a)   if the offence was in relation to his capacity as organiser of the demonstration, to imprisonment for a term not exceeding 51 weeks, to a fine not exceeding level 4 on the standard scale, or to both,

(b)   otherwise, to a fine not exceeding level 3 on the standard scale.

(4)   A person who is guilty of the offence of inciting another to—

(a)   do anything which would constitute an offence mentioned in subsection (1), (2) or (3), or

(b)   fail to do anything where the failure would constitute such an offence,

is liable on summary conviction to imprisonment for a term not exceeding 51 weeks, to a fine not exceeding level 4 on the standard scale, or to both, notwithstanding section 45(3) of the Magistrates' Courts Act 1980 (c. 43).

(5)   A constable in uniform may arrest without warrant anyone he reasonably believes is committing an offence mentioned in subsections (1) to (4).

This subsection ceases to have effect on the coming into force of section 110.

137   Loudspeakers in designated area

(1)   Subject to subsection (2), a loudspeaker shall not be operated, at any time or for any purpose, in a street in the designated area.

(2)   Subsection (1) does not apply to the operation of a loudspeaker—

(a)   in case of emergency,

    (b)   for police, fire and rescue authority or ambulance purposes,

    (c)   by the Environment Agency, a water undertaker or a sewerage undertaker in the exercise of any of its functions,

    (d)   by a local authority within its area,

    (e)   for communicating with persons on a vessel for the purpose of directing the movement of that or any other vessel,

    (f)   if the loudspeaker forms part of a public telephone system,

    (g)   if the loudspeaker is in or fixed to a vehicle and subsection (3) applies,

    (h)   otherwise than on a highway, by persons employed in connection with a transport undertaking used by the public, but only if the loudspeaker is operated solely for making announcements to passengers or prospective passengers or to other persons so employed,

    (i)   in accordance with a consent granted by a local authority under Schedule 2 to the Noise and Statutory Nuisance Act 1993 (c. 40).

(3)   This subsection applies if the loudspeaker referred to in subsection (2)(g) —

    (a)   is operated solely for the entertainment of or for communicating with the driver or a passenger of the vehicle (or, if the loudspeaker is or forms part of the horn or similar warning instrument of the vehicle, solely for giving warning to other traffic), and

    (b)   is so operated as not to give reasonable cause for annoyance to persons in the vicinity.

(4)   A person who operates or permits the operation of a loudspeaker in contravention of subsection (1) is guilty of an offence and is liable on summary conviction to —

    (a)   a fine not exceeding level 5 on the standard scale, together with

    (b)   a further fine not exceeding £50 for each day on which the offence continues after the conviction.

(5)   In this section —

    "local authority" means a London borough council (and, in subsection (2)(d), the Greater London Authority),

    "street" means a street within the meaning of section 48(1) of the New Roads and Street Works Act 1991 (c. 22) which is for the time being open to the public,

    "the designated area" means the area specified in an order under section 138,

    "vessel" includes a hovercraft within the meaning of the Hovercraft Act 1968 (c. 59).

(6)   In Schedule 2 to the Noise and Statutory Nuisance Act 1993 (consent to the operation of loudspeakers in streets or roads), in paragraph 1(1), at the end add "or of section 137(1) of the Serious Organised Crime and Police Act 2005".

138   The designated area

(1)   The Secretary of State may by order specify an area as the designated area for the purposes of sections 132 to 137.

(2)   The area may be specified by description, by reference to a map or in any other way.

(3)   No point in the area so specified may be more than one kilometre in a straight line from the point nearest to it in Parliament Square.

Anti-social behaviour

139   Orders about anti-social behaviour etc.

(1)   The Crime and Disorder Act 1998 (c. 37) is amended as provided in subsections (2) to (9).

(2)   In section 1 (anti-social behaviour orders), after subsection (10B) insert —

   "(10C)   In proceedings for an offence under subsection (10), a copy of the original anti-social behaviour order, certified as such by the proper officer of the court which made it, is admissible as evidence of its having been made and of its contents to the same extent that oral evidence of those things is admissible in those proceedings."

(3)   The existing text of section 1A (power of Secretary of State to add to relevant authorities) is to be subsection (1) of that section, and after that subsection add —

   "(2)   The Secretary of State may by order —

      (a)   provide that a person or body of any other description specified in the order is, in such cases and circumstances as may be prescribed by the order, to be a relevant authority for the purposes of such of sections 1 above and 1B, 1CA and 1E below as are specified in the order; and

      (b)   prescribe the description of persons who are to be "relevant persons" in relation to that person or body."

(4)   In section 1C (orders about anti-social behaviour on conviction in criminal proceedings) —

      (a)   after subsection (4) insert —

         "(4A)   The court may adjourn any proceedings in relation to an order under this section even after sentencing the offender.

         (4B)   If the offender does not appear for any adjourned proceedings, the court may further adjourn the proceedings or may issue a warrant for his arrest.

         (4C)   But the court may not issue a warrant for the offender's arrest unless it is satisfied that he has had adequate notice of the time and place of the adjourned proceedings.",

      (b)   in subsection (9), after "(10)" insert ", (10C)".

(5)   Section 1D (interim orders) is amended as provided in subsections (6) to (9).

(6)   For subsections (1) and (2) substitute —

   "(1)   This section applies where —

      (a)   an application is made for an anti-social behaviour order;

      (b)   an application is made for an order under section 1B;

      (c)   a request is made by the prosecution for an order under section 1C; or

    (d) the court is minded to make an order under section 1C of its own motion.

  (2) If, before determining the application or request, or before deciding whether to make an order under section 1C of its own motion, the court considers that it is just to make an order under this section pending the determination of that application or request or before making that decision, it may make such an order."

 (7) In subsection (4)(c), for "main application" substitute "application or request mentioned in subsection (1), or on the court's making a decision as to whether or not to make an order under section 1C of its own motion."

 (8) In subsection (5), at the beginning insert "In relation to cases to which this section applies by virtue of paragraph (a) or (b) of subsection (1),".

 (9) After subsection (5) add —

  "(6) In relation to cases to which this section applies by virtue of paragraph (c) or (d) of subsection (1) —

    (a) subsections (6) and (10) to (12) of section 1 apply for the purposes of the making and effect of orders under this section as they apply for the purposes of the making and effect of anti-social behaviour orders; and

    (b) section 1CA applies for the purposes of the variation or discharge of an order under this section as it applies for the purposes of the variation or discharge of an order under section 1C."

 (10) In section 14A of the Football Spectators Act 1989 (c. 37) (banning orders on conviction of an offence), after subsection (4) insert —

  "(4A) The court may adjourn any proceedings in relation to an order under this section even after sentencing the offender.

  (4B) If the offender does not appear for any adjourned proceedings, the court may further adjourn the proceedings or may issue a warrant for his arrest.

  (4C) But the court may not issue a warrant for the offender's arrest unless it is satisfied that he has had adequate notice of the time and place of the adjourned proceedings."

140 Variation and discharge of anti-social behaviour orders made on conviction

 (1) The Crime and Disorder Act 1998 (c. 37) is amended as follows.

 (2) In section 1 (anti-social behaviour orders), in subsection (1A), after "1B" insert ", 1CA".

 (3) In section 1C (orders on conviction), omit subsections (6) to (8).

 (4) After section 1C insert —

  "1CA Variation and discharge of orders under section 1C

  (1) An offender subject to an order under section 1C may apply to the court which made it for it to be varied or discharged.

(2) If he does so, he must also send written notice of his application to the Director of Public Prosecutions.

(3) The Director of Public Prosecutions may apply to the court which made an order under section 1C for it to be varied or discharged.

(4) A relevant authority may also apply to the court which made an order under section 1C for it to be varied or discharged if it appears to it that —

    (a) in the case of variation, the protection of relevant persons from anti-social acts by the person subject to the order would be more appropriately effected by a variation of the order;

    (b) in the case of discharge, that it is no longer necessary to protect relevant persons from anti-social acts by him by means of such an order.

(5) If the Director of Public Prosecutions or a relevant authority applies for the variation or discharge of an order under section 1C, he or it must also send written notice of the application to the person subject to the order.

(6) In the case of an order under section 1C made by a magistrates' court, the references in subsections (1), (3) and (4) to the court by which the order was made include a reference to any magistrates' court acting in the same local justice area as that court.

(7) No order under section 1C shall be discharged on an application under this section before the end of the period of two years beginning with the day on which the order takes effect, unless —

    (a) in the case of an application under subsection (1), the Director of Public Prosecutions consents, or

    (b) in the case of an application under subsection (3) or (4), the offender consents."

(5) In section 3 of the Prosecution of Offences Act 1985 (c. 23) (functions of the Director of Public Prosecutions), in subsection (2), after paragraph (fa) insert —

    "(fb) where it appears to him appropriate to do so, to have the conduct of applications under section 1CA(3) of the Crime and Disorder Act 1998 for the variation or discharge of orders made under section 1C of that Act;

    (fc) where it appears to him appropriate to do so, to appear on any application under section 1CA of that Act made by a person subject to an order under section 1C of that Act for the variation or discharge of the order."

141 Anti-social behaviour orders etc: reporting restrictions

(1) The Crime and Disorder Act 1998 (c. 37) is amended as follows.

(2) In section 1 (anti-social behaviour orders) —

    (a) after subsection (10C) (inserted by section 139(2) of this Act), insert —

        "(10D) In relation to proceedings brought against a child or a young person for an offence under subsection (10) —

            (a) section 49 of the Children and Young Persons Act 1933 (restrictions on reports of proceedings in which children

> and young persons are concerned) does not apply in respect of the child or young person against whom the proceedings are brought;
>
> (b) section 45 of the Youth Justice and Criminal Evidence Act 1999 (power to restrict reporting of criminal proceedings involving persons under 18) does so apply.
>
> (10E) If, in relation to any such proceedings, the court does exercise its power to give a direction under section 45 of the Youth Justice and Criminal Evidence Act 1999, it shall give its reasons for doing so.",
>
> (b) in subsection (12), before the definition of "the commencement date" insert—
>
> > ""child" and "young person" shall have the same meaning as in the Children and Young Persons Act 1933;".

(3) In section 1C (orders about anti-social behaviour on conviction in criminal proceedings), in subsection (9), after "(10C)" (inserted by section 139(4)(b) of this Act) insert ", (10D), (10E)".

(4) Subject to paragraph 2(2) of Schedule 2 to the Youth Justice and Criminal Evidence Act 1999 (c. 23), until section 45 of that Act comes into force, the references to it in section 1(10D)(b) and (10E) of the Crime and Disorder Act 1998 (c. 37) (inserted by subsection (2) of this section) shall be read as references to section 39 of the Children and Young Persons Act 1933 (c. 12).

142 Contracting out of local authority functions relating to anti-social behaviour orders

(1) In the Crime and Disorder Act 1998 after section 1E (consultation requirements relating to individual support orders) insert—

"1F   Contracting out of local authority functions

> (1) The Secretary of State may by order provide that a relevant authority which is a local authority may make arrangements with a person specified (or of a description specified) in the order for the exercise of any function it has under sections 1 to 1E above—
>
> > (a) by such a person, or
> >
> > (b) by an employee of his.
>
> (2) The order may provide—
>
> > (a) that the power of the relevant authority to make the arrangements is subject to such conditions as are specified in the order;
> >
> > (b) that the arrangements must be subject to such conditions as are so specified;
> >
> > (c) that the arrangements may be made subject to such other conditions as the relevant authority thinks appropriate.
>
> (3) The order may provide that the arrangements may authorise the exercise of the function—
>
> > (a) either wholly or to such extent as may be specified in the order or arrangements;
> >
> > (b) either generally or in such cases or areas as may be so specified.

(4) An order may provide that the person with whom arrangements are made in pursuance of the order is to be treated as if he were a public body for the purposes of section 1 of the Local Authorities (Goods and Services) Act 1970.

(5) The Secretary of State must not make an order under this section unless he first consults —

     (a) the National Assembly for Wales, if the order relates to a relevant authority in Wales;

     (b) such representatives of local government as he thinks appropriate;

     (c) such other persons as he thinks appropriate.

(6) Any arrangements made by a relevant authority in pursuance of an order under this section do not prevent the relevant authority from exercising the function to which the arrangements relate.

(7) The following provisions of the Deregulation and Contracting Out Act 1994 apply for the purposes of arrangements made in pursuance of an order under this section as they apply for the purposes of an authorisation to exercise functions by virtue of an order under section 70(2) of that Act —

     (a) section 72 (effect of contracting out);

     (b) section 73 (termination of contracting out);

     (c) section 75 and Schedule 15 (provision relating to disclosure of information);

     (d) paragraph 3 of Schedule 16 (authorised persons to be treated as officers of local authority).

(8) For the purposes of subsection (7), any reference in the provisions specified in paragraphs (a) to (d) to a person authorised to exercise a function must be construed as a reference to a person with whom an arrangement is made for the exercise of the function in pursuance of an order under this section.

(9) Relevant authorities and any person with whom arrangements are made in pursuance of an order under this section must have regard to any guidance issued by the Secretary of State for the purposes of this section.

(10) An order under this section may make different provision for different purposes.

(11) An order under this section may contain —

     (a) such consequential, supplemental or incidental provisions (including provision modifying any enactment), or

     (b) such transitional provisions or savings,

as the person making the order thinks appropriate.

(12) Each of the following is a local authority —

     (a) a local authority within the meaning of section 270 of the Local Government Act 1972;

     (b) the Common Council of the City of London;

     (c) the Council of the Isles of Scilly."

(2) In subsection (1) of section 1A of that Act (definition of relevant authority) (as re-numbered by section 139(3) of this Act) for "and 1E" substitute ", 1E and 1F".

(3) In section 114(3) of that Act (orders and regulations) after "section" insert "1F,".

143 Special measures for witnesses in proceedings for anti-social behaviour orders etc.

After section 1H of the Crime and Disorder Act 1998 (c. 37) (as amended by the Drugs Act 2005 (c. 17)) insert—

"1I Special measures for witnesses

(1) This section applies to the following proceedings—

  (a) any proceedings in a magistrates' court on an application for an anti-social behaviour order,

  (b) any proceedings in a magistrates' court or the Crown Court so far as relating to the issue whether to make an order under section 1C, and

  (c) any proceedings in a magistrates' court so far as relating to the issue whether to make an order under section 1D.

(2) Chapter 1 of Part 2 of the Youth Justice and Criminal Evidence Act 1999 (special measures directions in the case of vulnerable and intimidated witnesses) shall apply in relation to any such proceedings as it applies in relation to criminal proceedings, but with—

  (a) the omission of the provisions of that Act mentioned in subsection (3) (which make provision appropriate only in the context of criminal proceedings), and

  (b) any other necessary modifications.

(3) The provisions are—

  (a) section 17(4),

  (b) section 21(1)(b) and (5) to (7),

  (c) section 22(1)(b) and (2)(b) and (c),

  (d) section 27(10), and

  (e) section 32.

(4) Any rules of court made under or for the purposes of Chapter 1 of Part 2 of that Act shall apply in relation to proceedings to which this section applies—

  (a) to such extent as may be provided by rules of court, and

  (b) subject to such modifications as may be so provided.

(5) Section 47 of that Act (restrictions on reporting special measures directions etc.) applies, with any necessary modifications, in relation to—

  (a) a direction under section 19 of the Act as applied by this section, or

  (b) a direction discharging or varying such a direction,

and sections 49 and 51 of that Act (offences) apply accordingly."

Parental compensation orders

144 Parental compensation orders

Schedule 10 is to have effect.

PART 5

MISCELLANEOUS

Protection of activities of certain organisations

145 Interference with contractual relationships so as to harm animal research organisation

(1) A person (A) commits an offence if, with the intention of harming an animal research organisation, he—

    (a) does a relevant act, or

    (b) threatens that he or somebody else will do a relevant act,

in circumstances in which that act or threat is intended or likely to cause a second person (B) to take any of the steps in subsection (2).

(2) The steps are—

    (a) not to perform any contractual obligation owed by B to a third person (C) (whether or not such non-performance amounts to a breach of contract);

    (b) to terminate any contract B has with C;

    (c) not to enter into a contract with C.

(3) For the purposes of this section, a "relevant act" is—

    (a) an act amounting to a criminal offence, or

    (b) a tortious act causing B to suffer loss or damage of any description;

but paragraph (b) does not include an act which is actionable on the ground only that it induces another person to break a contract with B.

(4) For the purposes of this section, "contract" includes any other arrangement (and "contractual" is to be read accordingly).

(5) For the purposes of this section, to "harm" an animal research organisation means—

    (a) to cause the organisation to suffer loss or damage of any description, or

    (b) to prevent or hinder the carrying out by the organisation of any of its activities.

(6) This section does not apply to any act done wholly or mainly in contemplation or furtherance of a trade dispute.

(7) In subsection (6) "trade dispute" has the same meaning as in Part 4 of the Trade Union and Labour Relations (Consolidation) Act 1992 (c. 52), except that section 218 of that Act shall be read as if—

    (a) it made provision corresponding to section 244(4) of that Act, and

    (b) in subsection (5), the definition of "worker" included any person falling within paragraph (b) of the definition of "worker" in section 244(5).

146   Intimidation of persons connected with animal research organisation

(1)   A person (A) commits an offence if, with the intention of causing a second person (B) to abstain from doing something which B is entitled to do (or to do something which B is entitled to abstain from doing) —

    (a)   A threatens B that A or somebody else will do a relevant act, and

    (b)   A does so wholly or mainly because B is a person falling within subsection (2).

(2)   A person falls within this subsection if he is —

    (a)   an employee or officer of an animal research organisation;

    (b)   a student at an educational establishment that is an animal research organisation;

    (c)   a lessor or licensor of any premises occupied by an animal research organisation;

    (d)   a person with a financial interest in, or who provides financial assistance to, an animal research organisation;

    (e)   a customer or supplier of an animal research organisation;

    (f)   a person who is contemplating becoming someone within paragraph (c), (d) or (e);

    (g)   a person who is, or is contemplating becoming, a customer or supplier of someone within paragraph (c), (d), (e) or (f);

    (h)   an employee or officer of someone within paragraph (c), (d), (e), (f) or (g);

    (i)   a person with a financial interest in, or who provides financial assistance to, someone within paragraph (c), (d), (e), (f) or (g);

    (j)   a spouse, civil partner, friend or relative of, or a person who is known personally to, someone within any of paragraphs (a) to (i);

    (k)   a person who is, or is contemplating becoming, a customer or supplier of someone within paragraph (a), (b), (h), (i) or (j); or

    (l)   an employer of someone within paragraph (j).

(3)   For the purposes of this section, an "officer" of an animal research organisation or a person includes —

    (a)   where the organisation or person is a body corporate, a director, manager or secretary;

    (b)   where the organisation or person is a charity, a charity trustee (within the meaning of the Charities Act 1993 (c. 10));

    (c)   where the organisation or person is a partnership, a partner.

(4)   For the purposes of this section —

    (a)   a person is a customer or supplier of another person if he purchases goods, services or facilities from, or (as the case may be) supplies goods, services or facilities to, that other; and

    (b)   "supplier" includes a person who supplies services in pursuance of any enactment that requires or authorises such services to be provided.

(5)   For the purposes of this section, a "relevant act" is —

    (a)   an act amounting to a criminal offence, or

    (b)   a tortious act causing B or another person to suffer loss or damage of any description.

(6) The Secretary of State may by order amend this section so as to include within subsection (2) any description of persons framed by reference to their connection with—

    (a) an animal research organisation, or

    (b) any description of persons for the time being mentioned in that subsection.

(7) This section does not apply to any act done wholly or mainly in contemplation or furtherance of a trade dispute.

(8) In subsection (7) "trade dispute" has the meaning given by section 145(7).

147 Penalty for offences under sections 145 and 146

(1) A person guilty of an offence under section 145 or 146 is liable—

    (a) on summary conviction, to imprisonment for a term not exceeding 12 months or to a fine not exceeding the statutory maximum, or to both;

    (b) on conviction on indictment, to imprisonment for a term not exceeding five years or to a fine, or to both.

(2) No proceedings for an offence under either of those sections may be instituted except by or with the consent of the Director of Public Prosecutions.

148 Animal research organisations

(1) For the purposes of sections 145 and 146 "animal research organisation" means any person or organisation falling within subsection (2) or (3).

(2) A person or organisation falls within this subsection if he or it is the owner, lessee or licensee of premises constituting or including—

    (a) a place specified in a licence granted under section 4 or 5 of the 1986 Act,

    (b) a scientific procedure establishment designated under section 6 of that Act, or

    (c) a breeding or supplying establishment designated under section 7 of that Act.

(3) A person or organisation falls within this subsection if he or it employs, or engages under a contract for services, any of the following in his capacity as such—

    (a) the holder of a personal licence granted under section 4 of the 1986 Act,

    (b) the holder of a project licence granted under section 5 of that Act,

    (c) a person specified under section 6(5) of that Act, or

    (d) a person specified under section 7(5) of that Act.

(4) The Secretary of State may by order amend this section so as to include a reference to any description of persons whom he considers to be involved in, or to have a direct connection with persons who are involved in, the application of regulated procedures.

(5) In this section—

    "the 1986 Act" means the Animals (Scientific Procedures) Act 1986 (c. 14);

    "organisation" includes any institution, trust, undertaking or association of persons;

    "premises" includes any place within the meaning of the 1986 Act;

"regulated procedures" has the meaning given by section 2 of the 1986 Act.

149   Extension of sections 145 to 147

(1)   The Secretary of State may by order provide for sections 145, 146 and 147 to apply in relation to persons or organisations of a description specified in the order as they apply in relation to animal research organisations.

(2)   The Secretary of State may, however, only make an order under this section if satisfied that a series of acts has taken place and —

    (a)   that those acts were directed at persons or organisations of the description specified in the order or at persons having a connection with them, and

    (b)   that, if those persons or organisations had been animal research organisations, those acts would have constituted offences under section 145 or 146.

(3)   In this section "organisation" and "animal research organisation" have the meanings given by section 148.

Vehicle registration and insurance and road traffic offences

150   Offence in respect of incorrectly registered vehicles

(1)   After section 43B of the Vehicle Excise and Registration Act 1994 (c. 22) insert —

"Offence in respect of incorrectly registered vehicles

43C   Offence of using an incorrectly registered vehicle

    (1)   A person is guilty of an offence if, on a public road or in a public place, he uses a vehicle to which subsection (2) applies and in respect of which —

        (a)   the name and address of the keeper are not recorded in the register, or

        (b)   any of the particulars recorded in the register are incorrect.

    (2)   This subsection applies to a vehicle if —

        (a)   vehicle excise duty is chargeable in respect of it, or

        (b)   it is an exempt vehicle in respect of which regulations under this Act require a nil licence to be in force.

    (3)   It is a defence for a person charged with an offence under subsection (1) to show (as the case may be) —

        (a)   that there was no reasonable opportunity, before the material time, to furnish the name and address of the keeper of the vehicle, or

        (b)   that there was no reasonable opportunity, before the material time, to furnish particulars correcting the incorrect particulars.

    (4)   It is also a defence for a person charged with an offence under subsection (1) to show —

        (a)   that he had reasonable grounds for believing, or that it was reasonable for him to expect, that the name and address of the keeper or the other particulars of registration (as the case may be) were correctly recorded in the register, or

 (b) that any exception prescribed in regulations under this section is met.

(5) A person guilty of an offence under this section is liable on summary conviction to a fine not exceeding level 3 on the standard scale.

(6) The Secretary of State may make regulations prescribing, varying or revoking exceptions for the purposes of subsection (4)(b).

(7) In this section—

  "keeper", in relation to a vehicle, means the person by whom it is kept at the material time;

  "the register" means the register kept by the Secretary of State under Part 2."

(2) In Schedule 3 to the Road Traffic Offenders Act 1988 (c. 53) (fixed penalty offences) after the entry relating to section 43 of the Vehicle Excise and Registration Act 1994 insert—

"Section 43C of that Act	Using an incorrectly registered vehicle."

151 Power of constables etc. to require production of registration documents in respect of a vehicle

After section 28 of the Vehicle Excise and Registration Act 1994 (c. 22) insert—

"Power of constables etc. to require production of documents

28A Power of constables etc. to require production of registration documents

(1) A person using a vehicle in respect of which a registration document has been issued must produce the document for inspection on being so required by—

 (a) a constable, or

 (b) a person authorised by the Secretary of State for the purposes of this section (an "authorised person").

(2) An authorised person exercising the power conferred by subsection (1) must, if so requested, produce evidence of his authority to exercise the power.

(3) A person is guilty of an offence if he fails to comply with subsection (1).

(4) Subsection (3) does not apply if any of the following conditions is satisfied.

(5) The first condition is that—

 (a) the person produces the registration document, in person, at a police station specified by him at the time of the request, and

 (b) he does so within 7 days after the date on which the request was made or as soon as is reasonably practicable.

(6)   The second condition is that—

     (a)   the vehicle is subject to a lease or hire agreement,

     (b)   the vehicle is not registered in the name of the lessee or hirer under that agreement and is not required to be so registered,

     (c)   the person produces appropriate evidence of the agreement to the constable or authorised person at the time of the request or he produces such evidence in person, at a police station specified by him at the time of the request—

         (i)   within 7 days after the date of the request, or

         (ii)   as soon as is reasonably practicable, and

     (d)   the person has reasonable grounds for believing, or it is reasonable for him to expect, that the person from whom the vehicle has been leased or hired is able to produce, or require the production of, the registration document.

(7)   In subsection (6)(c) "appropriate evidence" means—

     (a)   a copy of the agreement, or

     (b)   such other documentary evidence of the agreement as is prescribed in regulations under this section.

(8)   The third condition is that any exception prescribed in regulations under this section is met.

(9)   Where a requirement is imposed under subsection (1) by an authorised person, a testing station provided under section 52(2) of the Road Traffic Act 1988 may be specified under subsection (5)(a) or (6)(c) instead of a police station.

(10)   A person accused of an offence under this section is not entitled to the benefit of an exception conferred by or under this section unless evidence is adduced that is sufficient to raise an issue with respect to that exception, but where evidence is so adduced it is for the prosecution to prove beyond reasonable doubt that the exception does not apply.

(11)   A person guilty of an offence under this section is liable on summary conviction to a fine not exceeding level 2 on the standard scale.

(12)   The Secretary of State may make regulations—

     (a)   prescribing descriptions of evidence for the purposes of subsection (7);

     (b)   prescribing, varying or revoking exceptions for the purposes of subsection (8).

(13)   In this section "registration document" means a registration document issued in accordance with regulations under section 22(1)(e)."

152   Power to seize etc. vehicles driven without licence or insurance

After section 165 of the Road Traffic Act 1988 (c. 52) insert—

"165A Power to seize vehicles driven without licence or insurance

(1)   Subsection (5) applies if any of the following conditions is satisfied.

(2)   The first condition is that—

      (a)   a constable in uniform requires, under section 164, a person to produce his licence and its counterpart for examination,

      (b)   the person fails to produce them, and

      (c)   the constable has reasonable grounds for believing that a motor vehicle is or was being driven by the person in contravention of section 87(1).

(3)   The second condition is that—

      (a)   a constable in uniform requires, under section 165, a person to produce evidence that a motor vehicle is not or was not being driven in contravention of section 143,

      (b)   the person fails to produce such evidence, and

      (c)   the constable has reasonable grounds for believing that the vehicle is or was being so driven.

(4)   The third condition is that—

      (a)   a constable in uniform requires, under section 163, a person driving a motor vehicle to stop the vehicle,

      (b)   the person fails to stop the vehicle, or to stop the vehicle long enough, for the constable to make such lawful enquiries as he considers appropriate, and

      (c)   the constable has reasonable grounds for believing that the vehicle is or was being driven in contravention of section 87(1) or 143.

(5)   Where this subsection applies, the constable may—

      (a)   seize the vehicle in accordance with subsections (6) and (7) and remove it;

      (b)   enter, for the purpose of exercising a power falling within paragraph (a), any premises (other than a private dwelling house) on which he has reasonable grounds for believing the vehicle to be;

      (c)   use reasonable force, if necessary, in the exercise of any power conferred by paragraph (a) or (b).

(6)   Before seizing the motor vehicle, the constable must warn the person by whom it appears that the vehicle is or was being driven in contravention of section 87(1) or 143 that he will seize it—

      (a)   in a section 87(1) case, if the person does not produce his licence and its counterpart immediately;

      (b)   in a section 143 case, if the person does not provide him immediately with evidence that the vehicle is not or was not being driven in contravention of that section.

But the constable is not required to give such a warning if the circumstances make it impracticable for him to do so.

(7)   If the constable is unable to seize the vehicle immediately because the person driving the vehicle has failed to stop as requested or has driven off, he may seize it at any time within the period of 24 hours beginning with the time at which the condition in question is first satisfied.

(8)   The powers conferred on a constable by this section are exercisable only at a time when regulations under section 165B are in force.

(9)   In this section—

(a)   a reference to a motor vehicle does not include an invalid carriage;

(b)   a reference to evidence that a motor vehicle is not or was not being driven in contravention of section 143 is a reference to a document or other evidence within section 165(2)(a);

(c)   "counterpart" and "licence" have the same meanings as in section 164;

(d)   "private dwelling house" does not include any garage or other structure occupied with the dwelling house, or any land appurtenant to the dwelling house.

165B   Retention etc. of vehicles seized under section 165A

(1)   The Secretary of State may by regulations make provision as to —

    (a)   the removal and retention of motor vehicles seized under section 165A; and

    (b)   the release or disposal of such motor vehicles.

(2)   Regulations under subsection (1) may, in particular, make provision —

    (a)   for the giving of notice of the seizure of a motor vehicle under section 165A to a person who is the registered keeper, the owner or the driver of that vehicle;

    (b)   for the procedure by which a person who claims to be the registered keeper or the owner of a motor vehicle seized under section 165A may seek to have it released;

    (c)   for requiring the payment, by the registered keeper, owner or driver of the vehicle, of fees, charges or costs in relation to the removal and retention of such a motor vehicle and to any application for its release;

    (d)   as to the circumstances in which a motor vehicle seized under section 165A may be disposed of;

    (e)   as to the destination —

        (i)   of any fees or charges payable in accordance with the regulations;

        (ii)   of the proceeds (if any) arising from the disposal of a motor vehicle seized under section 165A;

    (f)   for the delivery to a local authority, in circumstances prescribed by or determined in accordance with the regulations, of any motor vehicle seized under section 165A.

(3)   Regulations under subsection (1) must provide that a person who would otherwise be liable to pay any fee or charge under the regulations is not liable to pay it if —

    (a)   he was not driving the motor vehicle at the time in question, and

    (b)   he did not know that the vehicle was being driven at that time, had not consented to its being driven and could not, by the taking of reasonable steps, have prevented it from being driven.

(4)   Regulations under subsection (1) may make different provision for different cases.

(5)   In this section —

    "local authority" —

        (a)   in relation to England, means —

        (i)   a county council,

        (ii) the council of a district comprised in an area for which there is no county council,

        (iii) a London borough council,

        (iv) the Common Council of the City of London, or

        (v) Transport for London;

   (b) in relation to Wales, means the council of a county or county borough; and

   (c) in relation to Scotland, means a council constituted under section 2 of the Local Government etc. (Scotland) Act 1994;

"registered keeper", in relation to a motor vehicle, means the person in whose name the vehicle is registered under the Vehicle Excise and Registration Act 1994."

153 Disclosure of information about insurance status of vehicles

(1) The Secretary of State may by regulations make provision for and in connection with requiring MIIC to make available relevant vehicle insurance information to PITO for it to process with a view to making the processed information available for use by constables.

(2) "Relevant vehicle insurance information" means information relating to vehicles the use of which has been (but no longer is) insured under a policy of insurance, or security in respect of third party risks, complying with the requirements of Part 6 of the Road Traffic Act 1988 (c. 52).

(3) The regulations may in particular—

   (a) require all relevant vehicle insurance information or any particular description of such information to be made available to PITO,

   (b) determine the purposes for which information processed from such information by PITO may be made available for use by constables, and

   (c) determine the circumstances in which any of the processed information which has been made available for use by constables may be further disclosed by them.

(4) In this section—

"information" means information held in any form,

"MIIC" means the Motor Insurers' Information Centre (a company limited by guarantee and incorporated under the Companies Act 1985 (c. 6) on 8th December 1998), and

"PITO" means the Police Information Technology Organisation.

154 Power to require specimens of breath at roadside or at hospital etc.

(1) Section 6D of the Road Traffic Act 1988 (preliminary tests for drink and drugs: arrest) is amended as follows.

(2) After subsection (1) insert—

"(1A) The fact that specimens of breath have been provided under section 7 of this Act by the person concerned does not prevent subsection (1) above having effect if the constable who imposed on him the requirement to provide the specimens has reasonable cause to believe that the device used to analyse the specimens has not produced a reliable indication of the proportion of alcohol in the breath of the person."

(3)   After subsection (2) insert—

"(2A)   A person arrested under this section may, instead of being taken to a police station, be detained at or near the place where the preliminary test was, or would have been, administered, with a view to imposing on him there a requirement under section 7 of this Act."

(4)   Section 7 of that Act (provision of specimens for analysis) is amended as follows.

(5)   For subsection (2) substitute—

"(2)   A requirement under this section to provide specimens of breath can only be made—

(a)   at a police station,

(b)   at a hospital, or

(c)   at or near a place where a relevant breath test has been administered to the person concerned or would have been so administered but for his failure to co-operate with it.

(2A)   For the purposes of this section "a relevant breath test" is a procedure involving the provision by the person concerned of a specimen of breath to be used for the purpose of obtaining an indication whether the proportion of alcohol in his breath or blood is likely to exceed the prescribed limit.

(2B)   A requirement under this section to provide specimens of breath may not be made at or near a place mentioned in subsection (2)(c) above unless the constable making it—

(a)   is in uniform, or

(b)   has imposed a requirement on the person concerned to co-operate with a relevant breath test in circumstances in which section 6(5) of this Act applies.

(2C)   Where a constable has imposed a requirement on the person concerned to co-operate with a relevant breath test at any place, he is entitled to remain at or near that place in order to impose on him there a requirement under this section.

(2D)   If a requirement under subsection (1)(a) above has been made at a place other than at a police station, such a requirement may subsequently be made at a police station if (but only if)—

(a)   a device or a reliable device of the type mentioned in subsection (1)(a) above was not available at that place or it was for any other reason not practicable to use such a device there, or

(b)   the constable who made the previous requirement has reasonable cause to believe that the device used there has not produced a reliable indication of the proportion of alcohol in the breath of the person concerned."

(6)   In subsection (3) (circumstances in which requirement to provide a specimen of blood or urine may be made)—

(a) in paragraph (b) (breath-testing device not available etc.) insert at the beginning "specimens of breath have not been provided elsewhere and", and

(b) in paragraph (bb) (police station breath-testing device has not provided a reliable indication of alcohol level) for "at the police station" substitute "(at the police station or elsewhere)".

(7) In section 8 of that Act (choice of specimens of breath) after subsection (2) insert—

"(2A) If the person who makes a claim under subsection (2) above was required to provide specimens of breath under section 7 of this Act at or near a place mentioned in subsection (2)(c) of that section, a constable may arrest him without warrant."

(8) In section 9(1) of that Act (protection for hospital patients) for "for a laboratory test" substitute "under section 7 of this Act".

(9) Section 10 of that Act (detention of persons affected by alcohol or a drug) is amended as follows.

(10) In subsection (1) (detention at a police station)—

(a) for "until it appears to the constable" substitute "(or, if the specimen was provided otherwise than at a police station, arrested and taken to and detained at a police station) if a constable has reasonable grounds for believing", and

(b) for "not be committing" substitute "commit".

(11) In subsection (2) (grounds for detention) for "A person shall not be detained in pursuance of this section if it appears to a" substitute "Subsection (1) above does not apply to the person if it ought reasonably to appear to the".

(12) After that subsection insert—

"(2A) A person who is at a hospital as a patient shall not be arrested and taken from there to a police station in pursuance of this section if it would be prejudicial to his proper care and treatment as a patient."

155 Payments by Secretary of State to police authorities in relation to the prevention, detection and enforcement of certain traffic offences

(1) The Secretary of State may make payments in respect of the whole or any part of the expenditure of a police authority in relation to—

(a) the prevention and detection of offences to which subsection (3) applies, or

(b) any enforcement action or proceedings in respect of such offences or any alleged such offences.

(2) Payments under this section shall be made at such times, in such manner and subject to such conditions as the Secretary of State may determine.

(3) This subsection applies to offences committed in England and Wales under the following provisions—

Road Traffic Act 1988 (c. 52)

section 14 (requirements regarding seat belts: adults);

section 15(2) and (4) (restriction on carrying children not wearing seat belts in motor vehicles);

section 42 (motor vehicles and trailers: other construction and use requirements) in relation to the construction and use requirements imposed by the following regulations—

(a) regulations 54, 57, 104 and 110 of the Road Vehicles (Construction and Use) Regulations 1986 (S.I. 1986/1078);

(b) regulations 11(1) and 25 of the Road Vehicles Lighting Regulations 1989 (S.I. 1989/1796);

section 47 (obligatory test certificates for motor vehicles);

section 87(1) (drivers of motor vehicles to have driving licences);

section 143 (users of motor vehicles to be insured or secured against third-party risks);

section 163 (power of police to stop vehicles);

section 172 (duty to give information as to the identity of driver etc. in certain circumstances);

Vehicle Excise and Registration Act 1994 (c. 22)

section 33 (not exhibiting vehicle licence);

section 42 (not fixing registration mark);

section 43 (obscured registration mark);

section 43C (using an incorrectly registered vehicle);

section 59 (regulations: offences) in relation to the requirements imposed by regulation 11 of the Road Vehicles (Display of Registration Marks) Regulations 2001 (S.I. 2001/561).

(4) The Secretary of State may by order amend the list of offences in subsection (3) so as to add, modify or omit any entry.

(5) In subsection (3) "construction and use requirements" has the meaning given by section 41(7) of the Road Traffic Act 1988 (c. 52).

156 Payments by Scottish Ministers to police authorities etc. in relation to the prevention, detection and enforcement of certain traffic offences

(1) The Scottish Ministers may make payments in respect of the whole or any part of the expenditure of a police authority or joint police board (within the meaning of the Police (Scotland) Act 1967 (c. 77)) in relation to—

(a) the prevention and detection of offences to which subsection (3) applies, or

(b) any enforcement action or proceedings in respect of such offences or any alleged such offences.

(2) Payments under this section shall be made at such times, in such manner and subject to such conditions as the Scottish Ministers may determine.

(3) This subsection applies to offences committed in Scotland under the following provisions—

Road Traffic Act 1988 (c. 52)

section 14 (requirements regarding seat belts: adults);

section 15(2) and (4) (restriction on carrying children not wearing seat belts in motor vehicles);

section 42 (motor vehicles and trailers: other construction and use requirements) in relation to the construction and use requirements imposed by the following regulations—

(a) regulations 54, 57, 104 and 110 of the Road Vehicles (Construction and Use) Regulations 1986 (S.I. 1986/1078);

(b) regulations 11(1) and 25 of the Road Vehicles Lighting Regulations 1989 (S.I. 1989/1796);

section 47 (obligatory test certificates for motor vehicles);

section 87(1) (drivers of motor vehicles to have driving licences);

section 143 (users of motor vehicles to be insured or secured against third-party risks);

section 163 (power of police to stop vehicles);

section 172 (duty to give information as to the identity of driver etc. in certain circumstances);

Vehicle Excise and Registration Act 1994 (c. 22)

section 33 (not exhibiting vehicle licence);

section 42 (not fixing registration mark);

section 43 (obscured registration mark);

section 43C (using an incorrectly registered vehicle);

section 59 (regulations: offences) in relation to the requirements imposed by regulation 11 of the Road Vehicles (Display of Registration Marks) Regulations 2001 (S.I. 2001/561).

(4) The Scottish Ministers may by order amend the list of offences in subsection (3) so as to add, modify or omit any entry.

(5) In subsection (3) "construction and use requirements" has the meaning given by section 41(7) of the Road Traffic Act 1988 (c. 52).

(6) In section 95 of the Road Traffic Offenders Act 1988 (c. 53) (destination of fines imposed in respect of road traffic offences etc.) insert—

"(3) There shall be paid into the Scottish Consolidated Fund all fixed penalties imposed in respect of offences, committed in Scotland, to which section 156(3) of the Serious Organised Crime and Police Act 2005 applies."

Local policing information

157 Publication of local policing information

After section 8 of the Police Act 1996 (c. 16) insert—

"8A Local policing summaries

(1) As soon as possible after the end of each financial year, every police authority established under section 3 shall issue a report for members of the public in the authority's area on matters relating to the policing of that area for the year.

(2) Such a report is referred to in this section as a "local policing summary".

(3) The Secretary of State may by order specify matters which are to be included in a local policing summary.

(4)   A police authority shall arrange —

    (a)   for every local policing summary issued by it under this section to be published in such manner as appears to it to be appropriate, and

    (b)   for a copy of every such summary to be sent, by whatever means appear to the authority to be appropriate, to each person liable to pay any tax, precept or levy to or in respect of the authority.

(5)   It shall be the duty of a police authority, in preparing and publishing a local policing summary, to have regard to any guidance given by the Secretary of State about the form and content of local policing summaries and the manner of their publication.

(6)   Before making an order under subsection (3), and before giving any such guidance as is referred to in subsection (5), the Secretary of State must consult —

    (a)   persons whom he considers to represent the interests of police authorities,

    (b)   persons whom he considers to represent the interests of chief officers of police, and

    (c)   such other persons as he thinks fit.

(7)   This section shall apply in relation to the Metropolitan Police Authority as it applies to a police authority established under section 3.

(8)   A statutory instrument containing an order under subsection (3) shall be subject to annulment in pursuance of a resolution of either House of Parliament."

Other miscellaneous police matters

158   Responsibilities in relation to the health and safety etc. of police

(1)   In section 51A of the Health and Safety at Work etc. Act 1974 (c. 37) (application of Part 1 of that Act to police) after subsection (2) insert —

"(2A)   For the purposes of this Part the relevant officer, as defined by subsection (2)(a) or (c) above, shall be treated as a corporation sole.

(2B)   Where, in a case in which the relevant officer, as so defined, is guilty of an offence by virtue of this section, it is proved —

    (a)   that the officer-holder personally consented to the commission of the offence,

    (b)   that he personally connived in its commission, or

    (c)   that the commission of the offence was attributable to personal neglect on his part,

the office-holder (as well as the corporation sole) shall be guilty of the offence and shall be liable to be proceeded against and punished accordingly.

(2C)   In subsection (2B) above "the office-holder", in relation to the relevant officer, means an individual who, at the time of the consent, connivance or neglect —

(a) held the office or other position mentioned in subsection (2) above as the office or position of that officer; or

(b) was for the time being responsible for exercising and performing the powers and duties of that office or position.

(2D) The provisions mentioned in subsection (2E) below (which impose the same liability for unlawful conduct of constables on persons having their direction or control as would arise if the constables were employees of those persons) do not apply to any liability by virtue of this Part.

(2E) Those provisions are—

(a) section 39 of the Police (Scotland) Act 1967;

(b) section 88(1) of the Police Act 1996;

(c) section 97(9) of that Act;

(d) paragraph 7(1) of Schedule 8 to the Police Act 1997;

(e) paragraph 14(1) of Schedule 3 to the Criminal Justice and Police Act 2001;

(f) section 28 of the Serious Organised Crime and Police Act 2005.

(2F) In the application of this section to Scotland—

(a) subsection (2A) shall have effect as if for the words "corporation sole" there were substituted "distinct juristic person (that is to say, as a juristic person distinct from the individual who for the time being is the office-holder)";

(b) subsection (2B) shall have effect as if for the words "corporation sole" there were substituted "juristic person"; and

(c) subsection (2C) shall have effect as if for the words "subsection (2B)" there were substituted "subsections (2A) and (2B)"."

(2) For subsection (2) of each of the following sections of the Employment Rights Act 1996 (c. 18)—

(a) section 49A (right of police officers not to suffer detriment in relation to health and safety issues), and

(b) section 134A (right of police officers not to be unfairly dismissed in relation to health and safety issues),

substitute the subsection set out in subsection (3) of this section.

(3) The subsection to be substituted is—

"(2) In this section "the relevant officer", in relation to—

(a) a person holding the office of constable, or

(b) a person holding an appointment as a police cadet,

means the person who under section 51A of the Health and Safety at Work etc. Act 1974 is to be treated as his employer for the purposes of Part 1 of that Act."

(4) The following provisions of the Police Reform Act 2002 (c. 30) (which relate to duties and rights in relation to the health and safety of police) cease to have effect—

(a) section 95, and

(b) in Schedule 8, the reference to section 5 of the Police (Health and Safety) Act 1997 (c. 42).

(5)   The amendments made by subsections (1) to (3) have effect for the purposes of any proceedings in or before a court or tribunal that are commenced on or after the day on which this Act is passed as if the amendments had come into force on 1st July 1998.

(6)   For the purposes of proceedings commenced against a person in his capacity by virtue of this section as a corporation sole (or, in Scotland, as a distinct juristic person) anything done by or in relation to that person before the passing of this Act shall be deemed to have been done by or in relation to that person in that capacity.

(7)   No person shall be liable by virtue of section 51A(2B) of the Health and Safety at Work etc. Act 1974 (c. 37) in respect of anything occurring before the passing of this Act.

159   Investigations: accelerated procedure in special cases

Schedule 11 (which makes provision for an accelerated procedure for certain investigations into the conduct of police officers) has effect.

160   Investigations: deaths and serious injuries during or after contact with the police

Schedule 12 (which makes provision for the investigation of deaths and serious injuries which occur during or after contact with persons serving with the police) has effect.

Royal Parks etc.

161   Abolition of Royal Parks Constabulary

(1)   The Royal Parks Constabulary is abolished.

(2)   Every relevant person shall cease to be a park constable on the appointed day.

(3)   Subsection (2) is not to be taken as terminating the Crown employment of any relevant person.

(4)   In this section, section 162 and Schedule 13 —

        "appointed day" means such day as the Secretary of State may by order appoint for the purposes of this section,

        "Crown employment" has the same meaning as in the Employment Rights Act 1996 (c. 18), and

        "relevant person" means a person who immediately before the appointed day is serving as a park constable with the Royal Parks Constabulary.

(5)   Schedule 13 (which provides for transfers to the Metropolitan Police Authority and makes amendments) has effect.

162   Regulation of specified parks

(1)   From the appointed day the Parks Regulation Act 1872 (c. 15) does not apply to the specified parks.

(2) But from the appointed day section 2 of the Parks Regulation (Amendment) Act 1926 (c. 36) applies in relation to the specified parks in the same way as it applies in relation to parks to which the Parks Regulation Act 1872 applies.

(3) The Secretary of State must ensure that copies of any regulations made under section 2 of the Parks Regulation (Amendment) Act 1926 (c. 36) which are in force in relation to a specified park are displayed in a suitable position in that park.

(4) In this section "specified park" means a park, garden, recreation ground, open space or other land in the metropolitan police district—

   (a) which is specified in an order made by the Secretary of State before the appointed day, and

   (b) to which the Parks Regulation Act 1872 (c. 15) then applied by virtue of section 1 of the Parks Regulation (Amendment) Act 1926.

Criminal record checks

163 Criminal record certificates

(1) Sections 113 and 115 of the Police Act 1997 (c. 50) (criminal record certificates) are omitted.

(2) Before section 114 of that Act insert—

"113A Criminal record certificates

   (1) The Secretary of State must issue a criminal record certificate to any individual who—

      (a) makes an application in the prescribed manner and form, and

      (b) pays in the prescribed manner any prescribed fee.

   (2) The application must—

      (a) be countersigned by a registered person, and

      (b) be accompanied by a statement by the registered person that the certificate is required for the purposes of an exempted question.

   (3) A criminal record certificate is a certificate which—

      (a) gives the prescribed details of every relevant matter relating to the applicant which is recorded in central records, or

      (b) states that there is no such matter.

   (4) The Secretary of State must send a copy of a criminal record certificate to the registered person who countersigned the application.

   (5) The Secretary of State may treat an application under this section as an application under section 113B if—

      (a) in his opinion the certificate is required for a purpose prescribed under subsection (2) of that section,

      (b) the registered person provides him with the statement required by that subsection, and

      (c) the applicant consents and pays to the Secretary of State the amount (if any) by which the fee payable in relation to an application under that section exceeds the fee paid in relation to the application under this section.

(6)   In this section—

"central records" means such records of convictions and cautions held for the use of police forces generally as may be prescribed;

"exempted question" means a question in relation to which section 4(2)(a) or (b) of the Rehabilitation of Offenders Act 1974 (effect of rehabilitation) has been excluded by an order of the Secretary of State under section 4(4) of that Act;

"relevant matter" means—

(a)   a conviction within the meaning of the Rehabilitation of Offenders Act 1974, including a spent conviction, and

(b)   a caution.

113B   Enhanced criminal record certificates

(1)   The Secretary of State must issue an enhanced criminal record certificate to any individual who—

(a)   makes an application in the prescribed manner and form, and

(b)   pays in the prescribed manner any prescribed fee.

(2)   The application must—

(a)   be countersigned by a registered person, and

(b)   be accompanied by a statement by the registered person that the certificate is required for a prescribed purpose.

(3)   An enhanced criminal record certificate is a certificate which—

(a)   gives the prescribed details of every relevant matter relating to the applicant which is recorded in central records and any information provided in accordance with subsection (4), or

(b)   states that there is no such matter or information.

(4)   Before issuing an enhanced criminal record certificate the Secretary of State must request the chief officer of every relevant police force to provide any information which, in the chief officer's opinion—

(a)   might be relevant for the purpose described in the statement under subsection (2), and

(b)   ought to be included in the certificate.

(5)   The Secretary of State must also request the chief officer of every relevant police force to provide any information which, in the chief officer's opinion—

(a)   might be relevant for the purpose described in the statement under subsection (2),

(b)   ought not to be included in the certificate, in the interests of the prevention or detection of crime, and

(c)   can, without harming those interests, be disclosed to the registered person.

(6)   The Secretary of State must send to the registered person who countersigned the application—

(a)   a copy of the enhanced criminal record certificate, and

(b)   any information provided in accordance with subsection (5).

(7)   The Secretary of State may treat an application under this section as an application under section 113A if in his opinion the certificate is not required for a purpose prescribed under subsection (2).

(8) If by virtue of subsection (7) the Secretary of State treats an application under this section as an application under section 113A, he must refund to the applicant the amount (if any) by which the fee paid in relation to the application under this section exceeds the fee payable in relation to an application under section 113A.

(9) In this section—

"central records", "exempted question", and "relevant matter" have the same meaning as in section 113A;

"relevant police force", in relation to an application under this section, means a police force which is a relevant police force in relation to that application under regulations made by the Secretary of State.

(10) For the purposes of this section references to a police force include any of the following—

(a) the Royal Navy Regulating Branch;

(b) the Royal Marines Police;

(c) the Royal Military Police;

(d) the Royal Air Force Police;

(e) the Ministry of Defence Police;

(f) the National Criminal Intelligence Service;

(g) the National Crime Squad;

(h) the British Transport Police;

(i) the Civil Nuclear Constabulary;

(j) the States of Jersey Police Force;

(k) the salaried police force of the Island of Guernsey;

(l) the Isle of Man Constabulary;

(m) a body with functions in any country or territory outside the British Islands which correspond to those of a police force in any part of the United Kingdom,

and any reference to the chief officer of a police force includes the person responsible for the direction of a body mentioned in this subsection.

(11) For the purposes of this section each of the following must be treated as if it were a police force—

(a) the Commissioners for Her Majesty's Revenue and Customs (and for this purpose a reference to the chief officer of a police force must be taken to be a reference to any one of the Commissioners);

(b) the Serious Organised Crime Agency (and for this purpose a reference to the chief officer of a police force must be taken to be a reference to the Director General of the Agency);

(c) such other department or body as is prescribed (and regulations may prescribe in relation to the department or body the person to whom a reference to the chief officer is to be taken to be).

113C Criminal record certificates: suitability relating to children

(1) If an application under section 113A or 113B is accompanied by a children's suitability statement the criminal record certificate or enhanced criminal record certificate (as the case may be) must also state—

    (a)   whether the applicant is included in a specified children's list;

    (b)   if he is included in such a list, such details of his inclusion as may be prescribed;

    (c)   whether he is subject to a specified children's direction;

    (d)   if he is subject to such a direction, the grounds on which it was given and such details as may be prescribed of the circumstances in which it was given.

(2)   A children's suitability statement is a statement by the registered person that the certificate is required for the purpose of considering—

    (a)   the applicant's suitability to be employed, supplied to work, found work or given work in a position (whether paid or unpaid) within subsection (5),

    (b)   the applicant's suitability to be a foster parent or to adopt a child,

    (c)   the applicant's suitability to be a child's special guardian for the purposes of sections 14A and 14C of the Children Act 1989,

    (d)   the applicant's suitability to have a child placed with him by virtue of section 70 of the Children (Scotland) Act 1995 or by virtue of section 5(2), (3) and (4) of the Social Work (Scotland) Act 1968, or

    (e)   the suitability of a person living in the same household as the applicant to be a person mentioned in paragraph (b) or (c) or to have a child placed with him as mentioned in paragraph (d).

(3)   Each of the following is a specified children's list—

    (a)   the list kept under section 1 of the Protection of Children Act 1999;

    (b)   the list kept under section 1(1) of the Protection of Children (Scotland) Act 2003;

    (c)   the list kept under Article 3 of the Protection of Children and Vulnerable Adults (Northern Ireland) Order 2003;

    (d)   any list kept for the purposes of regulations under Article 70(2)(e) or 88A(2)(b) of the Education and Libraries (Northern Ireland) Order 1986;

    (e)   any such other list as the Secretary of State specifies by order if he thinks that the list corresponds to a list specified in paragraphs (a) to (c) and is kept in pursuance of a country or territory outside the United Kingdom.

(4)   Each of the following is a specified children's direction—

    (a)   a direction under section 142 of the Education Act 2002;

    (b)   anything which the Secretary of State specifies by order which he thinks corresponds to such a direction and which is done for the purposes of the law of Scotland or of Northern Ireland or of a country or territory outside the United Kingdom.

(5)   A position falls within this subsection if it is any of the following—

    (a)   a child care position within the meaning of the Protection of Children Act 1999;

    (b)   a child care position within the meaning of the Protection of Children (Scotland) Act 2003;

(c) a child care position within the meaning of Chapter 1 of Part 2 of the Protection of Children and Vulnerable Adults (Northern Ireland) Order 2003;

(d) a position, employment or further employment in which may be prohibited or restricted by regulations under Article 70(2)(e) or 88A(2)(b) of the Education and Libraries (Northern Ireland) Order 1986;

(e) a position which involves work to which section 142 of the Education Act 2002 applies;

(f) a position of such other description as may be prescribed.

(6) An order under subsection (4)(b) may make such modifications of subsection (1)(d) as the Secretary of State thinks necessary or expedient in consequence of the order.

113D Criminal record certificates: suitability relating to adults

(1) If an application under section 113A or 113B is accompanied by an adults' suitability statement the criminal record certificate or enhanced criminal record certificate (as the case may be) must also state —

(a) whether the applicant is included in a specified adults' list;

(b) if he is included in such a list, such details of his inclusion as may be prescribed.

(2) An adults' suitability statement is a statement by the registered person that the certificate is required for the purpose of considering the applicant's suitability to be employed, supplied to work, found work or given work in a position (whether paid or unpaid) falling within subsection (4).

(3) Each of the following is a specified adults' list —

(a) the list kept under section 81 of the Care Standards Act 2000;

(b) the list kept under Article 35 of the Protection of Children and Vulnerable Adults (Northern Ireland) Order 2003;

(c) any such other list as the Secretary of State specifies by order if he thinks that the list corresponds to a list specified in paragraph (a) or (b) and is kept in pursuance of the law of Scotland or of a country or territory outside the United Kingdom.

(4) A position falls within this subsection if it is any of the following —

(a) a care position within the meaning of Part 7 of the Care Standards Act 2000;

(b) a care position within the meaning of Part 3 of the Protection of Children and Vulnerable Adults (Northern Ireland) Order 2003;

(c) a position concerned with providing a care service (as defined by section 2(1) of the Regulation of Care (Scotland) Act 2001);

(d) a position of such other description as may be prescribed.

113E Criminal record certificates: specified children's and adults' lists: urgent cases

(1) Subsection (2) applies to an application under section 113A or 113B if —

(a) it is accompanied by a children's suitability statement,

(b)   the registered person requests an urgent preliminary response, and

(c)   the applicant pays in the prescribed manner such additional fee as is prescribed in respect of the application.

(2)   The Secretary of State must notify the registered person—

(a)   if the applicant is not included in a specified children's list, of that fact;

(b)   if the applicant is included in such a list, of the details prescribed for the purposes of section 113C(1)(b) above;

(c)   if the applicant is not subject to a specified children's direction, of that fact;

(d)   if the applicant is subject to such a direction, of the grounds on which the direction was given and the details prescribed for the purposes of section 113C(1)(d) above.

(3)   Subsection (4) applies to an application under section 113A or 113B if—

(a)   it is accompanied by an adults' suitability statement,

(b)   the registered person requests an urgent preliminary response, and

(c)   the applicant pays in the prescribed manner such additional fee as is prescribed in respect of the application.

(4)   The Secretary of State must notify the registered person either—

(a)   that the applicant is not included in a specified adults' list, or

(b)   that a criminal record certificate or enhanced criminal record certificate will be issued in due course.

(5)   In this section—

"criminal record certificate" has the same meaning as in section 113A;

"enhanced criminal record certificate" has the same meaning as in section 113B;

"children's suitability statement", "specified children's direction" and "specified children's list" have the same meaning as in section 113C;

"adults' suitability statement" and "specified adults' list" have the same meaning as in section 113D.

113F   Criminal record certificates: supplementary

(1)   References in sections 113C(2) and 113D(2) to considering the applicant's suitability to be employed, supplied to work, found work or given work in a position falling within section 113C(5) or 113D(4) include references to considering—

(a)   for the purposes of Part 10A of the Children Act 1989 (child minding and day care in England and Wales), the applicant's suitability to look after or be in regular contact with children under the age of eight;

(b)   for the purposes of that Part of that Act, in the case of an applicant for or holder of a certificate under section 79W of that Act, or a person prescribed under subsection (4) of that section, his suitability to look after children within the meaning of that section;

(c)   the applicant's suitability to be registered for child minding or providing day care under section 71 of the Children Act 1989 or Article 118 of the Children (Northern Ireland) Order 1995 (child minding and day care);

(d)   for the purposes of section 3 of the Teaching and Higher Education Act 1998 (registration of teachers with the General Teaching Council for England or the General Teaching Council for Wales) or of section 6 of the Teaching Council (Scotland) Act 1965 (registration of teachers with the General Teaching Council for Scotland), the applicant's suitability to be a teacher;

(e)   the applicant's suitability to be registered under Part 2 of the Care Standards Act 2000 (establishments and agencies);

(f)   the applicant's suitability to be registered under Part 4 of that Act (social care workers);

(g)   the applicant's suitability to be registered under Part 1 of the Regulation of Care (Scotland) Act 2001 (applications by persons seeking to provide a care service);

(h)   the applicant's suitability to be registered under Part 3 of that Act (social workers and other social service workers);

(i)   the applicant's application to have a care service, consisting of the provision of child minding or the day care of children, registered under Part 1 of that Act (care services);

(j)   the applicant's suitability to be registered under Part 1 of the Health and Personal Social Services Act (Northern Ireland) 2001 (social care workers);

(k)   the applicant's suitability to be registered under Part 3 of the Health and Personal Social Services (Quality, Improvement and Regulation) (Northern Ireland) Order 2003 (regulation of establishments and agencies).

(2)   The power to make an order under section 113C or 113D is exercisable by statutory instrument, but no such order may be made unless a draft of the order has been laid before and approved by a resolution by each House of Parliament.

(3)   If the power mentioned in subsection (2) is exercised by the Scottish Ministers, the reference in that subsection to each House of Parliament must be construed as a reference to the Scottish Parliament."

(3)   Schedule 14 (which makes consequential amendments to Part 5 of the Police Act 1997 (c. 50)) has effect.

(4)   If section 115(1) of the Adoption and Children Act 2002 (c. 38) comes into force before the preceding provisions of this section, the Secretary of State may by order apply Part 5 of the Police Act 1997 subject to such modifications as he thinks necessary or expedient for the purpose of enabling a certificate or statement to be issued under section 113 or 115 of that Act of 1997 in connection with consideration by a court of whether to make a special guardianship order under section 14A of the Children Act 1989 (c. 41).

164   Criminal records checks: verification of identity

(1)   Section 118 of the Police Act 1997 (evidence of identity) is amended as follows.

(2)   In subsection (1) after "117" insert "or 120".

(3)   After subsection (2) insert—

    "(2A)   For the purpose of verifying evidence of identity supplied in pursuance of subsection (1) the Secretary of State may obtain such information as he thinks is appropriate from data held —

        (a)   by the United Kingdom Passport Agency;

        (b)   by the Driver and Vehicle Licensing Agency;

        (c)   by Driver and Vehicle Licensing Northern Ireland;

        (d)   by the Secretary of State in connection with keeping records of national insurance numbers;

        (e)   by such other persons or for such purposes as is prescribed."

165   Certain references to police forces

(1)   In section 119 of the Police Act 1997 (c. 50) (sources of information),

    (a)   in subsection (3) for "the prescribed fee" substitute "such fee as he thinks appropriate";

    (b)   after subsection (5) insert—

        "(6)   For the purposes of this section references to a police force include any body mentioned in subsections (10)(a) to (i) and (11) of section 113B and references to a chief officer must be construed accordingly."

(7)   In the case of such a body the reference in subsection (3) to the appropriate police authority must be construed as a reference to such body as is prescribed."

(2)   In each version of section 120A of that Act (as inserted respectively by section 134(1) of the Criminal Justice and Police Act 2001 (c. 16) and section 70 of the Criminal Justice (Scotland) Act 2003 (asp 7)), after subsection (5) insert—

        "(6)   For the purposes of this section references to a police force include any body mentioned in subsections (10)(a) to (i) and (11) of section 113B and references to a chief officer must be construed accordingly."

(3)   In section 124A of that Act (offences relating to disclosure of information) (inserted by section 328 of and paragraphs 1 and 11 of Schedule 35 to the Criminal Justice Act 2003 (c. 44)), after subsection (5) insert —

        "(6)   For the purposes of this section the reference to a police force includes any body mentioned in subsections (10)(a) to (i) and (11) of section 113B and the reference to a chief officer must be construed accordingly."

166   Further amendments to Police Act 1997 as it applies to Scotland

(1)   In section 120A of the Police Act 1997 (as inserted by section 70 of the Criminal Justice (Scotland) Act 2003 (asp 7)), in subsection (5), for the words "the prescribed fee" to the end substitute "such fee as they consider appropriate".

(2)   In section 126 of that Act of 1997 after subsection (2) insert—

        "(3)   In the application of this Part to Scotland references to the Secretary of State must be construed as references to the Scottish Ministers.

(4)   Subsection (3) does not apply to section 118(2A)(c) or 124A(1) and (2)."

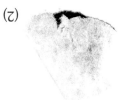

167   Part 5 of the Police Act 1997: Northern Ireland

The amendments made by Schedule 35 to the Criminal Justice Act 2003 (c. 44) to Part 5 of the Police Act 1997 (c. 50) extend to Northern Ireland as well as to England and Wales, and accordingly in section 337(5) of that Act of 2003 (extent) —

(a)   after "section 315" insert —
     "section 328;";

(b)   after "Schedule 5" insert —
     "Schedule 35."

168   Part 5 of the Police Act 1997: Channel Islands and Isle of Man

(1)   Her Majesty may by Order in Council extend any provision of Part 5 of the Police Act 1997 (certificates of criminal records etc.), with such modifications as appear to Her Majesty in Council to be appropriate, to any of the Channel Islands or the Isle of Man.

(2)   An order under this section may make such consequential, incidental, supplementary, transitory or transitional provision or savings as Her Majesty in Council thinks appropriate.

Witness summonses

169   Powers of Crown Court and Magistrates' Court to issue witness summons

(1)   In section 2(1) of the Criminal Procedure (Attendance of Witnesses) Act 1965 (c. 69) (issue of witness summons on application to Crown Court) for paragraph (b) substitute —
     "(b)   it is in the interests of justice to issue a summons under this section to secure the attendance of that person to give evidence or to produce the document or thing."

(2)   In section 97 of the Magistrates' Courts Act 1980 (c. 43) (summons to witness) for subsection (1) substitute —

     "(1)   Where a justice of the peace is satisfied that —
          (a)   any person in England or Wales is likely to be able to give material evidence, or produce any document or thing likely to be material evidence, at the summary trial of an information or hearing of a complaint by a magistrates' court, and
          (b)   it is in the interests of justice to issue a summons under this subsection to secure the attendance of that person to give evidence or produce the document or thing,
     the justice shall issue a summons directed to that person requiring him to attend before the court at the time and place appointed in the summons to give evidence or to produce the document or thing."

(3)   In section 97A(1) of that Act (summons as to committal proceedings) for paragraph (b) substitute —
     "(b)   it is in the interests of justice to issue a summons under this section to secure the attendance of that person to give evidence or to produce the document or other exhibit, and".

(4)   In paragraph 4(1) of Schedule 3 to the Crime and Disorder Act 1998 (c. 37)

(power of justice to take depositions etc.) for paragraph (b) substitute—

> "(b)   it is in the interests of justice to issue a summons under this paragraph to secure the attendance of the witness to have his evidence taken as a deposition or to produce the document or other exhibit."

(5)   In section 51A(1) of the Judicature (Northern Ireland) Act 1978 (c. 23) (issue of witness summons on application to Crown Court) for paragraph (b) substitute—

> "(b)   it is in the interests of justice to issue a summons under this section to secure the attendance of that person to give evidence or to produce the document or thing."

170   Powers of courts-martial etc. to issue warrants of arrest in respect of witnesses

(1)   Section 25 of the Armed Forces Act 2001 (c. 19) (powers to compel attendance of witnesses) is amended as follows.

(2)   In subsection (1) (which inserts a new section 101A in the Army Act 1955 (3 & 4 Eliz. 2 c. 18)), in subsection (1) of the new section 101A, for paragraph (b) substitute—

> "(b)   that it is in the interests of justice that the person should attend to give evidence or to produce the document or other thing, and".

(3)   In subsection (2) (which inserts a new section 101A in the Air Force Act 1955 (3 & 4 Eliz. 2 c. 19)), in subsection (1) of the new section 101A, for paragraph (b) substitute—

> "(b)   that it is in the interests of justice that the person should attend to give evidence or to produce the document or other thing, and".

(4)   In subsection (3) (which inserts a new section 65A in the Naval Discipline Act 1957), in subsection (1) of the new section 65A, for paragraph (b) substitute—

> "(b)   that it is in the interests of justice that the person should attend to give evidence or to produce the document or other thing, and".

Private Security Industry Act 2001: Scotland

171   Private Security Industry Act 2001: Scottish extent

(1)   Schedule 15 amends the Private Security Industry Act 2001 (c. 12) in relation to its extent to Scotland.

(2)   In Schedule 2 to the Scottish Public Services Ombudsman Act 2002 (asp 11) (persons liable to investigation) after paragraph 90 add—

> "91   The Security Industry Authority."

PART 6

FINAL PROVISIONS

172 Orders and regulations

(1) Any power of the Secretary of State to make an order or regulations under this Act, and any power of the Scottish Ministers to make an order under this Act, is exercisable by statutory instrument.

(2) Any such power—
  (a) may be exercised so as to make different provision for different cases or descriptions of case or different purposes or areas, and
  (b) includes power to make such incidental, supplementary, consequential, transitory, transitional or saving provision as the Secretary of State considers appropriate (or, in the case of an order made by the Scottish Ministers, as they consider appropriate).

(3) Subject to subsections (4) and (5), orders or regulations made by the Secretary of State under this Act are to be subject to annulment in pursuance of a resolution of either House of Parliament.

(4) Subsection (3) does not apply to any order under section 1(3), 161(4) or 178.

(5) Subsection (3) also does not apply to—
  (a) any order under section 33(2)(f);
  (b) any order under section 52;
  (c) any order under section 61(4);
  (d) any order under section 76(4);
  (e) any order under section 82(6);
  (f) any order under section 87(5);
  (g) any order under section 89(5);
  (h) any order under section 96(1);
  (i) any order under section 97(1);
  (j) any order under section 146(6), 148(4) or 149;
  (k) any order under section 173 which amends or repeals any provision of an Act;
and no such order may be made by the Secretary of State (whether alone or with other provisions) unless a draft of the statutory instrument containing the order has been laid before, and approved by a resolution of, each House of Parliament.

(6) Subject to subsections (7) and (8), orders made by the Scottish Ministers under this Act are to be subject to annulment in pursuance of a resolution of the Scottish Parliament.

(7) Subsection (6) does not apply to any order under section 178.

(8) Subsection (6) also does not apply to—
  (a) any order under section 52;
  (b) any order under section 61(5);
  (c) any order under section 77(4);
  (d) any order under section 87(6);
  (e) any order under section 89(6);

    (f)   any order under section 96(1);

    (g)   any order under section 173 which amends or repeals any provision of an Act;

and no such order may be made by the Scottish Ministers (whether alone or with other provisions) unless a draft of the statutory instrument containing the order has been laid before, and approved by a resolution of, the Scottish Parliament.

173 Supplementary, incidental, consequential etc. provision

(1)   The Secretary of State may by order make—

    (a)   such supplementary, incidental or consequential provision, or

    (b)   such transitory, transitional or saving provision,

as he considers appropriate for the general purposes, or any particular purpose, of this Act, or in consequence of, or for giving full effect to, any provision made by this Act.

(2)   An order under subsection (1) may amend, repeal, revoke or otherwise modify any enactment (including this Act).

(3)   The power to make an order under subsection (1) includes power to repeal or revoke an enactment which is spent.

(4)   Before exercising the power conferred by subsection (1) in relation to an enactment which extends to Scotland, the Secretary of State must consult the Scottish Ministers.

(5)   The power conferred by subsection (1) is exercisable by the Scottish Ministers (rather than by the Secretary of State) where the provision to be made is—

    (a)   for the general purposes of this Act and would be within the legislative competence of the Scottish Parliament if it were included in an Act of that Parliament; or

    (b)   for the purposes of, in consequence of, or for giving full effect to—

        (i)   section 77, 156, 171 or Schedule 15,

        (ii)   so far as extending to Scotland, any provision mentioned in section 178(4),

        (iii)   so far as relating as mentioned in section 178(5), section 174(2) and Schedule 17,

        (iv)   so far as having effect as mentioned in section 178(6)(a), section 96.

(6)   But an order under—

    (a)   paragraph (b)(i) of subsection (5) in relation to section 171 or Schedule 15, or

    (b)   paragraph (b)(iv) of that subsection,

may be made only after consulting the Secretary of State.

(7)   Nothing in this Act affects the generality of the power conferred by this section.

174 Minor and consequential amendments, repeals and revocations

(1)   Schedule 16 makes provision for remaining minor and consequential amendments (search warrants).

(2)   Schedule 17 makes provision for the repeal and revocation of enactments (including enactments which are spent).

175   Penalties for offences: transitional modification for England and Wales

(1)   This section contains transitional modifications in respect of penalties for certain offences committed in England or Wales.

(2)   In relation to an offence committed before the commencement of section 154(1) of the Criminal Justice Act 2003 (c. 44) (general limit on magistrates' court's power to impose imprisonment), the references in the following provisions to periods of imprisonment of 12 months are to be read as references to periods of imprisonment of 6 months—

> section 67(5)(b);
> section 86(2)(b);
> section 88(3)(b);
> section 147(1)(a).

(3)   In relation to an offence committed before the commencement of section 281(5) of the Criminal Justice Act 2003 (alteration of penalties for summary offences), the references in the following provisions of this Act to periods of imprisonment of 51 weeks are to be read as references to the periods of imprisonment specified in respect of those provisions as follows—

Section	Modified period of imprisonment
section 51(4)(a)	6 months
section 51(5)(a)	1 month
section 57(4)(a)	6 months
section 57(5)(a)	1 month
section 67(4)(a)	6 months
section 79(10)(a)(i)	6 months
section 112(5)	4 months
section 128(5)(a)	6 months
section 136(1)	3 months
section 136(3)(a)	3 months
section 136(4)	3 months

176   Expenses

(1)   There shall be paid out of money provided by Parliament—

(a)   any expenditure incurred by the Secretary of State by virtue of this Act;

(b)   any increase attributable to this Act in the sums payable out of money so provided under any other enactment.

(2) Subsection (1)(a) does not apply to any expenditure of the Secretary of State under section 155.

177   Interpretation

(1) In this Act "SOCA" means the Serious Organised Crime Agency.

(2) In this Act "enactment" includes—
   (a) an enactment contained in or made under an Act of the Scottish Parliament or Northern Ireland legislation, and
   (b) an enactment comprised in subordinate legislation (within the meaning of the Interpretation Act 1978 (c. 30)).

(3) In this Act references to enactments include enactments passed or made after the passing of this Act.

(4) Subsections (2) and (3) apply except where the context otherwise requires.

178   Commencement

(1) The following provisions come into force on the day on which this Act is passed—
   (a) sections 117(7) (and section 117(6) so far as relates to it), 158, 167, 172, 173, 176, 177, this section and section 179, and
   (b) Part 1 of Schedule 17 and (so far as it relates to that Part of that Schedule) section 174(2).

(2) Section 163(4) comes into force at the end of the period of three months beginning with the day on which this Act is passed.

(3) Sections 77 and 156 come into force on such day as the Scottish Ministers may by order appoint.

(4) So far as they extend to Scotland—
   (a) Chapter 1 of Part 2,
   (b) sections 79 to 81,
   (c) Chapter 4 of Part 2 (including Schedule 5),
   (d) sections 163 to 166, and
   (e) Schedule 14,
come into force on such day as the Scottish Ministers may by order appoint.

(5) So far as they relate—
   (a) to sections 113 and 115 of the Police Act 1997 (c. 50) as those sections apply to Scotland;
   (b) to section 125 of that Act, to the Regulation of Care (Scotland) Act 2001 (asp 8), to the Protection of Children (Scotland) Act 2003 (asp 5) and to the Criminal Justice (Scotland) Act 2003 (asp 7),
section 174(2) and Schedule 17 come into force on such day as the Scottish Ministers may by order appoint.

(6) The following provisions come into force on such day as the Scottish Ministers may by order appoint after consulting the Secretary of State—
   (a) section 96 so far as it has effect for the purpose of conferring functions on the Scottish Ministers, and
   (b) section 171 and Schedule 15.

(7) The following provisions come into force on such day as the Secretary of State may by order appoint after consulting the Scottish Ministers −
  (a) sections 95, 98(2), 99(2) and (3), 100, 101 and 107, and
  (b) paragraphs 1 and 6 of Schedule 6, and section 109 so far as relating to those paragraphs.

(8) Otherwise, this Act comes into force on such day as the Secretary of State may by order appoint.

(9) Different days may be appointed for different purposes or different areas.

(10) The Secretary of State may by order make such provision as he considers appropriate for transitory, transitional or saving purposes in connection with the coming into force of any provision of this Act.

(11) The power conferred by subsection (10) is exercisable by the Scottish Ministers (rather than the Secretary of State) in connection with any provision of this Act which comes into force by order made by the Scottish Ministers.

179 Short title and extent

(1) This Act may be cited as the Serious Organised Crime and Police Act 2005.

(2) Subject to the following provisions, this Act extends to England and Wales only.

(3) The following extend also to Scotland −
  (a) sections 1 to 54, 57 and 58,
  (b) sections 60 to 68, 70, 79 to 96, 98 to 106, 107(1) and (4) and 108,
  (c) section 123,
  (d) section 131,
  (e) sections 150 to 153, 156(6), 158, 163(1) and (2), 164, 165(1) and (2), 166(2), 167 and 171(1),
  (f) sections 172, 173, 176 to 178 and this section,
  (g) Schedules 1, 3, 5 and 15.

(4) The following extend to Scotland only −
  (a) section 77 and 107(3),
  (b) sections 129 and 130(3),
  (c) sections 156(1) to (5), 166(1) and 171(2).

(5) The following extend also to Northern Ireland −
  (a) sections 1 to 54, 57 and 58,
  (b) sections 68, 71 to 75, 79 to 106, 107(1), (2) and (4) and 108,
  (c) section 123(1),
  (d) sections 128, 131 and 144,
  (e) sections 150(1), 151, 163(1) and (2), 164, 165, 166(2) and 167,
  (f) sections 172, 173, 176 to 178 and this section,
  (g) Schedules 1, 3 and 5.

(6) The following extend to Northern Ireland only −
  (a) section 55(2),
  (b) section 78,
  (c) section 130(2),

      (d)   Part 2 of Schedule 10.

(7)   The following have the same extent as the enactments to which they relate—

      (a)   section 55(1) and Schedule 2,

      (b)   section 59 and Schedule 4,

      (c)   section 109 and Schedule 6,

      (d)   section 154,

      (e)   section 159 and Schedule 11,

      (f)   section 160 and Schedule 12,

      (g)   section 161(5) (so far as it has effect for the purposes of Part 2 of Schedule 13) and that Part of that Schedule,

      (h)   section 163(3) and Schedule 14,

      (i)   sections 169(5) and 170,

      (j)   (subject to subsection (8)) section 174(2) and Schedule 17.

(8)   So far as Schedule 17 contains a repeal or revocation of an enactment which corresponds to the repeal or revocation of that enactment by another provision of this Act, that Schedule and section 174(2) have the same extent as that other provision.

(9)   So far as they relate to any provision of this Act which extends to any place outside the United Kingdom, sections 172, 173, 177, 178 and this section also extend there.

(10)   Subsection (2) does not apply to the following—

      (a)   section 168, or

      (b)   any provision of Schedule 7 which makes provision as to its extent.

SCHEDULES

SCHEDULE 1

Section 1

THE SERIOUS ORGANISED CRIME AGENCY

PART 1

THE BOARD OF SOCA

Membership

1   (1) SOCA shall consist of —

   (a) a chairman,

   (b) such number of ex-officio members as SOCA may from time to time determine, and

   (c) such number of other members ("ordinary members") as the Secretary of State may so determine.

   (2) The following limits apply for the purposes of sub-paragraph (1) —

   (a) the number of ex-officio members determined under sub-paragraph (1)(b) must not at any time exceed such number as may for the time being be specified by the Secretary of State,

   (b) the number of ordinary members determined under sub-paragraph (1)(c) must not at any time be less than the number of ex-officio members for the time being determined under sub-paragraph (1)(b), and

   (c) the total of the numbers determined under sub-paragraph (1)(b) and (c) must not at any time be less than four.

   (3) The chairman and the ordinary members are to be appointed by the Secretary of State.

   (4) Before appointing a person to hold office as chairman the Secretary of State must consult the Scottish Ministers.

   (5) For the purposes of this Schedule the "ex-officio members" are —

   (a) the Director-General of SOCA (see paragraph 9), and

   (b) such other employees of SOCA as may for the time being be appointed by the Director General after consulting the chairman.

   (6) References in any enactment to members of SOCA are (unless the context otherwise requires) references to any of its members mentioned in sub-paragraph (1).

Tenure of office: chairman and ordinary members

2   The chairman and the ordinary members shall hold and vacate office as such in accordance with the terms of their respective appointments.
This is subject to paragraphs 3 and 4.

3   (1)   An appointment of a person to hold office as chairman or ordinary member shall be for a term not exceeding five years.

       (2)   A person holding office as chairman or ordinary member may at any time resign that office by giving notice in writing to the Secretary of State.

4   The Secretary of State may by notice in writing remove a person from office as chairman or ordinary member if satisfied that —

          (a)   he has without reasonable excuse failed, for a continuous period of three months, to carry out his functions as chairman or ordinary member;

          (b)   he has without reasonable excuse been absent from three consecutive meetings of SOCA;

          (c)   he has been convicted (whether before or after his appointment) of a criminal offence;

          (d)   he is an undischarged bankrupt or his estate has been sequestrated and he has not been discharged;

          (e)   he is the subject of a bankruptcy restrictions order or an interim order under Schedule 4A to the Insolvency Act 1986 (c. 45) or an order to the like effect made under any corresponding enactment in force in Scotland or Northern Ireland;

          (f)   he has made a composition or arrangement with, or granted a trust deed for, his creditors;

          (g)   he has failed to comply with the terms of his appointment; or

          (h)   he is otherwise unable or unfit to carry out his functions as chairman or ordinary member.

5   A person who ceases to be the chairman or an ordinary member is eligible for re-appointment, except where he is removed from office under paragraph 4.

Remuneration, pensions etc. of chairman and ordinary members

6   (1)   SOCA shall pay to the chairman and each of the ordinary members such remuneration and allowances as may be determined by the Secretary of State.

       (2)   SOCA shall, if required to do so by the Secretary of State —

          (a)   pay such pension, allowances or gratuities as may be determined by the Secretary of State to or in respect of a person who is or has been the chairman or an ordinary member, or

          (b)   make such payments as may be so determined towards provision for the payment of a pension, allowances or gratuities to or in respect of such a person.

       (3)   If the Secretary of State determines that there are special circumstances which make it right for a person ceasing to hold office as chairman or ordinary member to receive compensation, SOCA shall pay to him a sum by

Serious Organised Crime and Police Act 2005 (c. 15)
Schedule 1 – The Serious Organised Crime Agency
Part 1 – The Board of SOCA

141

way of compensation of such amount as may be determined by the Secretary of State.

(4) Service as chairman of SOCA shall be included among the kinds of service to which a scheme under section 1 of the Superannuation Act 1972 (c. 11) can apply, and accordingly in Schedule 1 to that Act (in which those kinds of service are listed) insert at the appropriate place—

"Chairman of the Serious Organised Crime Agency."

(5) SOCA must pay to the Minister for the Civil Service, at such times as he may direct, such sums as he may determine in respect of any increase attributable to sub-paragraph (4) in the sums payable out of money provided by Parliament under that Act.

Termination of office of ex-officio members

7 (1) The Director General ceases to be an ex-officio member of SOCA on ceasing to be Director General.

(2) Any other ex-officio member of SOCA ceases to be such a member—
   (a) on ceasing to be an employee of SOCA, or
   (b) if the Director General by notice in writing revokes his appointment as ex-officio member.

(3) Before revoking an appointment under sub-paragraph (2)(b) the Director General must consult the chairman of SOCA.

(4) An ex-officio member other than the Director General may at any time resign his office as ex-officio member by giving notice in writing to the Director General.

PART 2

DIRECTOR GENERAL AND OTHER STAFF

SOCA's staff

8 (1) SOCA shall have—
   (a) a Director General (see paragraph 9), and
   (b) such other employees as SOCA may appoint.

(2) SOCA may make arrangements for persons to be seconded to SOCA to serve as members of its staff.

(3) A member of a police force on temporary service with SOCA shall be under the direction and control of SOCA.

(4) References in any enactment to members of staff of SOCA are (unless the context otherwise requires) references to persons who either are employees of SOCA or have been seconded to SOCA to serve as members of its staff.

The Director General

9 (1) The Director General shall be—
   (a) appointed by the Secretary of State, and
   (b) employed by SOCA on such terms and conditions as the Secretary of State may determine.

142   *Serious Organised Crime and Police Act 2005 (c. 15)*
Schedule 1 — The Serious Organised Crime Agency
Part 2 — Director General and other staff

(2) But a person may not be so appointed for a term exceeding five years.

(3) Before appointing a person as Director General the Secretary of State must consult—

    (a)   the chairman of SOCA, and

    (b)   the Scottish Ministers.

(4) SOCA shall pay to its Director General such remuneration and allowances as the Secretary of State may determine.

Termination or suspension of appointment of Director General

10   (1) The Secretary of State may call on the Director General to retire or to resign from his office as Director General—

    (a)   in the interests of efficiency or effectiveness, or

    (b)   by reason of any misconduct by the Director General.

(2) But before doing so the Secretary of State must have complied with sub-paragraphs (3) to (6).

(3) The Secretary of State must give the Director General—

    (a)   an explanation in writing of the grounds on which the Secretary of State proposes to call upon the Director General to retire or resign as mentioned in sub-paragraph (1)(a) or (b), and

    (b)   an opportunity to make representations to the Secretary of State (including an opportunity to make them in person).

(4) The Secretary of State must consider any representations made by or on behalf of the Director General.

(5) The Secretary of State must send a copy of the explanation mentioned in sub-paragraph (3)(a) to the chairman of SOCA.

(6) The Secretary of State must consult—

    (a)   the chairman of SOCA, and

    (b)   the Scottish Ministers.

(7) If the Director General is, under sub-paragraph (1), called upon to retire or resign, he must retire or resign with effect from—

    (a)   such date as the Secretary of State may specify, or

    (b)   such earlier date as may be agreed between him and the Secretary of State.

(8) If the Secretary of State considers that it is necessary to do so for the maintenance of public confidence in SOCA, he may suspend the Director General from duty.

But before doing so the Secretary of State must have complied with sub-paragraph (6).

(9) Nothing in this paragraph affects any power of the Secretary of State to terminate or suspend the Director General's employment with SOCA in accordance with the terms and conditions of that employment.

Serious Organised Crime and Police Act 2005 (c. 15)
Schedule 1 — The Serious Organised Crime Agency
Part 2 — Director General and other staff

143

Delegation of functions of Director General

11 (1) Anything authorised or required to be done by the Director General may be done by any other member of SOCA's staff who is authorised for the purpose by the Director General (whether generally or specially).

(2) This paragraph does not apply in any case in relation to which specific provision for the delegation of any function of the Director General is made by this Act or any other enactment.

Remuneration and pensions of staff

12 (1) SOCA shall pay to its employees such remuneration and allowances as it may determine.

(2) Sub-paragraph (1) does not apply to the Director General (to whom paragraph 9(4) applies instead).

13 (1) SOCA may pay, or make payments in respect of, such pensions, allowances or gratuities to or in respect of its employees or former employees as it may determine.

(2) Employment with SOCA shall be included among the kinds of employment to which a scheme under section 1 of the Superannuation Act 1972 (c. 11) can apply, and accordingly in Schedule 1 to that Act (in which those kinds of employment are listed) insert at the appropriate place —

"Employment by the Serious Organised Crime Agency."

(3) If any person —

(a) on ceasing to be employed by SOCA becomes or continues to be one of its members, and

(b) was, by reference to his employment, a participant in a scheme under section 1 of that Act,

the Minister for the Civil Service may determine that his service as a member of SOCA is to be treated for the purposes of the scheme as if his service as a member were service as an employee of SOCA (whether or not any benefits are payable to or in respect of him by virtue of paragraph 6).

(4) SOCA shall pay to the Minister for the Civil Service, at such times as he may direct, such sums as he may determine in respect of any increase attributable to this paragraph in the sums payable out of money provided by Parliament under that Act.

Insurance

14 The Employers' Liability (Compulsory Insurance) Act 1969 (c. 57) does not require insurance to be effected by SOCA.

PART 3

COMMITTEES, PROCEDURE ETC.

Committees

15 (1) SOCA may establish committees.

(2) Any committee so established may establish one or more sub-committees.

144

Serious Organised Crime and Police Act 2005 (c. 15)
Schedule 1 — The Serious Organised Crime Agency
Part 3 — Committees, procedure etc.

(3) Any such committee or sub-committee must be a chaired by a member of SOCA.

(4) A person who is not a member of SOCA may be appointed to any such committee or sub-committee.

(5) If a member of any such committee or sub-committee is neither —

    (a) a member of SOCA, nor

    (b) a member of its staff,

SOCA may pay to him such remuneration and allowances as it may determine.

Delegation to committees and staff

16 (1) SOCA may, to such extent as it may determine, delegate any of its functions to any of its committees or to any members of its staff.

   (2) Any of SOCA's committees may, to such extent as the committee may determine, delegate any function conferred on it to any of its sub-committees or to any member of SOCA's staff.

Proceedings

17 (1) Subject to the following provisions of this paragraph, SOCA may regulate —

    (a) its own proceedings (including quorum), and

    (b) the procedure (including quorum) of its committees and sub-committees.

   (2) Any determination as to the quorum for meetings of SOCA or any of its committees or sub-committees must be made at a meeting of SOCA that is attended by both the chairman and the Director General.

   (3) The quorum for meetings of SOCA shall in the first instance be determined by a meeting of SOCA that is attended by at least five of its members.

18 (1) The validity of any proceedings of SOCA, or any of its committees or sub-committees, shall not be affected by —

    (a) any vacancy among the members of SOCA or the committee or sub-committee;

    (b) any defect in the appointment of any of those members or of the chairman or Director General; or

    (c) any vacancy in the office of the chairman or the Director General.

   (2) The proceedings to which this paragraph apply include those within sub-paragraph (2) (but not (3)) of paragraph 17.

Evidence

19 Any document purporting to be signed on behalf of SOCA shall be received in evidence and, unless the contrary is proved, be taken to be so signed.

Serious Organised Crime and Police Act 2005 (c. 15)
Schedule 1 – The Serious Organised Crime Agency
Part 4 – General

145

PART 4

GENERAL

Status

20   SOCA is not to be regarded —

    (a)   as the servant or agent of the Crown, or

    (b)   as enjoying any status, immunity or privilege of the Crown;

and SOCA's property is not to be regarded as property of, or property held on behalf of, the Crown.

Incidental powers

21   (1) In connection with exercising its functions SOCA may (subject to the provisions of this Act) —

    (a)   enter into contracts and other agreements (whether legally binding or not);

    (b)   acquire and dispose of property (including land);

    (c)   borrow money; and

    (d)   do such other things as SOCA thinks necessary or expedient.

    (2) The power conferred by sub-paragraph (1)(b) includes accepting —

    (a)   gifts of money, and

    (b)   gifts or loans of other property,

on such terms as SOCA considers appropriate (which may include terms providing for the commercial sponsorship of any of SOCA's activities).

    (3) But SOCA may exercise the power conferred by sub-paragraph (1)(b) or (c) only with the consent of the Secretary of State.

    (4) Such consent may be given —

    (a)   with respect to a particular case or with respect to a class of cases;

    (b)   subject to such conditions as the Secretary of State considers appropriate.

SCHEDULE 2

Section 55

FUNCTIONS OF INDEPENDENT POLICE COMPLAINTS COMMISSION IN RELATION TO SOCA

1   The Police Reform Act 2002 (c. 30) has effect subject to the following amendments.

2   In section 9(3) (persons ineligible for appointment as members of the Independent Police Complaints Commission) —

    (a)   after paragraph (d) insert —

           "(da) he is or has been the chairman or a member of, or a member of the staff of, the Serious Organised Crime Agency;"; and

    (b)   in paragraph (e), omit "is or".

3   (1) Section 10 (general functions of the Commission) is amended as follows.

(2) In subsection (1) —

    (a)   at the end of paragraph (e) omit "and";

    (b)   in paragraph (f) omit "the National Criminal Intelligence Service, the National Crime Squad and"; and

    (c)   at the end of that paragraph insert "; and

          (g)   to carry out functions in relation to the Serious Organised Crime Agency which correspond to those conferred on the Commission in relation to police forces by paragraph (e) of this subsection."

(3) In subsection (3) —

    (a)   omit paragraph (a);

    (b)   after paragraph (b) insert —

          "(ba)   any agreement under section 26A of this Act (Serious Organised Crime Agency);"; and

    (c)   in paragraph (d) omit "the National Criminal Intelligence Service, the National Crime Squad or".

(4) In subsection (7), omit "or" at the end of paragraph (a) and at the end of paragraph (b) insert "or

          (c)   its function under subsection (1)(g),".

4   (1)   Section 11 (reports) is amended as follows.

    (2) In subsection (6), for paragraphs (b) and (c) substitute —

        "(b)   to the Serious Organised Crime Agency; and".

    (3) For subsection (8) substitute —

        "(8)   Where a report under subsection (3) relates to the Serious Organised Crime Agency, the Commission shall send a copy of that report to the Agency."

    (4) In subsection (10), for paragraphs (d) and (e) substitute —

        "(d)   the Serious Organised Crime Agency;".

5   (1)   Section 15 (general duties of police authorities etc.) is amended as follows.

    (2) After subsection (1) insert —

        "(1A)   It shall be the duty of the Serious Organised Crime Agency to ensure that it is kept informed, in relation to the Agency, about all matters falling within subsection (2)."

    (3) In subsection (3) —

        (a)   for paragraph (c) substitute —

            "(c)   a police authority or chief officer requires the Director General of the Serious Organised Crime Agency to provide a member of the staff of that Agency for appointment under any of those paragraphs,"; and

        (b)   for "or Director General to whom the requirement is addressed" substitute "to whom the requirement is addressed or of the Director General".

    (4) In subsection (4), at the end of paragraph (b) insert "and" and for paragraphs (c) and (d) substitute —

        "(c)   the Serious Organised Crime Agency,".

Serious Organised Crime and Police Act 2005 (c. 15)
Schedule 2 – Functions of Independent Police Complaints Commission in relation to SOCA

147

(5) In subsection (5), at the end of paragraph (b) insert "and" and for paragraphs (c) and (d) substitute—

> "(c)   the Serious Organised Crime Agency,".

(6) In subsection (6)—

  (a) for "the Directors General of the National Criminal Intelligence Service and of the National Crime Squad" substitute "the Serious Organised Crime Agency";

  (b) in paragraph (a), for "of that Service or Squad" substitute "a member of the staff of the Agency"; and

  (c) omit the words from "or, as the case may be" to the end of the subsection.

(7) In subsection (7), for the words from "and in this subsection" onwards substitute "and where the person whose conduct is under investigation was a member of the staff of the Serious Organised Crime Agency at the time of the conduct, "third force" means any police force other than the force to which the person carrying out the investigation belongs."

(8) After subsection (7) insert—

> "(8)   Where the person who requires assistance and co-operation under subsection (5) is a member of the staff of the Serious Organised Crime Agency, a chief officer of a third force may be required to give that assistance and co-operation only with the approval of the Director General of the Agency.
>
> In this subsection, "third force", in relation to an investigation, means any police force other than the force to which the person whose conduct is under investigation belonged at the time of the conduct.

>   (9)   Where—

>   (a) the person carrying out an investigation is not a member of the staff of the Serious Organised Crime Agency; and

>   (b) the person whose conduct is under investigation was not a member of the staff of the Agency at the time of the conduct,

> the Director General of the Agency may be required to give assistance and co-operation under subsection (5) only with the approval of the chief officer of the force to which the person requiring it belongs."

6   In section 16 (payment for assistance with investigations), for subsections (5) and (6) substitute—

> "(5)   In this section (subject to subsection (6))—

>   (a) references to a police force and to a police authority maintaining a police force include references to the Serious Organised Crime Agency; and

>   (b) in relation to that Agency, references to the chief officer are references to the Director General.

>   (6)   This section shall have effect in relation to cases in which assistance is required to be provided by the Serious Organised Crime Agency as if—

>   (a) the reference in subsection (3)(b) to police authorities generally included a reference to the Agency; and

148

Serious Organised Crime and Police Act 2005 (c. 15)
Schedule 2 — Functions of Independent Police Complaints Commission in relation to SOCA

        (b)   the reference in subsection (4)(b) to police authorities generally were a reference to the Agency."

7   Omit section 25 (NCIS and NCS).

8   After section 26 insert —

"26A Serious Organised Crime Agency

    (1)   The Commission and the Serious Organised Crime Agency must enter into an agreement for the establishment and maintenance in relation to members of the Agency's staff of procedures corresponding or similar to those provided for by or under this Part.

    (2)   An agreement under this section —
        (a)   must not be made or varied except with the approval of the Secretary of State; and
        (b)   must not be terminated unless —
            (i)   it is replaced by another such agreement, and
            (ii)   the Secretary of State approves.

    (3)   An agreement under this section may contain provision for enabling the Commission to bring and conduct, or otherwise participate or intervene in, any proceedings which are identified by the agreement as disciplinary proceedings in relation to members of the Agency's staff.

    (4)   An agreement under this section must not confer any function on the Commission in relation to so much of any complaint or conduct matter as relates to the direction and control of the Agency by the Director General or other members of the Agency.

    (5)   Procedures established in accordance with an agreement under this section shall have no effect in relation to anything done outside England and Wales by any member of the staff of the Agency."

9   In section 29(3) (interpretation) —
        (a)   for paragraph (b) substitute —
              "(b)   a member of the staff of the Serious Organised Crime Agency;"; and
        (b)   in paragraph (d), for "(temporary service otherwise than with NCIS or NCS)" substitute "(temporary service of various kinds)".

10   In section 108(7) (extent etc.), omit paragraph (e).

11   (1)   Schedule 3 (handling of complaints and conduct matters) is amended as follows.

    (2)   In paragraph 16(3), for paragraph (b) substitute —
              "(b)   a member of the staff of the Serious Organised Crime Agency,".

    (3)   In paragraph 17(2), for paragraph (b) substitute —
              "(b)   a member of the staff of the Serious Organised Crime Agency,".

SCHEDULE 3   Section 58

TRANSFERS TO SOCA

Interpretation

1   In this Schedule —

"the 1967 Act" means the Police (Scotland) Act 1967 (c. 77);

"the 1996 Act" means the Police Act 1996 (c. 16);

"the 1998 Act" means the Police (Northern Ireland) Act 1998 (c. 32);

"the Commissioners" means the Commissioners for Her Majesty's Revenue and Customs;

"immigration officer" means a person who is an immigration officer within the meaning of the Immigration Act 1971 (c. 77);

"NCIS" means the National Criminal Intelligence Service;

"NCS" means the National Crime Squad;

"relevant appointment" means an appointment under section 6, 9, 13, 14, 52, 55, 58 or 59 of, or Schedule 1 to, the Police Act 1997 (c. 50);

"transfer scheme" means a scheme made by the Secretary of State under this Schedule.

Staff

2   (1) A transfer scheme may provide for a person who —

(a)   holds a relevant appointment,

(b)   is an officer of Revenue and Customs, or

(c)   is an immigration officer,

to become an employee of SOCA.

(2) If the person had a contract of employment before becoming an employee of SOCA, the scheme may provide for that contract to have effect (subject to any necessary modifications) as if originally made between him and SOCA.

(3) If the person did not have a contract of employment, the scheme may provide for the terms and conditions of his relevant appointment or service as an officer of Revenue and Customs or an immigration officer to have effect (subject to any necessary modifications) as the terms and conditions of his contract of employment with SOCA.

(4) In this paragraph "relevant appointment" does not include an appointment held by a person engaged on relevant service within the meaning of —

(a)   section 38A of the 1967 Act,

(b)   section 97 of the 1996 Act, or

(c)   section 27 of the 1998 Act.

3   A transfer scheme may provide —

(a)   for relevant service within section 38A(1)(ba) of the 1967 Act to have effect from a time specified in the scheme as relevant service within section 38A(1)(bc) of that Act,

(b)   for relevant service within section 97(1)(ca) or (cb) of the 1996 Act to have effect from a time specified in the scheme as relevant service within section 97(1)(cf) of that Act,

       (c)   for relevant service within section 27(1)(b) of the 1998 Act to have effect from a time specified in the scheme as relevant service within section 27(1)(cb) of that Act.

4   (1) A transfer scheme may provide —

       (a)   for the secondment by virtue of which a person holds a relevant appointment to have effect as a secondment to SOCA, and

       (b)   for him to serve as a member of the staff of SOCA.

    (2) The scheme may make provision as to the terms and conditions which are to have effect as the terms and conditions of his secondment to SOCA.

5   (1) A transfer scheme may provide —

       (a)   for the transfer to SOCA of the rights, powers, duties and liabilities of the employer under or in connection with the contract of employment of a person who becomes a member of the staff of SOCA by virtue of the scheme,

       (b)   for anything done before that transfer by or in relation to the employer in respect of such a contract or the employee to be treated as having been done by or in relation to SOCA.

    (2) Sub-paragraph (1) applies with the necessary modifications in relation to a person who before becoming a member of the staff of SOCA —

       (a)   did not have a contract of employment, or

       (b)   held a relevant appointment by virtue of a secondment.

    (3) A transfer scheme may make provision for periods before a person became an employee of SOCA to count as periods of employment with SOCA (and for the operation of the scheme not to be treated as having interrupted the continuity of that employment).

6   (1) A transfer scheme may provide for a person who —

       (a)   holds a relevant appointment or is an officer of Revenue and Customs or an immigration officer, and

       (b)   would otherwise become a member of the staff of SOCA by the operation of the scheme,

    not to become a member of the staff of SOCA if he gives notice objecting to the operation of the scheme in relation to him.

    (2) A transfer scheme may provide for any person who would be treated (whether by an enactment or otherwise) as being dismissed by the operation of the scheme not to be so treated.

7   (1) A transfer scheme may provide for the termination of a relevant appointment.

    (2) The Secretary of State may make a payment of such amount (if any) as he may determine to the person who held the appointment.

Property, rights and liabilities etc.

8   (1) A transfer scheme may provide for the transfer to SOCA of property, rights and liabilities of any of the following —

       (a)   NCIS, its Service Authority and Director General,

       (b)   NCS, its Service Authority and Director General,

       (c)   the Commissioners, and

         (d)   the Secretary of State.

(2) The scheme may —

         (a)   create rights, or impose liabilities, in relation to property, rights and liabilities transferred by virtue of the scheme, and

         (b)   apportion property, rights and liabilities between the Commissioners, or the Secretary of State, and SOCA.

(3) The scheme may provide for things done by or in relation to persons to whom sub-paragraph (4) applies to be —

         (a)   treated as done by or in relation to SOCA or members of the staff of SOCA,

         (b)   continued by or in relation to SOCA or members of the staff of SOCA.

(4) This sub-paragraph applies to —

         (a)   NCIS, its members and Service Authority,

         (b)   NCS, its members and Service Authority,

         (c)   the Commissioners and officers of Revenue and Customs, and

         (d)   the Secretary of State and immigration officers.

(5) The scheme may in particular make provision about the continuation of legal proceedings.

9   A transfer scheme may provide for SOCA to make any payment which —

         (a)   before a day specified in the scheme could have been made out of the NCIS service fund or the NCS service fund, but

         (b)   is not a liability which can be transferred by virtue of paragraph 8.

Supplementary

10   (1) A transfer scheme may contain —

         (a)   further provision in connection with any of the matters to which paragraphs 2 to 9 relate,

         (b)   the provision mentioned in sub-paragraph (3).

(2) The provision which may be made under sub-paragraph (1)(a) includes provision as to the consequences of the termination of a person's appointment or employment by or by virtue of the scheme.

(3) The provision mentioned in this sub-paragraph is provision —

         (a)   for the Secretary of State, or any other person nominated by or in accordance with the scheme, to determine any matter requiring determination under or in consequence of the scheme, and

         (b)   as to the payment of fees charged, or expenses incurred, by any person nominated to determine any matter by virtue of paragraph (a).

11   (1) Before making a transfer scheme which contains any provision relating to persons who fall within paragraph (a), (b) or (c) of paragraph 2(1), the Secretary of State must consult such bodies appearing to represent the interests of those persons as he considers appropriate.

(2) Before making a transfer scheme which contains any provision relating to —

         (a)   officers of Revenue and Customs, or

      (b)   property, rights or liabilities of the Commissioners,
the Secretary of State must consult the Commissioners.

Power to make regulations

12   The Secretary of State may by regulations make —

      (a)   provision as to the consequences of the termination of a person's employment by a transfer scheme (including provision removing any entitlement to compensation which might otherwise arise in such circumstances);

      (b)   transitory, transitional or saving provision in connection with any provision which is (or in the future may be) included in a transfer scheme by virtue of paragraph 3.

SCHEDULE 4

Section 59

MINOR AND CONSEQUENTIAL AMENDMENTS RELATING TO SOCA

Explosives Act 1875 (c. 17)

1   (1)   Section 75 of the Explosives Act 1875 is amended as follows.

    (2)   In subsection (1) —

      (a)   after "chief officer of police," insert "the Director General of the Serious Organised Crime Agency,", and

      (b)   after "any officer of police," insert "designated person,".

    (3)   For subsection (2) substitute —

      "(2)   In subsection (1) "designated person" means a member of the staff of the Serious Organised Crime Agency who is for the time being designated under section 43 of the Serious Organised Crime and Police Act 2005 as a person having the powers of a constable (but this is subject to any limitation specified in such a person's designation under that section)."

Police (Property) Act 1897 (c. 30)

2   (1)   Section 2A of the Police (Property) Act 1897 (application to NCS) is amended as follows.

    (2)   For "National Crime Squad" (in each place) substitute "Serious Organised Crime Agency".

    (3)   In subsection (2) —

      (a)   in paragraph (a) for "member of that Squad" substitute "member of the staff of that Agency", and

      (b)   in paragraph (b) for "Squad" substitute "Agency".

    (4)   In subsection (3) —

      (a)   in paragraph (a) for "the Service Authority for that Squad" substitute "that Agency", and

      (b)   in paragraph (b) for "Squad" substitute "Agency".

Serious Organised Crime and Police Act 2005 (c. 15)
Schedule 4 – Minor and consequential amendments relating to SOCA

153

(5) In the heading, for "**NCS**" substitute "**SOCA**".

Army Act 1955 (3 & 4 Eliz. 2 c. 18)

3   In section 83BC(2) of the Army Act 1955 (police forces which may be advised by prosecuting authority) omit paragraph (k).

Air Force Act 1955 (3 & 4 Eliz. 2 c. 19)

4   In section 83BC(2) of the Air Force Act 1955 (police forces which may be advised by prosecuting authority) omit paragraph (k).

Naval Discipline Act 1957 (c. 53)

5   In section 52IJ(2) of the Naval Discipline Act 1957 (police forces which may be advised by prosecuting authority) omit paragraph (k).

Public Records Act 1958 (c. 51)

6   In Schedule 1 to the Public Records Act 1958 (definition of public records) in Part 2 of the Table at the end of paragraph 3—
     (a)   at the appropriate place insert—
            "Serious Organised Crime Agency."; and
     (b)   omit the entries relating to the Service Authorities for the National Crime Squad and the National Criminal Intelligence Service.

Trustee Investments Act 1961 (c. 62)

7   The Trustee Investments Act 1961 has effect subject to the following amendments.

8   In section 11(4) (local authority investment schemes)—
     (a)   in paragraph (a) omit ", the Service Authority for the National Crime Squad", and
     (b)   omit paragraph (e).

9   In Part 2 of Schedule 1 (narrower-range investments requiring advice) omit paragraph 9(da).

Offices, Shops and Railway Premises Act 1963 (c. 41)

10   In section 90(4) of the Offices, Shops and Railway Premises Act 1963 (persons taken to be employed for the purposes of the Act)—
     (a)   at the end of paragraph (c) insert "or"; and
     (b)   for paragraph (d) substitute—
            "(d)   a member of a police force seconded to the Serious Organised Crime Agency to serve as a member of its staff."

Parliamentary Commissioner Act 1967 (c. 13)

11   In Schedule 2 to the Parliamentary Commissioner Act 1967 (departments etc. subject to investigation) omit the entries relating to the Service Authorities

for the National Crime Squad and the National Criminal Intelligence Service.

Police (Scotland) Act 1967 (c. 77)

12 The Police (Scotland) Act 1967 has effect subject to the following amendments.

13 In section 33 (inspectors of constabulary), in subsections (3) and (4), omit "and the National Criminal Intelligence Service".

14 (1) Section 38A (constables engaged on service outside their force) is amended as follows.

  (2) In subsection (1) —
    (a) omit paragraph (ba), and
    (b) after paragraph (bb) insert —
      "(bc) relevant service as a member of the staff of the Serious Organised Crime Agency on which a person is engaged with the consent of the appropriate authority,".

  (3) In subsection (6)(a) for "(ba) or (bb), (e) or (f)" substitute "(bb), (bc), (e) or (f)".

15 In section 39(4) (liability for wrongful acts of constables) for "section 23 of the Police Act 1997" substitute "section 23 or 25 of the Serious Organised Crime and Police Act 2005".

16 In section 41(4)(a) (assaults on constables) omit "or by a member of the National Criminal Intelligence Service or of the National Crime Squad".

Leasehold Reform Act 1967 (c. 88)

17 In section 28(5) of the Leasehold Reform Act 1967 (bodies retaining or resuming land required for public services) omit paragraph (bc).

Firearms Act 1968 (c. 27)

18 In section 54(3)(c) of the Firearms Act 1968 (application of Parts 1 and 2 to crown servants) for "National Criminal Intelligence Service or the National Crime Squad" substitute "staff of the Serious Organised Crime Agency".

Employment Agencies Act 1973 (c. 35)

19 In section 13(7) of the Employment Agencies Act 1973 (interpretation), in paragraph (f), omit ", the Service Authority for the National Criminal Intelligence Service, the Service Authority for the National Crime Squad".

Health and Safety at Work etc. Act 1974 (c. 37)

20 In section 51A(2) of the Health and Safety at Work etc. Act 1974 (application of Part 1 of the Act to the police) for paragraph (b) substitute —
    "(b) in relation to a member of a police force seconded to the Serious Organised Crime Agency to serve as a member of its staff, means that Agency, and".

Serious Organised Crime and Police Act 2005 (c. 15)
Schedule 4 — Minor and consequential amendments relating to SOCA

155

District Courts (Scotland) Act 1975 (c. 20)

21   In section 12(1) of the District Courts (Scotland) Act 1975 (restriction of functions of justices who are councillors etc.) after "authority" insert "or a member of staff of the Serious Organised Crime Agency".

House of Commons Disqualification Act 1975 (c. 24)

22   The House of Commons Disqualification Act 1975 has effect subject to the following amendments.

23   In section 1(1) (disqualification for membership of House of Commons) omit paragraph (da).

24   (1)   Schedule 1 (disqualifying offices) is amended as follows.

      (2)   In Part 2—
         (a)   at the appropriate place insert—
             "The Serious Organised Crime Agency."; and
         (b)   omit the entries relating to the Service Authorities for the National Crime Squad and the National Criminal Intelligence Service.

      (3)   In Part 3, at the appropriate place insert—
             "Member of the staff of the Serious Organised Crime Agency."

Northern Ireland Assembly Disqualification Act 1975 (c. 25)

25   The Northern Ireland Assembly Disqualification Act 1975 has effect subject to the following amendments.

26   In section 1(1) (disqualification for membership of Assembly) omit paragraph (da).

27   (1)   Schedule 1 (disqualifying offices) is amended as follows.

      (2)   In Part 2—
         (a)   at the appropriate place insert—
             "The Serious Organised Crime Agency."; and
         (b)   omit the entries relating to the Service Authorities for the National Crime Squad and the National Criminal Intelligence Service.

      (3)   In Part 3, at the appropriate place insert—
             "Member of the staff of the Serious Organised Crime Agency."

Sex Discrimination Act 1975 (c. 65)

28   In section 17 of the Sex Discrimination Act 1975 (police), in subsection (7)—
         (a)   in the definition of "chief officer of police", omit paragraph (aa);
         (b)   in the definition of "police authority", omit paragraph (aa); and
         (c)   in the definition of "police fund", omit the words from ", in relation to" (in the second place where they occur) to "the Police Act 1997".

Police Pensions Act 1976 (c. 35)

29   The Police Pensions Act 1976 has effect subject to the following amendments.

30   In section 7(2) (payment of pensions and contributions), at the beginning of each of paragraphs (ca) to (cd), insert "an employee of SOCA and who immediately before he became an employee of SOCA was serving as".

31 (1) Section 11 (interpretation) is amended as follows.

  (2) In subsection (1), at the beginning of each of paragraphs (ba), (bb), (bc) and (bd), after "service" insert "as an employee of SOCA by a person who immediately before he became an employee of SOCA was serving".

  (3) In subsection (2) for paragraphs (c) and (d) substitute —

    "(c) in relation to any such service as is mentioned in paragraph (ba), (bb), (bc) or (bd) of subsection (1) or any service of the kind described in section 97(1)(cf) of the Police Act 1997 or section 38A(1)(bc) of the Police (Scotland) Act 1967, it means SOCA;".

  (4) In subsection (5), in the definition of "central service" —

    (a) in paragraph (a) omit "(ca), (cb)," and after "(cc)" insert ", (cf)", and

    (b) in paragraph (b) for "(ba) or (bb)" substitute "(bb) or (bc)".

  (5) After the definition of "pension rights" in that subsection add —

    ""SOCA" means the Serious Organised Crime Agency."

32   Paragraphs 30 and 31 (and the corresponding entry in Schedule 17) do not affect the operation of the Police Pensions Act 1976 in relation to any person's service of any of the following kinds —

    (a) service as the Director General of the National Criminal Intelligence Service;

    (b) service as the Director General of the National Crime Squad;

    (c) service as a police member of the National Criminal Intelligence Service appointed under subsection (1)(b) of section 9 of the Police Act 1997 (c. 50) by virtue of subsection (2)(a) of that section;

    (d) service as a police member of the National Crime Squad appointed under subsection (1)(b) of section 55 of the Police Act 1997 by virtue of subsection (2)(a) of that section;

    (e) relevant service within paragraph (ca) or (cb) of section 97(1) of the Police Act 1996 (c. 16);

    (f) relevant service within section 38A(1)(ba) of the Police (Scotland) Act 1967 (c. 77).

Race Relations Act 1976 (c. 74)

33   The Race Relations Act 1976 has effect subject to the following amendments.

34 (1) Section 76B (other police bodies) is amended as follows.

  (2) Omit subsection (1).

  (3) In subsection (2) omit the word "also".

  (4) After subsection (2) insert —

    "(2A) Constables serving with the Serious Organised Crime Agency do not constitute a body of constables for the purposes of subsection (2)."

35   In Schedule 1A (bodies and other persons subject to general statutory duty) —

         (a)   in Part 1 omit paragraphs 59 and 60,

         (b)   in Part 2 at the appropriate place under the heading "Other Bodies, Etc" insert —

                       "The Serious Organised Crime Agency."; and

         (c)   in Part 3 omit the entry relating to the Director General of the National Crime Squad.

Sex Discrimination (Northern Ireland) Order 1976 (S.I. 1976/1042 (N.I. 15))

36   The Sex Discrimination (Northern Ireland) Order 1976 has effect subject to the following amendments.

37   In Article 84(8) (police officers) for "section 23 of the Police Act 1997" substitute "section 23 or 24 of the Serious Organised Crime and Police Act 2005".

38   In Article 85 (other police bodies), for paragraph (6) substitute —

         "(6)   In this Article in relation to any body of constables —

            (a)   "chief officer of police" means the person who has the direction and control of the body;

            (b)   "police authority" means the authority by which the members of the body are paid; and

            (c)   "police fund" means money provided by that authority."

Health and Safety at Work (Northern Ireland) Order 1978 (S.I. 1978/1039 (N.I. 9))

39   In Article 47A(2) of the Health and Safety at Work (Northern Ireland) Order 1978 (application of Part II of the Order to the police) omit sub-paragraph (b).

Law Reform (Miscellaneous Provisions) (Scotland) Act 1980 (c. 55)

40   In Part 1 of Schedule 1 to the Law Reform (Miscellaneous Provisions) (Scotland) Act 1980 (persons ineligible for jury service) in Group B, after paragraph (nb) insert —

            "(nc)   members of staff of the Serious Organised Crime Agency;".

Stock Transfer Act 1982 (c. 41)

41   In Schedule 1 to the Stock Transfer Act 1982 (securities specified for the purposes of the Act) in paragraph 7(1) —

         (a)   at the end of paragraph (b) insert "or"; and

         (b)   omit paragraph (bb) and the word "or" before it.

Road Traffic Regulation Act 1984 (c. 27)

42   (1)   Section 87 of the Road Traffic Regulation Act 1984 (exemption of fire, ambulance and police vehicles from speed limits) is amended as follows.

     (2)   The existing text of that section is to be subsection (1).

(3) After that subsection add —

> "(2) Subsection (1) above applies in relation to a vehicle being used —
>> (a) for Serious Organised Crime Agency purposes, or
>> (b) for training persons to drive vehicles for use for Serious Organised Crime Agency purposes,
>
> as it applies in relation to a vehicle being used for police purposes.
>
> (3) But (except where it is being used for training the person by whom it is being driven) subsection (1) above does not apply in relation to a vehicle by virtue of subsection (2) above unless it is being driven by a person who has been trained in driving vehicles at high speeds."

Police and Criminal Evidence Act 1984 (c. 60)

43   The Police and Criminal Evidence Act 1984 has effect subject to the following amendments.

44   In section 5 (reports of recorded searches and road checks) omit subsection (1A).

45   In section 55 (intimate searches) omit subsection (14A).

46   In section 63A(1A) (supplementary provision about fingerprints and samples) for paragraphs (b) and (c) substitute —

> "(b) the Serious Organised Crime Agency;".

Prosecution of Offences Act 1985 (c. 23)

47   In section 3(3) of the Prosecution of Offences Act 1985 (functions of Director of Public Prosecutions), in the definition of "police force", omit ", the National Crime Squad".

Ministry of Defence Police Act 1987 (c. 4)

48   The Ministry of Defence Police Act 1987 has effect subject to the following amendments.

49   In section 2B(3) (constables serving with other forces), in the definitions of "chief officer" and "relevant force", omit paragraphs (c) and (d).

50   After section 2B insert —

> **"2C   Constables serving with Serious Organised Crime Agency**
>
> (1) A member of the Ministry of Defence Police serving with the Serious Organised Crime Agency under arrangements to which subsection (2) applies shall —
>> (a) be under the direction and control of the Serious Organised Crime Agency, and
>> (b) continue to be a constable.
>
> (2) This subsection applies to arrangements made between —
>> (a) the Serious Organised Crime Agency, and
>> (b) the chief constable of the Ministry of Defence Police."

Serious Organised Crime and Police Act 2005 (c. 15)
Schedule 4 — Minor and consequential amendments relating to SOCA

159

Dartford-Thurrock Crossing Act 1988 (c. 20)

51   In section 19(a) of the Dartford-Thurrock Crossing Act 1988 (exemption from tolls) for sub-paragraph (ia) substitute—
        "(ia)   the Serious Organised Crime Agency;".

Road Traffic Act 1988 (c. 52)

52   The Road Traffic Act 1988 shall have effect subject to the following amendments.

53   (1) In section 124 (exemption from requirements regarding paid driving instruction) after subsection (1) insert—

        "(1A)   Section 123(1) and (2) also does not apply to the giving of instruction by a SOCA instructor in pursuance of arrangements made by the Director General of the Serious Organised Crime Agency.

        In this subsection "SOCA instructor" means a member of the staff of the Serious Organised Crime Agency whose duties consist of or include the giving instruction in the driving of motor cars to other members of the Agency's staff."

        (2) In subsection (2) of that section, omit the definitions of "chief officer of police", "police authority" and "police force".

54   In section 144(2) (exemption from requirement of third-party insurance or security) omit paragraph (ba).

Security Service Act 1989 (c. 5)

55   The Security Service Act 1989 has effect subject to the following amendments.

56   In section 1(4) (functions of the Security Service) for ", the National Criminal Intelligence Service, the National Crime Squad" substitute ", the Serious Organised Crime Agency".

57   In section 2(2)(c) (duties of the Director General)—
        (a)   for "the Director General of the National Criminal Intelligence Service" substitute "the Director General of the Serious Organised Crime Agency", and
        (b)   for ", the National Criminal Intelligence Service, the National Crime Squad" substitute ", the Serious Organised Crime Agency".

Official Secrets Act 1989 (c. 6)

58   In section 12(1)(e) of the Official Secrets Act 1989 (meaning of "Crown servant" in that Act) for "or of the National Criminal Intelligence Service or the National Crime Squad" substitute "or of the Serious Organised Crime Agency".

Aviation and Maritime Security Act 1990 (c. 31)

59   In section 22(4)(b) of the Aviation and Maritime Security Act 1990 (searches in harbour areas) omit sub-paragraph (iii) and the word "or" before it.

Tribunals and Inquiries Act 1992 (c. 53)

60   The Tribunals and Inquiries Act 1992 has effect subject to the following amendments.

61   In section 7(2) (removal of members of certain tribunals) after "36A" omit "(a) or (b)".

62   In Schedule 1 (tribunals under supervision of Council on Tribunals) in paragraph 36A omit "(a)" and sub-paragraph (b).

Criminal Appeal Act 1995 (c. 35)

63   (1) Section 22 of the Criminal Appeal Act 1995 (meaning of "public body" etc.) has effect subject to the following amendments.

      (2) In subsection (2) —

         (a)   in paragraph (a) omit ", the National Crime Squad",

         (b)   in paragraph (b) —

             (i)   at the end of sub-paragraph (i) insert "and",

             (ii)   omit sub-paragraph (ii), and

             (iii) at the end of sub-paragraph (iii) insert "and",

         (c)   in paragraph (c) for ", the City of London police force or the National Crime Squad" substitute "or the City of London police force", and

         (d)   omit paragraphs (d) and (e).

      (3) In subsection (4) for paragraph (aa) substitute —

         "(aa)   in relation to the Serious Organised Crime Agency, the Director General of that Agency,".

Disability Discrimination Act 1995 (c. 50)

64   The Disability Discrimination Act 1995 has effect subject to the following amendments.

65   (1) The section 64A (police) inserted by the Disability Discrimination Act 1995 (Amendment) Regulations 2003 (S.I. 2003/1673) is amended as follows.

      (2) In subsection (7) —

         (a)   in the definition of "chief officer of police", omit paragraph (b),

         (b)   in the definition of "police authority", omit paragraph (b), and

         (c)   in the definition of "police fund", omit paragraph (b).

66   In the section 64A (police) inserted by the Disability Discrimination Act 1995 (Amendment) Regulations (Northern Ireland) 2004 (S.R. 2004/55), in subsection (6)(a), for "section 23 of the Police Act 1997" substitute "section 23 or 24 of the Serious Organised Crime and Police Act 2005".

67   (1) The section 64B (other police bodies) inserted by the Disability Discrimination Act 1995 (Amendment) Regulations (Northern Ireland) 2004 is amended as follows.

      (2) For subsection (6) substitute —

         "(6)   Subject to subsection (8), in this section in relation to any body of constables —

Serious Organised Crime and Police Act 2005 (c. 15)
Schedule 4 – Minor and consequential amendments relating to SOCA

161

(a) "chief officer of police" means the person who has the direction and control of the body;

(b) "police authority" means the authority by which the members of the body are paid; and

(c) "police fund" means money provided by that authority."

Police Act 1996 (c. 16)

68   The Police Act 1996 has effect subject to the following amendments.

69   Omit section 23(8) (collaboration agreements).

70   Omit section 24(5) (mutual aid).

71   (1) Section 54 (appointment and functions of inspectors of constabulary) is amended as follows.

        (2) In subsection (2) omit "the National Criminal Intelligence Service and the National Crime Squad".

        (3) For subsection (2B) substitute –

              "(2B)   The Secretary of State may at any time require the inspectors of constabulary to carry out an inspection under this section of a police force maintained for any police area; and a requirement under this subsection may include a requirement for the inspection to be confined to a particular part of the force in question, to particular matters or to particular activities of that force."

72   In section 55 (publication of reports) omit subsection (7).

73   (1) Section 57 (common services) is amended as follows.

        (2) In subsection (3A) –
              (a) for "National Crime Squad" substitute "Serious Organised Crime Agency", and
              (b) for "Squad for the Squad" substitute "Agency for the Agency".

        (3) For subsection (4)(c) substitute –
              "(c)   if the regulations relate to the Serious Organised Crime Agency, that Agency."

74   Omit section 59(8) (police federations).

75   Omit section 60(2A) (regulations for police federations).

76   In section 61(1) (police negotiating board) omit paragraphs (aa) and (ba).

77   (1) Section 62 (functions of negotiating board with respect to regulations) is amended as follows.

        (2) In subsection (1) omit paragraphs (aa) and (ab).

        (3) Omit the subsection (1A) inserted by paragraph 82(2) of Schedule 9 to the Police Act 1997 (c. 50).

        (4) Omit subsections (1B) and (1C).

        (5) In subsection (2) for "subsection (1), (1A) or (1B)" substitute "subsection (1) or (1A)".

78   (1) Section 63 (police advisory boards) is amended as follows.

     (2) Omit subsections (1A) and (1B).

     (3) For subsection (3) substitute —

          "(3)   Before making —
                 (a)   regulations under section 50 or 52, other than regulations
                       with respect to any of the matters mentioned in section 61(1),
                       or
                 (b)   regulations under Part 2 of the Police Reform Act 2002,
                 the Secretary of State shall supply the Police Advisory Board for
                 England and Wales with a draft of the regulations, and take into
                 consideration any representations made by that Board."

79   In section 64 (membership of trade unions) omit subsections (4A) and (4B).

80   (1) Section 88 (liability for wrongful acts of constables) is amended as follows.

     (2) In subsection (5)(b) omit "or section 23 of the Police Act 1997".

     (3) After subsection (5) insert —

          "(5A) This section shall have effect where, by virtue of section 23 or 24 of
                 the Serious Organised Crime and Police Act 2005, a member of the
                 staff of the Serious Organised Crime Agency who is neither a
                 constable nor an employee of the police authority is provided to a
                 police force as if —
                 (a)   any unlawful conduct of his in the performance or purported
                       performance of his functions were unlawful conduct of a
                       constable under the direction and control of the chief officer
                       of police of that force; and
                 (b)   subsection (4) applied to him in the case of the police
                       authority maintaining that force."

81   In section 89(4)(a) (assaults on constables) omit "or by a member of the
          National Criminal Intelligence Service or of the National Crime Squad".

82   (1) Section 97 (police officers engaged on service outside their force) is amended
          as follows.

     (2) In subsection (1) —
          (a)   omit paragraphs (ca) and (cb),
          (b)   the paragraph (cd) inserted by paragraph 30(2) of Schedule 11 to the
                Proceeds of Crime Act 2002 (c. 29) is to be paragraph (ce), and
          (c)   after that paragraph insert —
                       "(cf)   temporary service as a member of the staff of the
                               Serious Organised Crime Agency on which a person
                               is engaged with the consent of the appropriate
                               authority;".

     (3) In subsection (6)(a) for the words from "paragraph" to "subsection (1)"
          substitute "paragraph (a), (aa), (b), (c), (cc), (cd), (ce), (cf), (d), (g) or (h) of
          subsection (1)".

     (4) In subsection (8) for the words from "paragraph" to "subsection (1)"
          substitute "paragraph (aa), (b), (c), (cc), (cd), (ce), (cf) or (d) of subsection (1)".

Serious Organised Crime and Police Act 2005 (c. 15)
Schedule 4 — Minor and consequential amendments relating to SOCA

163

83 (1) Section 98 (cross-border aid) is amended as follows.

    (2) In subsections (2) and (3) —

        (a) omit "or the Director General of the National Crime Squad", and

        (b) omit "or the National Crime Squad".

    (3) Omit subsection (3A).

    (4) In subsection (4) —

        (a) omit "or the National Crime Squad",

        (b) for "(2), (3) or (3A)" substitute "(2) or (3)", and

        (c) omit "or the Director General of the National Crime Squad".

    (5) In subsection (5) —

        (a) omit "or the National Crime Squad" (in both places), and

        (b) omit "or the Director General of the National Crime Squad".

    (6) Omit subsection (6A).

Employment Rights Act 1996 (c. 18)

84 The Employment Rights Act 1996 has effect subject to the following amendments.

85 In section 43KA(2) (application of Part 4A of that Act to the police) for paragraphs (b) and (c) substitute —

        "(b) in relation to a member of a police force seconded to the Serious Organised Crime Agency to serve as a member of its staff, that Agency; and".

86 In section 50(2) (right to time off for public duties) omit paragraph (ca).

87 In section 134A (application of section 100 of that Act to the police) after subsection (2) add —

        "(3) Subsection (1) does not apply to the holding of the office of constable by a member of a police force on secondment to the Serious Organised Crime Agency."

Juries (Northern Ireland) Order 1996 (S.I. 1996/1141 (N.I. 6))

88 In Schedule 2 to the Juries (Northern Ireland) Order 1996 omit the entry relating to members of the National Criminal Intelligence Service, members of the Service Authority for the National Criminal Intelligence Service and persons employed by the Authority.

Employment Rights (Northern Ireland) Order 1996 (S.I. 1996/1919 (N.I. 16))

89 The Employment Rights (Northern Ireland) Order 1996 has effect subject to the following amendments.

90 In Article 67KA(3) (application of Part VA of that Order to the police) omit sub-paragraph (b).

91 In Article 72A(2) (application of Article 68 of that Order to the police) omit sub-paragraph (b).

92   In Article 169A(2) (application of Article 132 of that Order to the police) omit sub-paragraph (b).

Police (Health and Safety) Act 1997 (c. 42)

93   In section 5(3) of the Police (Health and Safety) Act 1997—

        (a)   in the definition of "relevant authority" omit paragraphs (c) and (d),

        (b)   in the definition of "relevant fund" omit paragraphs (b) and (c), and

        (c)   in the definition of "responsible officer" omit paragraph (b).

Police Act 1997 (c. 50)

94   The Police Act 1997 has effect subject to the following amendments.

95   Omit sections 1 to 87 (provision about NCIS and NCS and their Service Authorities).

96   Omit sections 89 and 90 (general provision about NCS).

97   (1)   Section 93 (authorisations to interfere with property) is amended as follows.

     (2)   In subsection (1B) after "officer is a" insert "member of the staff of the Serious Organised Crime Agency,".

     (3)   In subsection (3) for paragraphs (b) and (c) substitute—

        "(b)   if the authorising officer is within subsection (5)(f), by a member of the staff of the Serious Organised Crime Agency,".

     (4)   In subsection (5) for paragraphs (f) and (g) substitute—

        "(f)   the Director General of the Serious Organised Crime Agency, or any member of the staff of that Agency who is designated for the purposes of this paragraph by that Director General;".

     (5)   In subsection (6) omit paragraphs (d) and (e).

98   (1)   Section 94 (authorisations in absence of authorising officer) is amended as follows.

     (2)   In subsection (1)—

        (a)   in paragraph (a) for "or (e)" substitute ", (e) or (f)",

        (b)   at the end of paragraph (a) insert "or",

        (c)   in paragraph (b) for ", (d) or (f)" substitute "or (d)", and

        (d)   omit paragraph (c) and the word "or" before it.

     (3)   In subsection (2) for paragraphs (e) and (ea) substitute—

        "(e)   where the authorising officer is within paragraph (f) of that subsection, by a person designated for the purposes of this section by the Director General of the Serious Organised Crime Agency;".

     (4)   Omit subsections (3) and (4)(c).

99   (1)   Section 95 (form and duration of authorisations) is amended as follows.

     (2)   In subsection (6) for "or (g)" substitute "or (f)".

     (3)   In subsection (7) for ", (d), (f) or (g)" substitute "or (d)".

Serious Organised Crime and Police Act 2005 (c. 15)
Schedule 4 – Minor and consequential amendments relating to SOCA

165

100 (1) Section 97 (authorisations requiring approval) is amended as follows.

    (2) In subsection (6A) –

        (a)   for ", (e) or (g)" substitute "or (e)", and

        (b)   for ", Chief Constable or, as the case may be, Director General" substitute "or, as the case may be, Chief Constable".

    (3) After subsection (6A) insert –

      "(6B)   The reference in subsection (6) to the authorising officer who gave the authorisation or in whose absence it was given shall be construed –

        (a)   in the case of an authorisation given by a person within paragraph (f) of section 93(5), as a reference to that person, and

        (b)   in the case of an authorisation given in the absence of such a person, as a reference to a member of the staff of the Serious Organised Crime Agency who is designated for the purposes of this section by the Director General of that Agency."

101   In section 105(3) (supplementary provision about appeals) for ", (d), (f) or (g)" substitute "or (d)".

102   In section 107(4)(b) (exclusions from Chief Commissioner's report) for "Service Authority for the National Criminal Intelligence Service or the Service Authority for the National Crime Squad" substitute "Serious Organised Crime Agency".

103 (1) Section 109 (Police Information Technology Organisation) is amended as follows.

    (2) In subsection (3) after "police forces," insert –

      "(aa)   the Serious Organised Crime Agency,".

    (3) In subsection (4) for "(a) or (b)" substitute "(a), (aa) or (b)".

104 (1) Section 111 (interpretation of Part 5) is amended as follows.

    (2) In subsection (1) –

        (a)   at the end of paragraph (a) insert "and", and

        (b)   omit paragraphs (c) and (d).

    (3) In subsection (2) –

        (a)   at the end of paragraph (b) insert "and", and

        (b)   omit paragraphs (d) and (e).

    (4) In subsection (3) –

        (a)   at the end of paragraph (a) insert "and", and

        (b)   omit paragraphs (c) and (d).

105   In section 137(2) (extent) omit paragraphs (b) and (c).

106   Omit Schedules 1 to 2A (Service Authorities for NCIS and NCS).

Race Relations (Northern Ireland) Order 1997 (S.I. 1997/869 (N.I. 6))

107   The Race Relations (Northern Ireland) Order 1997 has effect subject to the following amendments.

108   In Article 72A(8) (police officers) for "section 23 of the Police Act 1997" substitute "section 23 or 24 of the Serious Organised Crime and Police Act 2005".

109   In Article 72B (other police bodies), for paragraph (6) substitute —

"(6)   In this Article, in relation to any body of constables —
(a)   "chief officer of police" means the person who has the direction and control of the body;
(b)   "police authority" means the authority by which the members of the body are paid; and
(c)   "police fund" means money provided by that authority."

Police (Health and Safety) (Northern Ireland) Order 1997 (S.I. 1997/1774 (N.I. 16))

110   In Article 7(3) of the Police (Health and Safety) (Northern Ireland) Order 1997 —
(a)   in the definition of "the relevant authority", omit sub-paragraph (b),
(b)   in the definition of "the relevant fund", omit sub-paragraph (a), and
(c)   in the definition of "the responsible officer", omit sub-paragraph (b).

Audit Commission Act 1998 (c. 18)

111   In section 32(1) of the Audit Commission Act 1998 (documents to be sent by the Audit Commission to the Secretary of State), for the words from "relates to —" onwards substitute "relates to a police authority established under section 3 of the Police Act 1996."

Data Protection Act 1998 (c. 29)

112   In section 56(6) of the Data Protection Act 1998 (prohibition of requirement to produce certain records), in the first entry in the first column of the Table, for paragraphs (d) and (e) substitute —
"(d)   the Director General of the Serious Organised Crime Agency."

Police (Northern Ireland) Act 1998 (c. 32)

113   The Police (Northern Ireland) Act 1998 has effect subject to the following amendments.

114 (1) Section 27 (members of Police Service of Northern Ireland engaged on other police service) is amended as follows.

(2)   In subsection (1) —
(a)   omit paragraph (b), and
(b)   after paragraph (ca) insert —
"(cb)   seconded service as a member of the staff of the Serious Organised Crime Agency on which a member of the Police Service of Northern Ireland is engaged with the consent of the Chief Constable;".

(3)   In subsection (5)(b) for the words from "subsection (1)(aa)" to "or (j)" substitute "subsection (1)(aa), (c), (ca), (cb), (d), (e), (f), (h) or (j).

Serious Organised Crime and Police Act 2005 (c. 15)
Schedule 4 — Minor and consequential amendments relating to SOCA

167

(4) In subsection (7) for "(1)(b), (c) or (ca)" substitute "(1)(c), (ca) or (cb)".

115   In section 29(5) (liability for wrongful acts of constables) for "section 23 of the Police Act 1997" substitute "section 23 or 24 of the Serious Organised Crime and Police Act 2005".

116   In section 41 (inspectors of constabulary) for subsections (3) and (3A) substitute —

"(3A)   The Secretary of State may at any time require the inspectors to carry out an inspection under this section of the Police Service of Northern Ireland; and a requirement under this subsection may include a requirement for the inspection to be confined to a particular part of the Service, to particular matters or to particular activities of the Service."

117 (1) Section 42 (publication of reports of inspectors of constabulary) is amended as follows.

(2) In subsection (1) omit ", (3)".

(3) Omit subsection (7).

Crime and Disorder Act 1998 (c. 37)

118   Omit section 113 of the Crime and Disorder Act 1998 (deputy authorising officer under Part 3 of Police Act 1997).

Fair Employment and Treatment (Northern Ireland) Order 1998 (S.I. 1998/3162 (N.I. 21))

119   The Fair Employment and Treatment (Northern Ireland) Order 1998 has effect subject to the following amendments.

120   In Article 94(6) (police officers) for "section 23 of the Police Act 1997" substitute "section 23 or 24 of the Serious Organised Crime and Police Act 2005.

121   In Article 94A (other police bodies), for paragraph (6) substitute —

"(6)   In this Article, in relation to any body of constables —
    (a)   "chief officer of police" means the person who has the direction and control of the body;
    (b)   "police authority" means the authority by which the members of the body are paid; and
    (c)   "police fund" means money provided by that authority."

Immigration and Asylum Act 1999 (c. 33)

122   The Immigration and Asylum Act 1999 has effect subject to the following amendments.

123   In section 20(1) (supply of information to Secretary of State) for paragraphs (b) and (c) substitute —
    "(b)   the Serious Organised Crime Agency;".

124 (1) Section 21 (supply of information by Secretary of State) is amended as follows.

168

Serious Organised Crime and Police Act 2005 (c. 15)
Schedule 4 — Minor and consequential amendments relating to SOCA

(2) In subsection (1) for paragraphs (b) and (c) substitute —

"(b) the Serious Organised Crime Agency, for use for SOCA purposes;".

(3) For subsections (4) and (5) substitute —

"(4) "SOCA purposes" means any of the functions of the Serious Organised Crime Agency mentioned in section 2, 3 or 5 of the Serious Organised Crime and Police Act 2005."

Terrorism Act 2000 (c. 11)

125   The Terrorism Act 2000 has effect subject to the following amendments.

126   In section 19(7B) (duty to disclose information) —

(a) for "person" substitute "member of the staff of the Serious Organised Crime Agency", and

(b) for "the National Criminal Intelligence Service" substitute "that Agency".

127   In section 20(5) (permission to disclose information) —

(a) for "person" substitute "member of the staff of the Serious Organised Crime Agency", and

(b) for "the National Criminal Intelligence Service" substitute "that Agency".

128   In section 21A(14) (failure to disclose: regulated sector) —

(a) for "person" substitute "member of the staff of the Serious Organised Crime Agency", and

(b) for "the National Criminal Intelligence Service" substitute "that Agency".

129   In section 21B(7) (protected disclosures) —

(a) for "person" substitute "member of the staff of the Serious Organised Crime Agency", and

(b) for "the National Criminal Intelligence Service" substitute "that Agency".

130   In Schedule 14 (exercise of officers' powers), in paragraph 4(1), for paragraph (d) substitute —

"(d)   to the Serious Organised Crime Agency;".

Regulation of Investigatory Powers Act 2000 (c. 23)

131   The Regulation of Investigatory Powers Act 2000 has effect subject to the following amendments.

132 (1) Section 6 (application for issue of an interception warrant) is amended as follows.

(2) In subsection (2)(d) for "National Criminal Intelligence Service" substitute "Serious Organised Crime Agency".

(3) In subsection (3) after "specified in" insert "paragraph (a), (b), (c), (e), (f), (g), (h), (i) or (j)".

133 (1) In section 17(3) (exclusion of matters from legal proceedings) for paragraphs

Serious Organised Crime and Police Act 2005 (c. 15)
Schedule 4 — Minor and consequential amendments relating to SOCA

169

(c) and (d) substitute —

"(c) any member of the staff of the Serious Organised Crime Agency;".

(2) Sub-paragraph (1) does not affect the operation of section 17 in relation to conduct by any member of the National Criminal Intelligence Service or the National Crime Squad which took place before the commencement of this paragraph.

134 (1) In section 19(2) (unauthorised disclosures) for paragraphs (c) and (d) substitute —

"(c) every member of the staff of the Serious Organised Crime Agency;".

(2) Sub-paragraph (1) does not affect the operation of section 19 in relation to any person's service as a member of the National Criminal Intelligence Service or the National Crime Squad before the commencement of this paragraph.

135 (1) Section 25 (interpretation) is amended as follows.

(2) In subsection (1), in the definition of "relevant public authority", for paragraphs (b) and (c) substitute —

"(b) the Serious Organised Crime Agency;".

(3) After subsection (3) insert —

"(3A) References in this Chapter to an individual holding an office or position with the Serious Organised Crime Agency include references to any member of the staff of that Agency."

(4) For subsections (4) and (5) substitute —

"(4) The Secretary of State may by order —
(a) remove any person from the list of persons who are for the time being relevant public authorities for the purposes of this Chapter; and
(b) make such consequential amendments, repeals or revocations in this or any other enactment as appear to him to be necessary or expedient.

(5) The Secretary of State shall not make an order under this section —
(a) that adds any person to the list of persons who are for the time being relevant public authorities for the purposes of this Chapter, or
(b) that by virtue of subsection (4)(b) amends or repeals any provision of an Act,

unless a draft of the order has been laid before Parliament and approved by a resolution of each House."

136 In section 32(6) (authorisation of intrusive surveillance) for paragraphs (k) and (l) substitute —

"(k) the Director General of the Serious Organised Crime Agency and any member of the staff of that Agency who is designated for the purposes of this paragraph by that Director General;".

137 (1) Section 33 (rules for grant of authorisation) is amended as follows.

(2) In subsection (1) −

    (a)   omit ", the National Criminal Intelligence Service or the National Crime Squad", and

    (b)   omit ", Service or Squad".

(3) After subsection (1) insert −

    "(1A)   A person who is a designated person for the purposes of section 28 or 29 by reference to his office or position with the Serious Organised Crime Agency shall not grant an authorisation under that section except on an application made by a member of the staff of the Agency."

(4) In subsection (3) −

    (a)   omit ", the National Criminal Intelligence Service or the National Crime Squad", and

    (b)   omit (in both places) ", Service or Squad".

(5) After subsection (3) insert −

    "(3A)   The Director General of the Serious Organised Crime Agency or a person designated for the purposes of section 32(6)(k) by that Director General shall not grant an authorisation for the carrying out of intrusive surveillance except on an application made by a member of the staff of the Agency."

(6) In subsection (5)(a) for "the National Criminal Intelligence Service or the National Crime Squad," substitute "a member of the staff of the Serious Organised Crime Agency,".

(7) In subsection (6) −

    (a)   in paragraph (e) omit "and also of the National Criminal Intelligence Service", and

    (b)   omit paragraph (f).

138 (1) Section 34 (grant of authorisations in absence of senior officer) is amended as follows.

    (2) In subsection (1)(a) for "of the National Criminal Intelligence Service or of the National Crime Squad" substitute "a member of the staff of the Serious Organised Crime Agency".

    (3) In subsection (2)(a) for ", Service or Squad" substitute "or Agency".

    (4) In subsection (4) for paragraphs (j) and (k) substitute −

        "(j)   a person is entitled to act for the Director General of the Serious Organised Crime Agency if he is a person designated for the purposes of this paragraph by that Director General as a person entitled so to act in an urgent case;".

    (5) Omit subsection (5).

    (6) Omit subsection (6)(c).

139 (1) Section 35 (notification of certain authorisations) is amended as follows.

    (2) In subsection (1) for "police, customs" substitute "police, SOCA, customs".

    (3) In subsection (10) −

Serious Organised Crime and Police Act 2005 (c. 15)
Schedule 4 — Minor and consequential amendments relating to SOCA

171

    (a)   for "police, customs" substitute "police, SOCA, customs", and

    (b)   in paragraph (a) for ", the National Criminal Intelligence Service or the National Crime Squad" substitute "or the Serious Organised Crime Agency".

140 (1) Section 36 (approval required for authorisations to take effect) is amended as follows.

    (2) In subsection (1) for paragraphs (b) and (c) substitute —

        "(b)   a member of the staff of the Serious Organised Crime Agency;".

    (3) In subsection (6) —

        (a)   in paragraph (b) for "National Criminal Intelligence Service or the Director General of the National Crime Squad," substitute "Serious Organised Crime Agency,", and

        (b)   for paragraphs (d) and (e) substitute —

            "(d)   where the authorisation was granted by a person designated for the purposes of section 32(6)(k), or by a person entitled to act for the Director General of the Serious Organised Crime Agency by virtue of section 34(4)(j), that Director General;".

141   In section 37(1) (quashing of police and customs authorisations) for paragraphs (b) and (c) substitute —

        "(b)   a member of the staff of the Serious Organised Crime Agency;".

142   In section 40 (duty to provide information to Surveillance Commissioners) for paragraphs (b) and (c) substitute —

        "(b)   every member of the staff of the Serious Organised Crime Agency,".

143   In section 45(6) (cancellation of authorisations) —

        (a)   at the end of paragraph (b) insert "and", and

        (b)   omit paragraphs (d) and (e).

144   In section 46(3) (restriction on authorisations extending to Scotland) after paragraph (da) insert —

        "(db)   the Serious Organised Crime Agency;".

145   In section 49(1)(e) (notices requiring disclosure) after "the police" (in both places) insert ", SOCA".

146 (1) Section 51 (cases in which key required) is amended as follows.

    (2) In subsection (2) —

        (a)   for "the police, the customs" substitute "the police, SOCA, the customs", and

        (b)   after paragraph (a) insert —

            "(aa)   in the case of a direction by SOCA, except by or with the permission of the Director General of the Serious Organised Crime Agency;".

    (3) In subsection (3) after "of police," insert "the Director General of the Serious Organised Crime Agency,".

(4) In subsection (6) after "of police," insert "by the Director General of the Serious Organised Crime Agency,".

147   In section 54(3) (tipping-off) after "police" (in both places) insert "SOCA,".

148 (1) Section 55 (duties of specified authorities) is amended as follows.

   (2) In subsection (1) after paragraph (b) insert—
         "(ba)   the Director General of the Serious Organised Crime Agency;".

   (3) After subsection (3) insert—

       "(3A)   Paragraph 11 of Schedule 1 to the Serious Organised Crime and Police Act 2005 does not apply in relation to the duties of the Director General of the Serious Organised Crime Agency under this section."

149   In section 56(1) (interpretation)—
         (a)   in the definition of "chief officer of police" omit paragraphs (j) and (k),
         (b)   in paragraph (a) of the definition of "the police" after "constable" insert "(except a constable who is a member of the staff of the Serious Organised Crime Agency)", and
         (c)   after the definition of "section 49 notice" insert—
                   ""SOCA" means the Serious Organised Crime Agency or any member of the staff of the Serious Organised Crime Agency;".

150   In section 58(1) (co-operation with Commissioner) for paragraphs (b) and (c) substitute—
         "(b)   every member of the staff of the Serious Organised Crime Agency,".

151   In section 65(6) (the Tribunal) for paragraphs (d) and (e) substitute—
         "(d)   the Serious Organised Crime Agency; or".

152   In section 68(7) (disclosure to Tribunal) for paragraphs (b) and (c) substitute—
         "(b)   every member of the staff of the Serious Organised Crime Agency;".

153   In section 75(6) (authorisations under Part 3 of Police Act 1997) omit paragraph (b).

154 (1) Section 76A (foreign surveillance operations) is amended as follows.

   (2) In subsection (6)(a) for "National Criminal Intelligence Service" substitute "Serious Organised Crime Agency".

   (3) In subsection (11), in the definition of "United Kingdom officer"—
         (a)   in paragraph (b) for "National Criminal Intelligence Service" substitute "staff of the Serious Organised Crime Agency", and
         (b)   in paragraph (c) omit "the National Crime Squad or".

155 (1) In Schedule 1 (relevant authorities) for paragraphs 2 and 3 substitute—

       "2   The Serious Organised Crime Agency."

156 (1) Schedule 2 (persons having appropriate permission) is amended as follows.

Serious Organised Crime and Police Act 2005 (c. 15)
Schedule 4 – Minor and consequential amendments relating to SOCA

173

(2) In paragraph 2 –
    (a) in sub-paragraph (3) after "the police" insert ", SOCA", and
    (b) in sub-paragraph (5) after "Only the police" insert ", SOCA".

(3) In paragraph 4(2) after "the police," (in each place) insert "SOCA,".

(4) In paragraph 5(3)(b) after "police" insert ", SOCA".

(5) In paragraph 6 –
    (a) after sub-paragraph (3) insert –

> "(3A) A member of the staff of the Serious Organised Crime Agency does not by virtue of paragraph 1, 4 or 5 have the appropriate permission in relation to any protected information unless permission to give a section 49 notice in relation to that information has been granted –
>   (a) by the Director General; or
>   (b) by a member of the staff of the Agency of or above such level as the Director General may designate for the purposes of this sub-paragraph."; and

    (b) after sub-paragraph (5) add –

> "(6) In sub-paragraph (2) "constable" does not include a constable who is a member of the staff of the Serious Organised Crime Agency."

Football (Disorder) Act 2000 (c. 25)

157   Omit section 2 of the Football (Disorder) Act 2000 (disclosure of information by NCIS).

Freedom of Information Act 2000 (c. 36)

158   The Freedom of Information Act 2000 has effect subject to the following amendments.

159   In section 23(3) (bodies supplying information which is exempt) omit "and" at the end of paragraph (k) and after paragraph (l) add –
    "(m)   the Serious Organised Crime Agency."

160   In Schedule 1 (list of public authorities), in Part 6, omit the entries relating to the National Crime Squad and the Service Authority for the National Crime Squad.

Criminal Justice and Court Services Act 2000 (c. 43)

161   In section 71(1) and (2)(a) of the Criminal Justice and Court Services Act 2000 (access to driver licensing records) after "constables" insert "and members of the staff of the Serious Organised Crime Agency".

Criminal Justice and Police Act 2001 (c. 16)

162   The Criminal Justice and Police Act 2001 has effect subject to the following amendments.

163   In section 88(8) (functions of Central Police Training and Development

Authority) for paragraphs (a) and (b) substitute—
    "(a)   the Serious Organised Crime Agency;".

164 (1) Section 104 (vice-chairmen) is amended as follows.

     (2) Omit subsection (3).

     (3) In subsection (4)—
        (a)   at the end of paragraph (a) insert "and", and
        (b)   omit paragraph (c) and the word "and" before it.

     (4) Omit subsection (8).

165 (1) Section 107 (payment of allowances to authority members) is amended as follows.

     (2) Omit subsection (1)(c).

     (3) Omit subsection (4).

166   Omit sections 108 to 121 (provision about NCIS and NCS and their Service Authorities).

167   Omit section 138(6)(d) (extent).

Proceeds of Crime Act 2002 (c.29)

168   The Proceeds of Crime Act 2002 has effect subject to the following amendments.

169   In section 313(1) (restriction on performance by police of functions of the Director of the Assets Recovery Agency) omit paragraphs (c) and (d).

170   In section 330(5)(a) (required disclosure of information regarding money laundering) for "the Director General of the National Criminal Intelligence Service" substitute "the Director General of the Serious Organised Crime Agency".

171   In section 331(5)(a) (required disclosure of information regarding money laundering) for "the Director General of the National Criminal Intelligence Service" substitute "the Director General of the Serious Organised Crime Agency".

172   In section 332(5)(a) (required disclosure of information regarding money laundering) for "the Director General of the National Criminal Intelligence Service" substitute "the Director General of the Serious Organised Crime Agency".

173   In section 336 (giving of consent by a nominated officer) in subsections (2)(a), (3)(a) and (4)(a), for "the Director General of the National Criminal Intelligence Service" substitute "the Director General of the Serious Organised Crime Agency".

174   In section 340(13) (interpretation of references to constable) for "the Director General of the National Criminal Intelligence Service" substitute "the Director General of the Serious Organised Crime Agency".

175   In section 378(5) (interpretation of references to officers) for "the Director General of the National Criminal Intelligence Service" substitute "the Director General of the Serious Organised Crime Agency".

Serious Organised Crime and Police Act 2005 (c. 15)
Schedule 4 – Minor and consequential amendments relating to SOCA

175

176   In section 436(5) (persons permitted to disclose information to the Director of the Assets Recovery Agency) for paragraphs (b) and (c) substitute —
> "(b)   the Director General of the Serious Organised Crime Agency;".

177   In section 439(5) (persons permitted to disclose information to the Lord Advocate and Scottish Ministers) for paragraphs (b) and (c) substitute —
> "(b)   the Director General of the Serious Organised Crime Agency;".

178   In section 445(2)(b) (external investigations) for "the Director General of the National Criminal Intelligence Service" substitute "the Director General of the Serious Organised Crime Agency".

Police Reform Act 2002 (c. 30)

179   The Police Reform Act 2002 has effect subject to the following amendments.

180   Omit section 8 (powers of Secretary of State in relation to NCIS and NCS).

181 (1) Section 38 (exercise of police powers by civilian employees) is amended as follows.

(2) Omit subsection (3).

(3) In subsection (4) omit "or a Director General".

(4) In subsection (7) omit "or of a Service Authority".

182   In section 42 (supplementary provisions relating to exercise of police powers) omit subsections (4) and (8).

183 (1) Section 45 (code of practice relating to exercise of police powers) is amended as follows.

(2) In subsection (1) omit "and by Directors General".

(3) In subsection (3) omit paragraphs (a), (b), (d) and (e).

(4) In subsection (5) omit "or a Director General".

184   In section 47(1) (interpretation) omit the definitions of "Director General" and "Service Authority".

185 (1) Section 82 (police nationality requirements) is amended as follows.

(2) In subsection (1) omit paragraph (c).

(3) In subsection (2) —
(a)   at the end of paragraph (a) insert "or", and
(b)   omit paragraph (c) and the word "or" before it.

(4) In subsection (3) —
(a)   at the end of paragraph (c) insert "and", and
(b)   omit paragraph (d).

(5) In subsection (4) for ", Service or Squad" substitute "or Service".

186   Omit sections 85 to 91 (NCIS and NCS: general provisions).

187   Omit section 93 (quorum for NCIS and NCS service authorities).

188 (1) Section 102 (liability for wrongful acts of constables) is amended as follows.

     (2) In subsection (2) omit paragraphs (c) and (d).

     (3) In subsection (5) omit paragraphs (b) and (c).

189 (1) Section 103 (liability in respect of members of teams) is amended as follows.

     (2) Omit subsections (2) and (3).

     (3) In subsection (6) omit ", the NCIS service fund or the NCS service fund,".

190   In Schedule 4 (powers exercisable by police civilians), in paragraph 36(1), omit paragraph (b) and the word "and" before it.

Crime (International Co-operation) Act 2003 (c. 32)

191   Omit section 85 (liability of NCIS in respect of foreign officers) of the Crime (International Co-operation) Act 2003.

Courts Act 2003 (c. 39)

192   In section 41(6)(c) of the Courts Act 2003 (disqualification of lay justices who are members of local authorities) for ", the Service Authority for the National Criminal Intelligence Service or the Service Authority for the National Crime Squad" substitute "or the Serious Organised Crime Agency".

Sexual Offences Act 2003 (c. 42)

193   The Sexual Offences Act 2003 has effect subject to the following amendments.

194   In section 94(3) (supply of information for verification) for paragraphs (c) and (d) substitute —
              "(c)   the Serious Organised Crime Agency."

195   In section 95(2) (supply of information by Secretary of State) for paragraphs (b) and (c) substitute —
              "(b)   the Serious Organised Crime Agency."

Criminal Justice Act 2003 (c. 44)

196   In section 29(5) of the Criminal Justice Act 2003 (persons who may institute criminal proceedings by written charge) after paragraph (ca) insert —
              "(cb)   the Director General of the Serious Organised Crime Agency or a person authorised by him to institute criminal proceedings;".

Energy Act 2004 (c. 20)

197   The Energy Act 2004 has effect subject to the following amendments.

198   In section 59(3) (members of civil nuclear constabulary serving with other forces) —
              (a)   in the definition of "chief officer" omit paragraphs (c) and (d), and
              (b)   in the definition of "relevant force" omit paragraphs (c) and (d).

Serious Organised Crime and Police Act 2005 (c. 15)
Schedule 4 – Minor and consequential amendments relating to SOCA

177

199   After section 59 insert –

"59A Constables serving with Serious Organised Crime Agency

(1)   A member of the Constabulary serving with the Serious Organised Crime Agency under arrangements to which subsection (2) applies shall –

(a)   be under the direction and control of the Serious Organised Crime Agency, and

(b)   continue to be a constable.

(2)   This subsection applies to arrangements made between the Serious Organised Crime Agency and the chief constable."

Domestic Violence, Crime and Victims Act 2004 (c. 28)

200   In Schedule 9 to the Domestic Violence, Crime and Victims Act 2004 (authorities within remit of Commissioner for Victims and Witnesses) for paragraphs 13 and 14 substitute –

"13   The Serious Organised Crime Agency."

SCHEDULE 5   Section 82

PERSONS SPECIFIED FOR THE PURPOSES OF SECTION 82

1   A person who is or might be, or who has been, a witness in legal proceedings (whether or not in the United Kingdom).

2   A person who has complied with a disclosure notice given to him by virtue of section 62(1).

3   (1)   A person who has been given an immunity notice under section 71(1) if the notice continues to have effect in relation to him.

      (2)   A person who has been given a restricted use undertaking under section 72(1) if the undertaking continues to have effect in relation to him.

4   A person who is or has been a member of a jury.

5   A person who holds or has held judicial office (whether or not in the United Kingdom).

6   A person who is or has been a justice of the peace or who holds or has held a position comparable to that of a justice of the peace in a place outside the United Kingdom.

7   A person who is or has been a member of an international tribunal which has jurisdiction in criminal matters.

8   A person who conducts or has conducted criminal prosecutions (whether or not in the United Kingdom).

9   (1)   A person who is or has been the Director of Public Prosecutions for England and Wales.

(2) A person who is or has been a member of staff of the Crown Prosecution Service for England and Wales.

10 (1) A person who is or has been the Director or deputy Director of Public Prosecutions for Northern Ireland.

(2) A person who is or has been a person appointed under Article 4(3) of the Prosecution of Offences (Northern Ireland) Order 1972 (S.I. 1972/538 (N.I.1)) to assist the Director of Public Prosecutions for Northern Ireland.

11 A person who is or has been under the direction and control of the Lord Advocate in the Lord Advocate's capacity as head of the systems of criminal prosecution and investigation of deaths in Scotland.

12 (1) A person who is or has been the Director of Revenue and Customs Prosecutions.

(2) A person who is or has been a member of staff of the Revenue and Customs Prosecutions Office.

13 A person who is or has been a constable.

14 A person who is or has been designated under—
    (a) section 38(1) of the Police Reform Act 2002 (c. 30) (police powers for police authority employees);
    (b) section 30(1) of the Police (Northern Ireland) Act 2003 (c. 6) (police powers for designated police support staff).

15 A person who is a police custody and security officer (within the meaning of section 9(1A) of the Police (Scotland) Act 1967 (c. 77)) of a police authority in Scotland.

16 A person who—
    (a) is or has been an officer of Revenue and Customs;
    (b) is or has been a member of staff of Her Majesty's Customs and Excise.

17 A person who is or has been a person appointed as an immigration officer under paragraph 1 of Schedule 2 to the Immigration Act 1971 (c. 77).

18 A person who is or has been a member of staff of SOCA.

19 (1) A person who is or has been the Director General of the National Criminal Intelligence Service or the Director General of the National Crime Squad.

(2) A person who is or has been under the direction and control of the Director General of the National Criminal Intelligence Service or the Director General of the National Crime Squad.

20 (1) A person who is or has been the Director of the Scottish Drug Enforcement Agency.

(2) A person who is or has been under the direction and control of the Director of the Scottish Drug Enforcement Agency.

21 (1) A person who is or has been the Director of the Assets Recovery Agency.

(2) A person who is or has been a member of staff of the Assets Recovery Agency or a person with whom the Director of that Agency has made

arrangements for the provision of services under section 1(4) of the Proceeds of Crime Act 2002 (c. 29).

22 (1) A person who is or has been the head of the Civil Recovery Unit, that is to say of the organisation known by that name which acts on behalf of the Scottish Ministers in proceedings under Part 5 of the Proceeds of Crime Act 2002 (civil recovery of the proceeds etc. of unlawful conduct).

(2) A person who is or has been a member of staff of the Civil Recovery Unit.

23 (1) A person who is or has been a person appointed by virtue of section 246(1) of the Proceeds of Crime Act 2002 (c. 29) as an interim receiver.

(2) A person who assists or has assisted an interim receiver so appointed in the exercise of such functions as are mentioned in section 247 of that Act.

24 (1) A person who is or has been a person appointed by virtue of section 256(1) of the Proceeds of Crime Act 2002 as an interim administrator.

(2) A person who assists or has assisted an interim administrator so appointed in the exercise of such functions as are mentioned in section 257 of that Act.

25 (1) A person who is or has been the head of the Financial Crime Unit, that is to say of the organisation known by that name which, among other activities, acts on behalf of the Lord Advocate in proceedings under Part 3 of the Proceeds of Crime Act 2002 (confiscation: Scotland).

(2) A person who is or has been a member of staff of the Financial Crime Unit.

26 A person who is or has been a prison officer.

27 A person who is or has been a covert human intelligence source (within the meaning of section 26(8) of the Regulation of Investigatory Powers Act 2000 (c. 23) or of section 1(7) of the Regulation of Investigatory Powers (Scotland) Act 2000 (asp 11)).

28 A person—
  (a) who is a member of the family of a person specified in any of the preceding paragraphs;
  (b) who lives or has lived in the same household as a person so specified;
  (c) who has or has had a close personal relationship with a person so specified.

SCHEDULE 6

MINOR AND CONSEQUENTIAL AMENDMENTS RELATING TO CHAPTER 6 OF PART 2

Prescription and Limitation (Scotland) Act 1973 (c. 52)

1 In section 19B(3) of the Prescription and Limitation (Scotland) Act 1973 (actions for recovery of property obtained through unlawful conduct etc.) —
  (a) after paragraph (a) insert—
       "(aa) an application is made for a prohibitory property order, or", and
  (b) for "earlier" substitute "earliest".

Limitation Act 1980 (c. 58)

2   In section 27A(3) of the Limitation Act 1980 (time limits for bringing
         proceedings for recovery order: when proceedings are brought) —
         (a) after paragraph (a) insert —
                  "(aa) an application is made for a property freezing order,
                         or", and
         (b) for "earlier" substitute "earliest".

Limitation (Northern Ireland) Order 1989 (S.I. 1989/1339 (N.I. 11))

3   In Article 72A(3) of the Limitation (Northern Ireland) Order 1989 (time
         limits for bringing proceedings for recovery order: when proceedings are
         brought) —
         (a) after paragraph (a) insert —
                  "(aa) an application is made for a property freezing order,
                         or", and
         (b) for "earlier" substitute "earliest".

Proceeds of Crime Act 2002 (c. 29)

4   The Proceeds of Crime Act 2002 (c. 29) is amended as follows.

5   In section 82(f) (confiscation: England and Wales: property is free property
         if order under section 246 etc. applies to it) —
         (a) after "section" insert "245A," and
         (b) after "246," insert "255A, 256,".

6   In section 148(f) (confiscation: Scotland: property is free property if order
         under section 246 etc. applies to it) —
         (a) after "section" insert "245A," and
         (b) after "246," insert "255A, 256,".

7   In section 230(f) (confiscation: Northern Ireland: property is free property if
         order under section 246 etc. applies to it) —
         (a) after "section" insert "245A," and
         (b) after "246," insert "255A, 256,".

8   In section 241(2)(a) (conduct occurring outside the United Kingdom that is
         unlawful conduct for the purposes of Part 5) —
         (a) after "in a country" insert "or territory", and
         (b) for "of that country" substitute "applying in that country or
              territory".

9   In section 243 (proceedings for recovery orders in England and Wales or
         Northern Ireland), after subsection (4) insert —

         "(5) Nothing in sections 245A to 255 limits any power of the court apart
               from those sections to grant interim relief in connection with
               proceedings (including prospective proceedings) under this
               Chapter."

Serious Organised Crime and Police Act 2005 (c. 15)
Schedule 6 – Minor and consequential amendments relating to Chapter 6 of Part 2

181

10   Before section 248 (and its heading) insert the following heading—

"Property freezing orders and interim receiving orders: registration"

11   (1) Section 248 (registration: England and Wales) is amended as follows.

      (2) In subsection (1)(a), for "interim receiving orders" substitute "property freezing orders, and in relation to interim receiving orders,".

      (3) In subsection (1)(b), for "interim receiving orders" substitute "property freezing orders, and in relation to applications for interim receiving orders,".

      (4) In subsection (3), before "an interim receiving order" insert "a property freezing order or".

12   (1) Section 249 (registration: Northern Ireland) is amended as follows.

      (2) In subsection (1), after "applying for" insert "a property freezing order or".

      (3) In subsection (1)(b), for "an interim receiving order" substitute "a property freezing order, or an interim receiving order,".

      (4) After subsection (1) insert—

           "(1A) Upon being served with a copy of a property freezing order, the Registrar must, in respect of any registered land to which a property freezing order or an application for a property freezing order relates, make an entry inhibiting any dealing with the land without the consent of the High Court."

      (5) In subsection (3), after "entry made under subsection" insert "(1A) or".

      (6) In subsection (4)—
           (a)   after "Where" insert "a property freezing order or", and
           (b)   after "setting aside the" insert "property freezing order or".

13   Before section 250 (and its heading) insert the following heading—

"Interim receiving orders: further provisions"

14   (1) Section 252 (interim receiving orders: prohibition on dealings) is amended as follows.

      (2) For subsection (4) (restriction on exclusions for legal expenses) substitute—

           "(4) Where the court exercises the power to make an exclusion for the purpose of enabling a person to meet legal expenses that he has incurred, or may incur, in respect of proceedings under this Part, it must ensure that the exclusion—
                (a)   is limited to reasonable legal expenses that the person has reasonably incurred or that he reasonably incurs,
                (b)   specifies the total amount that may be released for legal expenses in pursuance of the exclusion, and
                (c)   is made subject to the required conditions (see section 286A) in addition to any conditions imposed under subsection (3).

    (4A)   The court, in deciding whether to make an exclusion for the purpose of enabling a person to meet legal expenses of his in respect of proceedings under this Part—

        (a)   must have regard (in particular) to the desirability of the person being represented in any proceedings under this Part in which he is a participant, and

        (b)   must, where the person is the respondent, disregard the possibility that legal representation of the person in any such proceedings might, were an exclusion not made, be funded by the Legal Services Commission or the Northern Ireland Legal Services Commission."

    (3)   In subsection (6) (power to make exclusions not to be exercised so as to prejudice enforcement authority's rights to recover property), after "must" insert ", subject to subsection (4A),".

15   In section 266 (recovery orders), after subsection (8) insert—

    "(8A)   A recovery order made by a court in England and Wales or Northern Ireland may provide for payment under section 280 of reasonable legal expenses that a person has reasonably incurred, or may reasonably incur, in respect of—

        (a)   the proceedings under this Part in which the order is made, or

        (b)   any related proceedings under this Part.

    (8B)   If regulations under section 286B apply to an item of expenditure, a sum in respect of the item is not payable under section 280 in pursuance of provision under subsection (8A) unless—

        (a)   the enforcement authority agrees to its payment, or

        (b)   the court has assessed the amount allowed by the regulations in respect of that item and the sum is paid in respect of the assessed amount."

16   In section 271(4) (certain payments to trustee for civil recovery to be reduced to take account of loss caused by interim receiving order etc.)—

    (a)   in paragraph (a), for "an interim receiving order or" substitute "a property freezing order, an interim receiving order, a prohibitory property order or an", and

    (b)   in paragraph (b), for "interim receiving order or interim administration order" substitute "order mentioned in paragraph (a)".

17   In section 272(5) (provision in recovery orders for compensation for loss caused by interim receiving order etc.)—

    (a)   in paragraph (a), for "an interim receiving order or" substitute "a property freezing order, an interim receiving order, a prohibitory property order or an", and

    (b)   in paragraph (b), for "interim receiving order or interim administration order" substitute "order mentioned in paragraph (a)".

18   In section 280(2) (application of realised proceeds of recovery order)—

Serious Organised Crime and Police Act 2005 (c. 15)
Schedule 6 — Minor and consequential amendments relating to Chapter 6 of Part 2

183

(a) after paragraph (a) insert—

"(aa) next, any payment of legal expenses which, after giving effect to section 266(8B), are payable under this subsection in pursuance of provision under section 266(8A) contained in the recovery order," and

(b) in paragraph (b), for "second" substitute "then".

19   In section 283 (compensation where interim receiving order etc. has applied)—

(a) in subsection (1), for "an interim receiving order or" substitute "a property freezing order, an interim receiving order, a prohibitory property order or an", and

(b) in subsection (5), for "interim receiving order or interim administration order" substitute "order mentioned in subsection (1)".

20   After section 286 insert—

"286A Legal expenses excluded from freezing: required conditions

(1) The Lord Chancellor may by regulations specify the required conditions for the purposes of section 245C(5) or 252(4).

(2) A required condition may (in particular)—

(a) restrict who may receive sums released in pursuance of the exclusion (by, for example, requiring released sums to be paid to professional legal advisers), or

(b) be made for the purpose of controlling the amount of any sum released in pursuance of the exclusion in respect of an item of expenditure.

(3) A required condition made for the purpose mentioned in subsection (2)(b) may (for example)—

(a) provide for sums to be released only with the agreement of the enforcement authority;

(b) provide for a sum to be released in respect of an item of expenditure only if the court has assessed the amount allowed by regulations under section 286B in respect of that item and the sum is released for payment of the assessed amount;

(c) provide for a sum to be released in respect of an item of expenditure only if—

(i) the enforcement authority agrees to its release, or

(ii) the court has assessed the amount allowed by regulations under section 286B in respect of that item and the sum is released for payment of the assessed amount.

(4) Before making regulations under this section, the Lord Chancellor must consult such persons as he considers appropriate.

286B Legal expenses: regulations for purposes of section 266(8B) or 286A(3)

(1) The Lord Chancellor may by regulations—

(a) make provision for the purposes of section 266(8B);

184
Serious Organised Crime and Police Act 2005 (c. 15)
Schedule 6 — Minor and consequential amendments relating to Chapter 6 of Part 2

    (b)   make provision for the purposes of required conditions that make provision of the kind mentioned in section 286A(3)(b) or (c).

  (2)   Regulations under this section may (in particular) —

    (a)   limit the amount of remuneration allowable to representatives for a unit of time worked;

    (b)   limit the total amount of remuneration allowable to representatives for work done in connection with proceedings or a step in proceedings;

    (c)   limit the amount allowable in respect of an item of expense incurred by a representative or incurred, otherwise than in respect of the remuneration of a representative, by a party to proceedings.

  (3)   Before making regulations under this section, the Lord Chancellor must consult such persons as he considers appropriate."

21   In section 287 (financial threshold for starting proceedings), in subsections (3) and (4) (threshold applies to applications made before proceedings started but does not apply after proceedings started or application made), for "an interim receiving order or" substitute "a property freezing order, an interim receiving order, a prohibitory property order or an".

22 (1)   Section 316(1) (interpretation of Part 5) is amended as follows.

  (2)   After the definition of "premises" insert —

        ""prohibitory property order" has the meaning given by section 255A(2);

        "property freezing order" has the meaning given by section 245A(2);".

  (3)   In paragraph (b) of the definition of "respondent", for "an interim receiving order or" substitute "a property freezing order, an interim receiving order, a prohibitory property order or an".

23   In section 432 (insolvency practitioners), in subsections (1)(b), (8)(a) and (9)(a), for "an interim receiving order made under section 246" substitute "a property freezing order made under section 245A, an interim receiving order made under section 246, a prohibitory property order made under section 255A".

SCHEDULE 7   Section 111

POWERS OF ARREST: SUPPLEMENTARY

PART 1

SPECIFIC REPEALS

Unlawful Drilling Act 1819 (60 Geo. 3 & 1 Geo. 4 c. 1)

1   In section 2 of the Unlawful Drilling Act 1819 (power to disperse unlawful meeting), omit ", or for any other person acting in their aid or assistance,".

Serious Organised Crime and Police Act 2005 (c. 15)
Schedule 7 — Powers of Arrest: supplementary
Part 1 — Specific repeals

185

Vagrancy Act 1824 (c. 83)

2   Section 6 of the Vagrancy Act 1824 (power to apprehend) shall cease to have effect.

Railway Regulation Act 1842 (c. 55)

3   Section 17 of the Railway Regulation Act 1842 (punishment of persons guilty of misconduct) shall cease to have effect.

Companies Clauses Consolidation Act 1845 (c. 16)

4   In section 156 of the Companies Clauses Consolidation Act 1845 (transient offenders), omit ", and all persons called by him to his assistance,".

Railways Clauses Consolidation Act 1845 (c. 20)

5   (1) The Railways Clauses Consolidation Act 1845 is amended as follows.

      (2) Section 104 (detention of offenders) shall cease to have effect.

      (3) Section 154 (transient offenders) shall cease to have effect.

Licensing Act 1872 (c. 94)

6   In section 12 of the Licensing Act 1872 (penalty on persons found drunk), omit "may be apprehended, and".

Public Stores Act 1875 (c. 25)

7   In section 12 of the Public Stores Act 1875 (powers of arrest and search), omit subsection (1).

London County Council (General Powers) Act 1894 (c. ccxii)

8   In section 7 of the London County Council (General Powers) Act 1894 (arrest for breach of byelaws), omit "and any person called to the assistance of such constable or person authorised".

London County Council (General Powers) Act 1900 (c. cclxviii)

9   In section 27 of the London County Council (General Powers) Act 1900 (arrest for breach of byelaws), omit "and any person called to the assistance of such constable or officer".

Licensing Act 1902 (c. 28)

10   (1) The Licensing Act 1902 is amended as follows.

      (2) In section 1 (apprehension of persons found drunk), omit "apprehended and".

      (3) In section 2 (being drunk in charge of a child), in subsection (1), omit "may be apprehended, and".

186   *Serious Organised Crime and Police Act 2005 (c. 15)*
Schedule 7 — Powers of Arrest: supplementary
Part 1 — Specific repeals

Protection of Animals Act 1911 (c. 27)

11   In section 12 of the Protection of Animals Act 1911 (powers of constables), omit subsection (1).

Official Secrets Act 1911 (c. 28)

12   Section 6 of the Official Secrets Act 1911 (power of arrest) shall cease to have effect.

Public Order Act 1936 (1 Edw. 8 & 1 Geo. 6 c. 6)

13   In section 7 of the Public Order Act 1936 (enforcement), omit subsection (3).

Street Offences Act 1959 (c. 57)

14   In section 1 of the Street Offences Act 1959 (loitering or soliciting for purposes of prostitution), omit subsection (3).

Criminal Justice Act 1967 (c. 80)

15   In section 91 of the Criminal Justice Act 1967 (drunkenness in a public place), in subsection (1), omit "may be arrested without warrant by any person and".

Ministry of Housing and Local Government Provisional Order Confirmation (Greater London Parks and Open Spaces) Act 1967 (c. xxix)

16   In Article 19 (power of detention) of the Order set out in the Schedule to the Ministry of Housing and Local Government Provisional Order Confirmation (Greater London Parks and Open Spaces) Act 1967, omit "and any person called to the assistance of such constable or officer".

Theft Act 1968 (c. 60)

17   In section 25 of the Theft Act 1968 (going equipped for stealing etc.), omit subsection (4).

Port of London Act 1968 (c. xxxii)

18   Section 170 of the Port of London Act 1968 (power of arrest) shall cease to have effect.

Criminal Law Act 1977 (c. 45)

19   (1) The Criminal Law Act 1977 is amended as follows.

        (2) In section 6 (violence for securing entry), omit subsection (6).

        (3) In section 7 (adverse occupation of residential premises), omit subsection (6).

        (4) In section 8 (trespassing with a weapon of offence), omit subsection (4).

        (5) In section 9 (trespassing on premises of foreign missions, etc.), omit subsection (7).

Serious Organised Crime and Police Act 2005 (c. 15)
Schedule 7 – Powers of Arrest: supplementary
Part 1 – Specific repeals

187

(6) In section 10 (obstruction of certain officers executing process), in subsection (5), omit "A constable in uniform,".

Theft Act 1978 (c. 31)

20   In section 3 of the Theft Act 1978 (making off without payment), omit subsection (4).

Animal Health Act 1981 (c. 22)

21   (1)   The Animal Health Act 1981 is amended as follows.

     (2)   In section 61 (powers of arrest as to rabies), omit subsection (1).

     (3)   In section 62 (entry and search under section 61), omit subsection (1).

Local Government (Miscellaneous Provisions) Act 1982 (c. 30)

22   In Schedule 3 to the Local Government (Miscellaneous Provisions) Act 1982 (control of sex establishments), omit paragraph 24.

Aviation Security Act 1982 (c. 36)

23   In section 28 of the Aviation Security Act 1982 (byelaws for designated airports), omit subsection (3).

Police and Criminal Evidence Act 1984 (c. 60)

24   (1)   The Police and Criminal Evidence Act 1984 is amended as follows.

     (2)   In section 118 (general interpretation), in subsection (1), omit the definition of "arrestable offence".

     (3)   Schedule 1A (specific offences which are arrestable offences) shall cease to have effect.

     (4)   In Schedule 2 (preserved powers of arrest), the following are omitted –
            the entry relating to the Military Lands Act 1892 (c. 43),
            the entry relating to the Protection of Animals Act 1911 (c. 27),
            the entry relating to the Public Order Act 1936 (1 Edw. 8 & 1 Geo. 6 c. 6),
            the entry relating to the Street Offences Act 1959 (c. 57),
            the entry relating to the Criminal Law Act 1977 (c. 45),
            the entry relating to the Animal Health Act 1981 (c. 22).

Sporting Events (Control of Alcohol etc.) Act 1985 (c. 57)

25   In section 7 of the Sporting Events (Control of Alcohol etc.) Act 1985 (powers of enforcement), in subsection (2), omit ", and may arrest such a person".

Public Order Act 1986 (c. 64)

26   (1)   The Public Order Act 1986 is amended as follows.

     (2)   In section 3 (affray), omit subsection (6).

188   *Serious Organised Crime and Police Act 2005 (c. 15)*
                                                    Schedule 7 — Powers of Arrest: supplementary
                                                                 Part 1 — Specific repeals

(3) In section 4 (fear or provocation of violence), omit subsection (3).

(4) In section 4A (intentional harassment, alarm or distress), omit subsection (4).

(5) In section 5 (harassment, alarm or distress), omit subsections (4) and (5).

(6) In section 12 (imposing conditions on public processions), omit subsection (7).

(7) In section 13 (prohibiting public processions), omit subsection (10).

(8) In section 14 (imposing conditions on public assemblies), omit subsection (7).

(9) In section 14B (offences in connection with trespassory assemblies), omit subsection (4).

(10) In section 14C (stopping persons from proceeding to trespassory assemblies), omit subsection (4).

(11) In section 18 (use of words or behaviour or display of written material), omit subsection (3).

Road Traffic Act 1988 (c. 52)

27 (1) The Road Traffic Act 1988 is amended as follows.

(2) In section 4 (driving etc. under influence of drink or drugs), omit subsections (6) to (8).

(3) In section 163 of the Road Traffic Act 1988 (power of police to stop vehicles), omit subsection (4).

(4) The repeal of section 4(8) extends also to Scotland.

Football Spectators Act 1989 (c. 37)

28 In section 2 of the Football Spectators Act 1989 (offences relating to unauthorised attendance at designated football matches), omit subsection (4).

Transport and Works Act 1992 (c. 42)

29 In section 30 of the Transport and Works Act 1992 (powers of arrest and entry), omit subsections (1) and (3).

Trade Union and Labour Relations (Consolidation) Act 1992 (c. 52)

30 In section 241 of the Trade Union and Labour Relations (Consolidation) Act 1992 (intimidation or annoyance), omit subsection (3).

Criminal Justice and Public Order Act 1994 (c. 33)

31 (1) The Criminal Justice and Public Order Act 1994 is amended as follows.

(2) In section 61 (power to remove trespassers on land), omit subsection (5).

(3) In section 62B (failure to comply with direction under section 62A), omit subsection (4).

Serious Organised Crime and Police Act 2005 (c. 15)
Schedule 7 – Powers of Arrest: supplementary
Part 1 – Specific repeals

189

(4) In section 63 (powers to remove persons attending or preparing for a rave), omit subsection (8).

(5) In section 65 (raves: powers to stop persons from proceeding), omit subsection (5).

(6) In section 68 (offence of aggravated trespass), omit subsection (4).

(7) In section 69 (powers to remove persons committing or participating in aggravated trespass), omit subsection (5).

(8) In section 76 (interim possession orders: trespassing during currency of order), omit subsection (7).

Reserve Forces Act 1996 (c. 14)

32   In Schedule 2 to the Reserve Forces Act 1996 (deserters and absentees without leave), omit paragraph 2(1).

Confiscation of Alcohol (Young Persons) Act 1997 (c. 33)

33   In section 1 of the Confiscation of Alcohol (Young Persons) Act 1997 (confiscation of alcohol), omit subsection (5).

Crime and Disorder Act 1998 (c. 37)

34   In section 31 of the Crime and Disorder Act 1998 (racially or religiously aggravated public order offences), omit subsections (2) and (3).

Criminal Justice and Police Act 2001 (c. 16)

35   In the Criminal Justice and Police Act 2001 –
          (a)   in section 42 (police directions stopping harassment etc. of a person in his home), omit subsection (8),
          (b)   in section 47 (application of offences relating to prostitution advertising to public structures), omit subsection (3).

Anti-social Behaviour Act 2003 (c. 38)

36   In the Anti-social Behaviour Act 2003 –
          (a)   in section 4 (closure of premises: offences), omit subsection (5),
          (b)   in section 32 (supplementary provisions about powers relating to dispersal of groups and removal of persons under 16 to their homes), omit subsection (3).

Hunting Act 2004 (c. 37)

37   Section 7 of the Hunting Act 2004 (arrest) shall cease to have effect.

PART 2

GENERAL REPEAL

38   So much of the enactments set out in the second column of the Table below as confers a power of arrest without warrant upon –
          (a)   a constable, or

190   *Serious Organised Crime and Police Act 2005 (c. 15)*
Schedule 7 — Powers of Arrest: supplementary
Part 2 — General repeal

(b)   persons in general (as distinct from persons of any description specified in or for the purposes of the enactment),

shall cease to have effect to the extent that it is not already spent.

Short title and chapter	Enactment affected
Unlawful Drilling Act 1819 (60 Geo. 3 & 1 Geo. 4 c. 1)	Section 2 (power to disperse unlawful meeting).
Military Lands Act 1892 (c. 43)	Section 17(2) (powers relating to breaches of byelaws).
London County Council (General Powers) Act 1894 (c. ccxii)	Section 7 (arrest for breach of byelaws).
London County Council (General Powers) Act 1900 (c. cclxviii)	Section 27 (arrest for breach of byelaws).
Ministry of Housing and Local Government Provisional Order Confirmation (Greater London Parks and Open Spaces) Act 1967 (c. xxix)	Article 19 (power of detention) of the Order set out in the Schedule.
Theft Act 1968 (c. 60)	In Schedule 1 (offences of taking or destroying fish), paragraph 2(4).
Lotteries and Amusements Act 1976 (c. 32)	In section 19 (search warrants), the second paragraph (b).
Animal Health Act 1981 (c. 22)	Section 60 (duties and authorities of constables).

PART 3

AMENDMENTS RELATING TO REFERENCES TO ARRESTABLE OFFENCES AND SERIOUS ARRESTABLE OFFENCES

Criminal Law Act 1826 (c. 64)

39   In section 28 of the Criminal Law Act 1826 (which confers power to order the payment of compensation to those who have helped apprehend an offender), for "an arrestable offence" substitute "an indictable offence".

Criminal Law Act 1967 (c. 58)

40   (1)   The Criminal Law Act 1967 is amended as follows.

(2)   In section 4 (penalties for assisting offenders) —

(a)   in subsection (1) —

(i)   for "an arrestable offence" substitute "a relevant offence",

(ii)   for "other arrestable offence" substitute "other relevant offence",

(b)   for subsection (1A) substitute —

"(1A)   In this section and section 5 below, "relevant offence" means —

(a)   an offence for which the sentence is fixed by law,

Serious Organised Crime and Police Act 2005 (c. 15)
Schedule 7 — Powers of Arrest: supplementary
Part 3 — Amendments relating to references to arrestable offences and serious arrestable offences

191

      (b)   an offence for which a person of 18 years or over (not previously convicted) may be sentenced to imprisonment for a term of five years (or might be so sentenced but for the restrictions imposed by section 33 of the Magistrates' Courts Act 1980).",

    (c)   in subsection (2), for "an arrestable offence" substitute "a relevant offence".

(3) In section 5 (penalties for concealing offences or giving false information), in subsection (1) —

    (a)   for "an arrestable offence" substitute "a relevant offence",

    (b)   for "other arrestable offence" substitute "other relevant offence".

Port of London Act 1968 (c. xxxii)

41   (1) The Port of London Act 1968 is amended as follows.

    (2) In section 2 (interpretation), omit the definition of "arrestable offence".

    (3) In section 156 (powers of constables), in subsection (2), for "arrestable", in each place where it occurs, substitute "indictable".

Solicitors Act 1974 (c. 47)

42   (1) The Solicitors Act 1974 is amended as follows.

    (2) In section 13A (imposition of conditions while practising certificates are in force), in subsection (2)(d), for sub-paragraph (ii) substitute —

        "(ii)   an indictable offence."

    (3) In section 13B (suspension of practising certificates where solicitors convicted of fraud or serious crime), in subsection (1)(a), for sub-paragraph (ii) substitute —

        "(ii)   an indictable offence; and".

Police and Criminal Evidence Act 1984 (c. 60)

43   (1) The Police and Criminal Evidence Act 1984 is amended as follows.

    (2) In section 4 (road checks) —

      (a)   for "a serious arrestable offence", in each place where it occurs, substitute "an indictable offence",

      (b)   in subsection (14), for "serious arrestable offence" substitute "indictable offence".

    (3) In section 8 (powers to authorise entry and search), for "a serious arrestable offence", in both places, substitute "an indictable offence".

    (4) In section 17 (entry for purpose of arrest etc.), in subsection (1)(b), for "arrestable" substitute "indictable".

    (5) In section 18 (entry and search after arrest), in subsection (1), for "arrestable", in both places, substitute "indictable".

    (6) In section 32 (search upon arrest), in subsection (2), for paragraph (b)

192   *Serious Organised Crime and Police Act 2005 (c. 15)*
Schedule 7 — Powers of Arrest: supplementary
Part 3 — Amendments relating to references to arrestable offences and serious arrestable offences

substitute —

"(b)   if the offence for which he has been arrested is an indictable offence, to enter and search any premises in which he was when arrested or immediately before he was arrested for evidence relating to the offence."

(7)   In section 42 (authorisation of continued detention), in subsection (1)(b), for "arrestable" substitute "indictable".

(8)   In section 43 (warrants of further detention), in subsection (4)(b), for "a serious arrestable offence" substitute "an indictable offence".

(9)   In section 56 (right to have someone informed when arrested) —

(a)   in each of subsections (2)(a) and (5)(a), for "a serious arrestable offence" substitute "an indictable offence",

(b)   in subsection (5A)(a), for "the serious arrestable offence" substitute "the indictable offence".

(10)   In section 58 (access to legal advice) —

(a)   in each of subsections (6)(a) and (8)(a), for "a serious arrestable offence" substitute "an indictable offence",

(b)   in subsection (8A)(a), for "the serious arrestable offence" substitute "the indictable offence".

(11)   In section 114A (power to apply Act to officers of Secretary of State), in subsection (2)(c), for "a serious arrestable offence", in both places, substitute "an indictable offence".

(12)   Section 116 (meaning of "serious arrestable offence") shall cease to have effect.

(13)   In Schedule 1 (special procedure material), in paragraph 2(a)(i), for "a serious arrestable offence" substitute "an indictable offence".

(14)   Schedule 5 (serious arrestable offences) shall cease to have effect.

Administration of Justice Act 1985 (c. 61)

44   In section 16 of the Administration of Justice Act 1985 (conditional licences for licensed conveyancers), in subsection (1)(ia), for "a serious arrestable offence (as defined by section 116 of the Police and Criminal Evidence Act 1984)" substitute "an indictable offence".

Housing Act 1985 (c. 68)

45   In Part 1 of Schedule 2 to the Housing Act 1985 (which sets out grounds upon which a court may, if it considers it reasonable, order possession of dwelling-houses let under secure tenancies), in Ground 2, in paragraph (b)(ii), for "arrestable" substitute "indictable".

Housing Act 1988 (c. 50)

46   In Part 2 of Schedule 2 to the Housing Act 1988 (which sets out grounds on which a court may order possession of dwelling-houses let on assured tenancies), in Ground 14, in paragraph (b)(ii), for "arrestable" substitute "indictable".

Serious Organised Crime and Police Act 2005 (c. 15)
Schedule 7 — Powers of Arrest: supplementary
Part 3 — Amendments relating to references to arrestable offences and serious arrestable offences

193

Criminal Justice and Public Order Act 1994 (c. 33)

47   (1) The Criminal Justice and Public Order Act 1994 is amended as follows.

    (2) In section 137 (cross-border powers of arrest etc.) —

        (a) in subsection (1), for "conditions applicable to this subsection are" substitute "condition applicable to this subsection is",

        (b) for subsection (4) substitute —

> "(4) The condition applicable to subsection (1) above is that it appears to the constable that it would have been lawful for him to have exercised the powers had the suspected person been in England and Wales.",

        (c) in subsection (9), for the definition of ""arrestable offence" and "designated police station"" substitute —

> ""arrestable offence" has the same meaning as in the Police and Criminal Evidence (Northern Ireland) Order 1989 ("the 1989 Order");
>
> "designated police station" has the same meaning as in the Police and Criminal Evidence Act 1984 or, in relation to Northern Ireland, as in the 1989 Order; and".

    (3) In section 138 (provisions supplementing section 137), in subsection (3), for "subsections (4)(b) and (6)(b)" substitute "subsection (6)(b)".

    (4) In section 140 (reciprocal powers of arrest), in subsection (1), for "section 24(6) or (7) or 25" substitute "section 24".

    (5) This paragraph extends to the whole of the United Kingdom.

Terrorism Act 2000 (c. 11)

48   (1) In Schedule 8 to the Terrorism Act 2000 (detention), in paragraph 8 (which relates to the rights of a person detained under Schedule 7 to or section 41 of that Act) —

        (a) in sub-paragraph (4), for "serious arrestable offence", in each place where it occurs, substitute "serious offence",

        (b) in sub-paragraph (9), for the words before paragraph (a) substitute "In this paragraph, references to a "serious offence" are (in relation to England and Wales) to an indictable offence, and (in relation to Northern Ireland) to a serious arrestable offence within the meaning of Article 87 of the Police and Criminal Evidence (Northern Ireland) Order 1989; but also include — ".

    (2) This paragraph extends to the whole of the United Kingdom.

International Criminal Court Act 2001 (c. 17)

49   (1) The International Criminal Court Act 2001 is amended as follows.

    (2) In section 33 (entry, search and seizure), in subsection (2), for "a serious arrestable offence" substitute "(in the case of Part 2 of the 1984 Act) to an indictable offence or (in the case of Part III of the 1989 Order) to a serious arrestable offence".

194   *Serious Organised Crime and Police Act 2005 (c. 15)*
                                         Schedule 7 – Powers of Arrest: supplementary
              Part 3 – Amendments relating to references to arrestable offences and serious arrestable offences

(3) In section 55 (meaning of "ancillary offence" under the law of England and Wales), in subsection (5), in each of paragraphs (a) and (b), for "an arrestable offence" substitute "a relevant offence".

(4) This paragraph extends to England and Wales and to Northern Ireland (but not to Scotland).

Armed Forces Act 2001 (c. 19)

50   In section 5 of the Armed Forces Act 2001 (power of judicial officer to authorise entry and search of certain premises), in subsection (2)(a), for "a serious arrestable offence for the purposes of the 1984 Act" substitute "an indictable offence".

          This paragraph has the same extent as the Armed Forces Act 2001.

Crime (International Co-operation) Act 2003 (c. 32)

51   (1) The Crime (International Co-operation) Act 2003 is amended as follows.

     (2) In section 16 (extension of statutory search powers in England and Wales and Northern Ireland), in subsection (1) –
          (a)   for "serious arrestable offences" substitute "indictable offences",
          (b)   in paragraph (b), for "a serious arrestable offence" substitute "an indictable offence".

     (3) In section 17 (warrants in England and Wales or Northern Ireland), in subsection (3) –
          (a)   for paragraph (b) substitute –
                    "(b)   the conduct constituting the offence which is the subject of the proceedings or investigation would (if it occurred in England and Wales) constitute an indictable offence, or (if it occurred in Northern Ireland) constitute an arrestable offence, and",
          (b)   in the definition of "arrestable offence", omit the words "the Police and Criminal Evidence Act 1984 (c. 60) or (as the case may be)".

     (4) This paragraph extends to the whole of the United Kingdom.

PART 4

OTHER AMENDMENTS

Game Laws (Amendment) Act 1960 (c. 36)

52   (1) The Game Laws (Amendment) Act 1960 is amended as follows.

     (2) In section 2 (power of police to enter on land), in subsection (1)(b), for "section 25" substitute "section 24".

     (3) In section 4 (further provisions as to seizure and forfeiture), in subsection (1), for "section 25" substitute "section 24".

Immigration Act 1971 (c. 77)

53   In section 28A of the Immigration Act 1971 (arrest without warrant), in each of subsections (1) and (9A), for "A constable or" substitute "An".

Serious Organised Crime and Police Act 2005 (c. 15)
Schedule 7 — Powers of Arrest: supplementary
Part 4 — Other amendments

195

Customs and Excise Management Act 1979 (c. 2)

54   In section 138 of the Customs and Excise Management Act 1979 (provisions about arrest), in subsection (4)(b), after "section 24" insert "or 24A".
      This paragraph has the same extent as that Act.

Animal Health Act 1981 (c. 22)

55   (1) The Animal Health Act 1981 is amended as follows.

      (2) In section 61 (powers of arrest as to rabies) —
          (a)   in subsection (2), after "applies" insert "for the purposes of section 17(1)(caa) of the Police and Criminal Evidence Act 1984",
          (b)   for the heading substitute "Powers of entry and search in relation to rabies offences".

      (3) For the heading to section 62 (entry and search under section 61) substitute "Entry and search in exercise of powers to seize animals".

Wildlife and Countryside Act 1981 (c. 69)

56   In section 19 of the Wildlife and Countryside Act 1981 (enforcement), in subsection (2), for "section 25" substitute "section 24".
      This paragraph extends also to Scotland.

Aviation Security Act 1982 (c. 36)

57   In section 13 of the Aviation Security Act 1982 (power to require aerodrome managers to promote searches at airports), in subsection (5)(a), for "25" substitute "24A".
      This paragraph has the same extent as that Act.

Police and Criminal Evidence Act 1984 (c. 60)

58   In section 17 of the Police and Criminal Evidence Act 1984 (entry for purpose of arrest etc.), in subsection (1) —
          (a)   for paragraph (c)(iiia) substitute —
                "(iiia)   section 4 (driving etc. when under influence of drink or drugs) or 163 (failure to stop when required to do so by constable in uniform) of the Road Traffic Act 1988;
                (iiib)   section 27 of the Transport and Works Act 1992 (which relates to offences involving drink or drugs);",
          (b)   after paragraph (ca) insert —
                "(caa)   of arresting a person for an offence to which section 61 of the Animal Health Act 1981 applies;".

Road Traffic Act 1988 (c. 52)

59   In section 184 of the Road Traffic Act 1988 (application of sections 5 to 10 of that Act to persons subject to service discipline), for subsection (2)

196   *Serious Organised Crime and Police Act 2005 (c. 15)*
                                              Schedule 7 — Powers of Arrest: supplementary
                                                              Part 4 — Other amendments

substitute —

> "(2)   A member of the provost staff may arrest a person for the time being subject to service discipline without warrant if he has reasonable cause to suspect that that person is or has been committing an offence under section 4.
>
> (2A)   The power conferred by subsection (2) is exercisable outside as well as within Great Britain."

This paragraph has the same extent as section 184 of that Act.

Aviation and Maritime Security Act 1990 (c. 31)

60   In section 22 of the Aviation and Maritime Security Act 1990 (power to require harbour authorities to promote searches in harbour areas), in subsection (10)(a), for "25" substitute "24A".

This paragraph has the same extent as that Act.

Deer Act 1991 (c. 54)

61   In section 12 of the Deer Act 1991 (powers of search, arrest and seizure), in subsection (2)(b), for "section 25" substitute "section 24".

Gangmasters (Licensing) Act 2004 (c. 11)

63   The Gangmasters (Licensing) Act 2004 is amended as follows —
        (a)   in section 14 (offences: supplementary), in subsection (1), for "section 24(4) and (5)" substitute "section 24A",
        (b)   in Schedule 2 (application of Act to Northern Ireland), in paragraph 14, for "section 24(4) and (5)" substitute "section 24A".

This paragraph has the same extent as that Act.

Asylum and Immigration (Treatment of Claimants, etc.) Act 2004 (c. 19)

62   The Asylum and Immigration (Treatment of Claimants, etc.) Act 2004 is amended as follows —
        (a)   in section 2 (entering U.K. without passport, etc.), in subsection (10), for "a constable or" substitute "an",
        (b)   in section 35 (deportation or removal: cooperation), in subsection (5), for "a constable or" substitute "an".

SCHEDULE 8   Section 122

POWERS OF DESIGNATED AND ACCREDITED PERSONS

PART 1

DESIGNATED PERSONS

1   Schedule 4 to the Police Reform Act 2002 (c. 30) (powers exercisable by police civilians) is amended as follows.

Serious Organised Crime and Police Act 2005 (c. 15)
Schedule 8 — Powers of designated and accredited persons
Part 1 — Designated persons

197

Community support officers

2   After paragraph 1 insert—

"*Power to require name and address*

1A (1) This paragraph applies if a designation applies it to any person.

   (2) Such a designation may specify that, in relation to that person, the application of sub-paragraph (3) is confined to one or more only (and not to all) relevant offences or relevant licensing offences, being in each case specified in the designation.

   (3) Subject to sub-paragraph (4), where that person has reason to believe that another person has committed a relevant offence in the relevant police area, or a relevant licensing offence (whether or not in the relevant police area), he may require that other person to give him his name and address.

   (4) The power to impose a requirement under sub-paragraph (3) in relation to an offence under a relevant byelaw is exercisable only in a place to which the byelaw relates.

   (5) A person who fails to comply with a requirement under sub-paragraph (3) is guilty of an offence and shall be liable, on summary conviction, to a fine not exceeding level 3 on the standard scale.

   (6) In its application to an offence which is an offence by reference to which a notice may be given to a person in exercise of the power mentioned in paragraph 1(2)(aa), sub-paragraph (3) of this paragraph shall have effect as if for the words "has committed a relevant offence in the relevant police area" there were substituted "in the relevant police area has committed a relevant offence".

   (7) In this paragraph, "relevant offence", "relevant licensing offence" and "relevant byelaw" have the meaning given in paragraph 2 (reading accordingly the references to "this paragraph" in paragraph 2(6))."

3   (1) Paragraph 2 (power to detain etc.) is amended as follows.

     (2) For sub-paragraph (2) substitute—

         "(2) A designation may not apply this paragraph to any person unless a designation also applies paragraph 1A to him."

     (3) In sub-paragraph (3)—
         (a) for "sub-paragraph (2)" substitute "paragraph 1A(3)",
         (b) at the end add the following new sentence—
             "This sub-paragraph does not apply if the requirement was imposed in connection with a relevant licensing offence mentioned in paragraph (a), (c) or (f) of sub-paragraph (6A) believed to have been committed on licensed premises (within the meaning of the Licensing Act 2003)."

     (4) After sub-paragraph (3) insert—

         "(3A) Where—

198   *Serious Organised Crime and Police Act 2005 (c. 15)*
Schedule 8 — Powers of designated and accredited persons
Part 1 — Designated persons

   (a) a designation applies this paragraph to any person ("the CSO"); and

   (b) by virtue of a designation under paragraph 1A the CSO has the power to impose a requirement under sub-paragraph (3) of that paragraph in relation to an offence under a relevant byelaw,

   the CSO shall also have any power a constable has under the relevant byelaw to remove a person from a place.

(3B) Where a person to whom this paragraph applies ("the CSO") has reason to believe that another person is committing an offence under section 3 or 4 of the Vagrancy Act 1824, and requires him to stop doing whatever gives rise to that belief, the CSO may, if the other person fails to stop as required, require him to wait with the CSO, for a period not exceeding thirty minutes, for the arrival of a constable."

(5) In sub-paragraph (4), after "(3)" insert "or (3B)".

(6) In sub-paragraph (5) —

   (a) omit paragraph (a),

   (b) in paragraph (b), after "(3)" insert "or (3B)".

(7) In sub-paragraph (6), after the paragraph (ab) inserted by paragraph 13(2) of Schedule 13 to this Act, insert —

   "(ac) an offence under section 3 or 4 of the Vagrancy Act 1824; or

   (ad) an offence under a relevant byelaw; or".

(8) After sub-paragraph (6) insert —

   "(6A) In this paragraph "relevant licensing offence" means an offence under any of the following provisions of the Licensing Act 2003 —

      (a) section 141 (otherwise than by virtue of subsection (2)(c) or (3) of that section);

      (b) section 142;

      (c) section 146(1);

      (d) section 149(1)(a), (3)(a) or (4)(a);

      (e) section 150(1);

      (f) section 150(2) (otherwise than by virtue of subsection (3)(b) of that section);

      (g) section 152(1) (excluding paragraph (b)).

   (6B) In this paragraph "relevant byelaw" means a byelaw included in a list of byelaws which —

      (a) have been made by a relevant body with authority to make byelaws for any place within the relevant police area; and

      (b) the chief officer of the police force for the relevant police area and the relevant body have agreed to include in the list.

   (6C) The list must be published by the chief officer in such a way as to bring it to the attention of members of the public in localities where the byelaws in the list apply.

   (6D) A list of byelaws mentioned in sub-paragraph (6B) may be amended from time to time by agreement between the chief officer

Serious Organised Crime and Police Act 2005 (c. 15) 199
Schedule 8 – Powers of designated and accredited persons
Part 1 – Designated persons

and the relevant body in question, by adding byelaws to it or removing byelaws from it, and the amended list shall also be published by the chief officer as mentioned in sub-paragraph (6C).

(6E) A relevant body for the purposes of sub-paragraph (6B) is—

(a) in England, a county council, a district council, a London borough council or a parish council; or in Wales, a county council, a county borough council or a community council;

(b) the Greater London Authority;

(c) Transport for London;

(d) a metropolitan county passenger transport authority established under section 28 of the Local Government Act 1985;

(e) any body specified in an order made by the Secretary of State.

(6F) An order under sub-paragraph (6E)(e) may provide, in relation to any body specified in the order, that the agreement mentioned in sub-paragraph (6B)(b) and (6D) is to be made between the chief officer and the Secretary of State (rather than between the chief officer and the relevant body)."

(9) Omit sub-paragraph (7).

(10) At the end add—

"(8) The application of any provision of this paragraph by paragraph 3(2), 3A(2) or 7A(8) has no effect unless a designation under this paragraph has applied this paragraph to the CSO in question."

4   After paragraph 2 insert—

"Powers to search individuals and to seize and retain items

2A (1) Where a designation applies this paragraph to any person, that person shall (subject to sub-paragraph (3)) have the powers mentioned in sub-paragraph (2) in relation to a person upon whom he has imposed a requirement to wait under paragraph 2(3) or (3B) (whether or not that person makes an election under paragraph 2(4)).

(2) Those powers are the same powers as a constable has under section 32 of the 1984 Act in relation to a person arrested at a place other than a police station—

(a) to search the arrested person if the constable has reasonable grounds for believing that the arrested person may present a danger to himself or others; and to seize and retain anything he finds on exercising that power, if the constable has reasonable grounds for believing that the person being searched might use it to cause physical injury to himself or to any other person;

(b) to search the arrested person for anything which he might use to assist him to escape from lawful custody; and to seize and retain anything he finds on exercising that power (other than an item subject to legal privilege) if the constable has reasonable grounds for believing that the

200

Serious Organised Crime and Police Act 2005 (c. 15)
Schedule 8 — Powers of designated and accredited persons
Part 1 — Designated persons

person being searched might use it to assist him to escape from lawful custody.

(3) If in exercise of the power conferred by sub-paragraph (1) the person to whom this paragraph applies seizes and retains anything by virtue of sub-paragraph (2), he must —

    (a) tell the person from whom it was seized where inquiries about its recovery may be made; and

    (b) comply with a constable's instructions about what to do with it."

5   In paragraph 3 (power to require name and address of person acting in anti-social manner), in sub-paragraph (2), for "sub-paragraph (2) of that paragraph" substitute "paragraph 1A(3)".

6   After paragraph 3 insert —

"Power to require name and address: road traffic offences

3A (1) Where a designation applies this paragraph to any person, that person shall, in the relevant police area, have the powers of a constable —

    (a) under subsection (1) of section 165 of the Road Traffic Act 1988 to require a person mentioned in paragraph (c) of that subsection who he has reasonable cause to believe has committed, in the relevant police area, an offence under subsection (1) or (2) of section 35 of that Act (including that section as extended by paragraphs 11B(4) and 12(2) of this Schedule) to give his name and address; and

    (b) under section 169 of that Act to require a person committing an offence under section 37 of that Act (including that section as extended by paragraphs 11B(4) and 12(2) of this Schedule) to give his name and address.

(2) Sub-paragraphs (3) to (5) of paragraph 2 apply in the case of a requirement imposed by virtue of sub-paragraph (1) as they apply in the case of a requirement under paragraph 1A(3).

(3) The reference in section 169 of the Road Traffic Act 1988 to section 37 of that Act is to be taken to include a reference to that section as extended by paragraphs 11B(4) and 12(2) of this Schedule."

7   In paragraph 4 (power to use reasonable force to detain person) —

    (a) in sub-paragraph (2)(b), after "paragraph" insert "1A or",

    (b) in sub-paragraph (3), for "paragraph 2(2)" substitute "paragraph 1A(3)".

8   After paragraph 7 insert —

"Search and seizure powers: alcohol and tobacco

7A (1) Where a designation applies this paragraph to any person ("the CSO"), the CSO shall have the powers set out below.

(2) Where —

    (a) in exercise of the powers referred to in paragraph 5 or 6 the CSO has imposed, under section 12(2) of the Criminal

Serious Organised Crime and Police Act 2005 (c. 15)
Schedule 8 – Powers of designated and accredited persons
Part 1 – Designated persons

201

Justice and Police Act 2001 or under section 1 of the Confiscation of Alcohol (Young Persons) Act 1997, a requirement on a person to surrender alcohol or a container for alcohol;

(b)   that person fails to comply with that requirement; and

(c)   the CSO reasonably believes that the person has alcohol or a container for alcohol in his possession,

the CSO may search him for it.

(3)   Where —

(a)   in exercise of the powers referred to in paragraph 7 the CSO has sought to seize something which by virtue of that paragraph he has a power to seize;

(b)   the person from whom he sought to seize it fails to surrender it; and

(c).   the CSO reasonably believes that the person has it in his possession,

the CSO may search him for it.

(4)   The power to search conferred by sub-paragraph (2) or (3) —

(a)   is to do so only to the extent that is reasonably required for the purpose of discovering whatever the CSO is searching for; and

(b)   does not authorise the CSO to require a person to remove any of his clothing in public other than an outer coat, jacket or gloves.

(5)   A person who without reasonable excuse fails to consent to being searched is guilty of an offence and shall be liable, on summary conviction, to a fine not exceeding level 3 on the standard scale.

(6)   A CSO who proposes to exercise the power to search a person under sub-paragraph (2) or (3) must inform him that failing without reasonable excuse to consent to being searched is an offence.

(7)   If the person in question fails to consent to being searched, the CSO may require him to give the CSO his name and address.

(8)   Sub-paragraph (3) of paragraph 2 applies in the case of a requirement imposed by virtue of sub-paragraph (7) as it applies in the case of a requirement under paragraph 1A(3); and sub-paragraphs (4) to (5) of paragraph 2 also apply accordingly.

(9)   If on searching the person the CSO discovers what he is searching for, he may seize it and dispose of it.

Powers to seize and detain: controlled drugs

7B   (1)   Where a designation applies this paragraph to any person ("the CSO"), the CSO shall, within the relevant police area, have the powers set out in sub-paragraphs (2) and (3).

(2)   If the CSO —

(a)   finds a controlled drug in a person's possession (whether or not he finds it in the course of searching the person by

202   *Serious Organised Crime and Police Act 2005 (c. 15)*
Schedule 8 – Powers of designated and accredited persons
Part 1 – Designated persons

virtue of a designation under any paragraph of this Schedule); and

    (b)   reasonably believes that it is unlawful for the person to be in possession of it,

the CSO may seize it and retain it.

(3)   If the CSO—

    (a)   finds a controlled drug in a person's possession (as mentioned in sub-paragraph (2)); or

    (b)   reasonably believes that a person is in possession of a controlled drug,

and reasonably believes that it is unlawful for the person to be in possession of it, the CSO may require him to give the CSO his name and address.

(4)   If in exercise of the power conferred by sub-paragraph (2) the CSO seizes and retains a controlled drug, he must—

    (a)   if the person from whom it was seized maintains that he was lawfully in possession of it, tell the person where inquiries about its recovery may be made; and

    (b)   comply with a constable's instructions about what to do with it.

(5)   A person who fails to comply with a requirement under sub-paragraph (3) is guilty of an offence and shall be liable, on summary conviction, to a fine not exceeding level 3 on the standard scale.

(6)   In this paragraph, "controlled drug" has the same meaning as in the Misuse of Drugs Act 1971.

7C (1)   Sub-paragraph (2) applies where a designation applies this paragraph to any person ("the CSO").

   (2)   If the CSO imposes a requirement on a person under paragraph 7B(3)—

    (a)   sub-paragraph (3) of paragraph 2 applies in the case of such a requirement as it applies in the case of a requirement under paragraph 1A(3); and

    (b)   sub-paragraphs (4) to (5) of paragraph 2 also apply accordingly."

9   After paragraph 8 insert—

"Entry to investigate licensing offences

8A (1)   Where a designation applies this paragraph to any person, that person shall have the powers of a constable under section 180 of the Licensing Act 2003 to enter and search premises other than clubs in the relevant police area, but only in respect of a relevant licensing offence (as defined for the purposes of paragraph 2).

   (2)   Except as mentioned in sub-paragraph (3), a person to whom this paragraph applies shall not, in exercise of the power conferred by sub-paragraph (1), enter any premises except in the company, and under the supervision, of a constable.

Serious Organised Crime and Police Act 2005 (c. 15) 203
Schedule 8 – Powers of designated and accredited persons
Part 1 – Designated persons

(3) The prohibition in sub-paragraph (2) does not apply in relation to premises in respect of which the person to whom this paragraph applies reasonably believes that a premises licence under Part 3 of the Licensing Act 2003 authorises the sale of alcohol for consumption off the premises."

10   After paragraph 11A insert—

"Power to control traffic for purposes other than escorting a load of exceptional dimensions

11B (1) Where a designation applies this paragraph to any person, that person shall have, in the relevant police area—

(a) the power of a constable engaged in the regulation of traffic in a road to direct a person driving or propelling a vehicle to stop the vehicle or to make it proceed in, or keep to, a particular line of traffic;

(b) the power of a constable in uniform engaged in the regulation of vehicular traffic in a road to direct a person on foot to stop proceeding along or across the carriageway.

(2) The purposes for which those powers may be exercised do not include the purpose mentioned in paragraph 12(1).

(3) Where a designation applies this paragraph to any person, that person shall also have, in the relevant police area, the power of a constable, for the purposes of a traffic survey, to direct a person driving or propelling a vehicle to stop the vehicle, to make it proceed in, or keep to, a particular line of traffic, or to proceed to a particular point on or near the road.

(4) Sections 35 and 37 of the Road Traffic Act 1988 (offences of failing to comply with directions of constable engaged in regulation of traffic in a road) shall have effect in relation to the exercise of the powers mentioned in sub-paragraphs (1) and (3), for the purposes for which they may be exercised and by a person whose designation applies this paragraph to him, as if the references to a constable were references to him.

(5) A designation may not apply this paragraph to any person unless a designation also applies paragraph 3A to him."

11   After paragraph 13 insert—

"Power to place traffic signs

13A (1) Where a designation applies this paragraph to any person, that person shall have, in the relevant police area, the powers of a constable under section 67 of the Road Traffic Regulation Act 1984 to place and maintain traffic signs.

(2) Section 36 of the Road Traffic Act 1988 (drivers to comply with traffic directions) shall apply to signs placed in the exercise of the powers conferred by virtue of sub-paragraph (1)."

204

Serious Organised Crime and Police Act 2005 (c. 15)
Schedule 8 — Powers of designated and accredited persons
Part 1 — Designated persons

12   After paragraph 15 insert—

"Photographing of persons arrested, detained or given fixed penalty notices

    15ZA   Where a designation applies this paragraph to any person, that person shall, within the relevant police area, have the power of a constable under section 64A(1A) of the 1984 Act (photographing of suspects etc.) to take a photograph of a person elsewhere than at a police station."

Investigating officers

13   In paragraph 16 (search warrants)—
    (a)   in paragraph (a), for "in the relevant police area" substitute "whether in the relevant police area or not",
    (b)   in paragraph (e), for "in respect of premises in the relevant police area" substitute ", but in respect of premises in the relevant police area only,".

14   After paragraph 16 insert—

    "16A   Where a designation applies this paragraph to any person—
        (a)   the persons to whom a warrant may be addressed under section 26 of the Theft Act 1968 (search for stolen goods) shall, in relation to persons or premises in the relevant police area, include that person; and
        (b)   in relation to such a warrant addressed to him, that person shall have the powers under subsection (3) of that section.

    16B   Where a designation applies this paragraph to any person, subsection (3), and (to the extent that it applies subsection (3)) subsection (3A), of section 23 of the Misuse of Drugs Act 1971 (powers to search and obtain evidence) shall have effect as if, in relation to premises in the relevant police area, the reference to a constable included a reference to that person."

15   In paragraph 17 (access to excluded and special procedure material)—
    (a)   in paragraph (b)(ii), at the end add "(in the case of a specific premises warrant) or any premises, whether in the relevant police area or not (in the case of an all premises warrant);",
    (b)   in paragraph (bc), for "in respect of premises in the relevant police area" substitute ", but in respect of premises in the relevant police area only,".

Detention officers

16   After paragraph 33 insert—

"Taking of impressions of footwear

    33A   Where a designation applies this paragraph to any person—
        (a)   he shall, at any police station in the relevant police area, have the powers of a constable under section 61A of the 1984 Act (impressions of footwear) to take impressions of a person's footwear without the appropriate consent; and

Serious Organised Crime and Police Act 2005 (c. 15)
Schedule 8 — Powers of designated and accredited persons
Part 1 — Designated persons

205

(b) the requirement by virtue of section 61A(5)(a) of the 1984 Act that a person must be informed by an officer that an impression of his footwear may be the subject of a speculative search shall be capable of being discharged, in the case of a person at such a station, by his being so informed by the person to whom this paragraph applies."

PART 2

ACCREDITED PERSONS

17 Schedule 5 to the Police Reform Act 2002 (c. 30) (powers exercisable by accredited persons) is amended as follows.

18 In paragraph 2 (power to require giving of name and address), in sub-paragraph (3), after paragraph (a) insert —

"(aa) an offence under section 3 or 4 of the Vagrancy Act 1824; or".

19 After paragraph 3 insert —

"Power to require name and address: road traffic offences

3A (1) An accredited person whose accreditation specifies that this paragraph applies to him shall, in the relevant police area, have the powers of a constable —

(a) under subsection (1) of section 165 of the Road Traffic Act 1988 to require a person mentioned in paragraph (c) of that subsection who he has reasonable cause to believe has committed, in the relevant police area, an offence under subsection (1) or (2) of section 35 of that Act (including that section as extended by paragraphs 8B(4) and 9(2) of this Schedule) to give his name and address; and

(b) under section 169 of that Act to require a person committing an offence under section 37 of that Act (including that section as extended by paragraphs 8B(4) and 9(2) of this Schedule) to give his name and address.

(2) The reference in section 169 of the Road Traffic Act 1988 to section 37 of that Act is to be taken to include a reference to that section as extended by paragraphs 8B(4) and 9(2) of this Schedule."

20 After paragraph 8A insert —

"Power to control traffic for purposes other than escorting a load of exceptional dimensions

8B (1) A person whose accreditation specifies that this paragraph applies to him shall have, in the relevant police area —

(a) the power of a constable engaged in the regulation of traffic in a road to direct a person driving or propelling a vehicle to stop the vehicle or to make it proceed in, or keep to, a particular line of traffic;

(b) the power of a constable in uniform engaged in the regulation of vehicular traffic in a road to direct a person on foot to stop proceeding along or across the carriageway.

206   *Serious Organised Crime and Police Act 2005 (c. 15)*
Schedule 8 — Powers of designated and accredited persons
Part 2 — Accredited persons

(2) The purposes for which those powers may be exercised do not include the purpose mentioned in paragraph 9(1).

(3) A person whose accreditation specifies that this paragraph applies to him shall also have, in the relevant police area, the power of a constable, for the purposes of a traffic survey, to direct a person driving or propelling a vehicle to stop the vehicle, to make it proceed in, or keep to, a particular line of traffic, or to proceed to a particular point on or near the road.

(4) Sections 35 and 37 of the Road Traffic Act 1988 (offences of failing to comply with directions of constable engaged in regulation of traffic in a road) shall have effect in relation to the exercise of the powers mentioned in sub-paragraphs (1) and (3), for the purposes for which they may be exercised and by a person whose accreditation specifies that this paragraph applies to him, as if the references to a constable were references to him.

(5) A person's accreditation may not specify that this paragraph applies to him unless it also specifies that paragraph 3A applies to him."

21   After paragraph 9 insert—

"Photographing of persons given fixed penalty notices

9ZA   An accredited person whose accreditation specifies that this paragraph applies to him shall, within the relevant police area, have the power of a constable under section 64A(1A) of the 1984 Act (photographing of suspects etc.) to take a photograph, elsewhere than at a police station, of a person to whom the accredited person has given a penalty notice (or as the case may be a fixed penalty notice) in exercise of any power mentioned in paragraph 1(2)."

SCHEDULE 9 Section 122

ADDITIONAL POWERS AND DUTIES OF DESIGNATED PERSONS

1   Schedule 4 to the Police Reform Act 2002 (c. 30) (powers exercisable by police civilians) is amended as follows.

Community Support Officers

2   In paragraph 2 (power to detain etc.), after sub-paragraph (4) insert—

"(4A) If a person has imposed a requirement under sub-paragraph (3) or (3B) on another person ("P"), and P does not make an election under sub-paragraph (4), the person imposing the requirement shall, if a constable arrives within the thirty-minute period, be under a duty to remain with the constable and P until he has transferred control of P to the constable.

(4B) If, following an election under sub-paragraph (4), the person imposing the requirement under sub-paragraph (3) or (3B) ("the

CSO") takes the person upon whom it is imposed ("P") to a police station, the CSO—

(a) shall be under a duty to remain at the police station until he has transferred control of P to the custody officer there;

(b) until he has so transferred control of P, shall be treated for all purposes as having P in his lawful custody; and

(c) for so long as he is at the police station, or in its immediate vicinity, in compliance with, or having complied with, his duty under paragraph (a), shall be under a duty to prevent P's escape and to assist in keeping P under control."

3   In paragraph 4 (power to use reasonable force to detain person)—

(a) in sub-paragraph (2)(b), after "relevant offences" insert "or relevant licensing offences",

(b) in sub-paragraph (3), after "making off" insert "and to keep him under control".

4   After paragraph 4 insert—

"4ZA   Where a designation applies this paragraph to any person, that person may, if he has imposed a requirement on any person to wait with him under paragraph 2(3B) or by virtue of paragraph 7A(8) or 7C(2)(a), use reasonable force to prevent that other person from making off and to keep him under control while he is either—

(a) subject to that requirement; or

(b) accompanying the designated person to a police station in accordance with an election made under paragraph 2(4).

4ZB   Where a designation applies this paragraph to any person, that person, if he is complying with any duty under sub-paragraph (4A) or (4B) of paragraph 2, may use reasonable force to prevent P (as identified in those sub-paragraphs) from making off (or escaping) and to keep him under control."

Investigating officers

5   In paragraph 22 (power to transfer persons into custody of investigating officers), in sub-paragraph (2)—

(a) in paragraph (b), after "duty" insert "to keep that person under control and",

(b) in paragraph (c), at the end add "and under his control".

6   After paragraph 22 insert—

"Powers in respect of detained persons

22A   Where a designation applies this paragraph to any person, he shall be under a duty, when in the course of his employment he is present at a police station—

(a) to assist any officer or other designated person to keep any person detained at the police station under control; and

(b) to prevent the escape of any such person,

and for those purposes shall be entitled to use reasonable force."

Detention officers

7   After paragraph 33A (inserted by paragraph 16 of Schedule 8 to this Act) insert—

"*Powers in respect of detained persons*

33B   Where a designation applies this paragraph to any person, he shall be under a duty, when in the course of his employment he is present at a police station—

(a)   to keep under control any person detained at the police station and for whom he is for the time being responsible;

(b)   to assist any officer or other designated person to keep any other person detained at the police station under control; and

(c)   to prevent the escape of any such person as is mentioned in paragraph (a) or (b),

and for those purposes shall be entitled to use reasonable force.

33C   Where a designation applies this paragraph to any person, he shall be entitled to use reasonable force when—

(a)   securing, or assisting an officer or another designated person to secure, the detention of a person detained at a police station in the relevant police area, or

(b)   escorting within a police station in the relevant police area, or assisting an officer or another designated person to escort within such a police station, a person detained there."

Escort officers

8   (1)   Paragraph 34 (power to take an arrested person to a police station) is amended as follows.

(2)   In sub-paragraph (1)(c)—

(a)   in paragraph (ii), after "duty" insert "to keep the person under control and",

(b)   in paragraph (iii), at the end add "and under his control".

(3)   After sub-paragraph (1)(c) add—

"(d)   a person who has taken another person to a police station in exercise of the power conferred by virtue of paragraph (a)—

(i)   shall be under a duty to remain at the police station until he has transferred control of the other person to the custody officer at the police station;

(ii)   until he has so transferred control of the other person, shall be treated for all purposes as having that person in his lawful custody;

(iii)   for so long as he is at the police station or in its immediate vicinity in compliance with, or having complied with, his duty under sub-paragraph (i), shall be under a duty to prevent the escape of the other person and to assist in keeping him under control; and

(iv) shall be entitled to use reasonable force for the purpose of complying with his duty under sub-paragraph (iii)."

9 (1) Paragraph 35 (escort of persons in police detention) is amended as follows.

(2) In sub-paragraph (3) —

    (a) in paragraph (b), after "duty" insert "to keep the person under control and",

    (b) in paragraph (c), at the end add "and under his control".

(3) After sub-paragraph (3) insert —

    "(3A) A person who has escorted another person to a police station or other place in accordance with an authorisation under sub-paragraph (1) or (2) —

        (a) shall be under a duty to remain at the police station or other place until he has transferred control of the other person to a custody officer or other responsible person there;

        (b) until he has so transferred control of the other person, shall be treated for all purposes as having that person in his lawful custody;

        (c) for so long as he is at the police station or other place, or in its immediate vicinity, in compliance with, or having complied with, his duty under paragraph (a), shall be under a duty to prevent the escape of the other person and to assist in keeping him under control; and

        (d) shall be entitled to use reasonable force for the purpose of complying with his duty under paragraph (c)."

Staff custody officers

10 After paragraph 35A (inserted by section 120(5) of this Act) insert —

"Powers in respect of detained persons

    35B Where a designation applies this paragraph to any person, he shall be under a duty, when in the course of his employment he is present at a police station —

        (a) to keep under control any person detained at the police station and for whom he is for the time being responsible;

        (b) to assist any officer or other designated person to keep any other person detained at the police station under control; and

        (c) to prevent the escape of any such person as is mentioned in paragraph (a) or (b),

and for those purposes shall be entitled to use reasonable force."

210   *Serious Organised Crime and Police Act 2005 (c. 15)*
                                    Schedule 10 — Parental compensation orders
                                              Part 1 — England and Wales

SCHEDULE 10   Section 144

PARENTAL COMPENSATION ORDERS

PART 1

ENGLAND AND WALES

1   The Crime and Disorder Act 1998 (c. 37) is amended as provided in paragraphs 2 to 5.

2   After section 13 insert—

"13A Parental compensation orders

(1)   A magistrates' court may make an order under this section (a "parental compensation order") if on the application of a local authority it is satisfied, on the civil standard of proof—

    (a)   that the condition mentioned in subsection (2) below is fulfilled with respect to a child under the age of 10; and

    (b)   that it would be desirable to make the order in the interests of preventing a repetition of the behaviour in question.

(2)   The condition is that the child has taken, or caused loss of or damage to, property in the course of—

    (a)   committing an act which, if he had been aged 10 or over, would have constituted an offence; or

    (b)   acting in a manner that caused or was likely to cause harassment, alarm or distress to one or more persons not of the same household as himself.

(3)   A parental compensation order is an order which requires any person specified in the order who is a parent or guardian of the child (other than a local authority) to pay compensation of an amount specified in the order to any person or persons specified in the order who is, or are, affected by the taking of the property or its loss or damage.

(4)   The amount of compensation specified may not exceed £5,000 in all.

(5)   The Secretary of State may by order amend subsection (4) above so as to substitute a different amount.

(6)   For the purposes of collection and enforcement, a parental compensation order is to be treated as if it were a sum adjudged to be paid on the conviction by the magistrates' court which made the order of the person or persons specified in the order as liable to pay the compensation.

(7)   In this section and sections 13B and 13C below, "local authority" has the same meaning as in the 1989 Act.

13B   Parental compensation orders: the compensation

(1)   When specifying the amount of compensation for the purposes of section 13A(3) above, the magistrates' court shall take into account—

    (a)   the value of the property taken or damaged, or whose loss was caused, by the child;

Serious Organised Crime and Police Act 2005 (c. 15)
Schedule 10 – *Parental compensation orders*
Part 1 – *England and Wales*

211

      (b)   any further loss which flowed from the taking of or damage to the property, or from its loss;

      (c)   whether the child, or any parent or guardian of his, has already paid any compensation for the property (and if so, how much);

      (d)   whether the child, or any parent or guardian of his, has already made any reparation (and if so, what it consisted of);

      (e)   the means of those to be specified in the order as liable to pay the compensation, so far as the court can ascertain them;

      (f)   whether there was any lack of care on the part of the person affected by the taking of the property or its loss or damage which made it easier for the child to take or damage the property or to cause its loss.

(2)   If property taken is recovered before compensation is ordered to be paid in respect of it—

      (a)   the court shall not order any such compensation to be payable in respect of it if it is not damaged;

      (b)   if it is damaged, the damage shall be treated for the purposes of making a parental compensation order as having been caused by the child, regardless of how it was caused and who caused it.

(3)   The court shall specify in the order how and by when the compensation is to be paid (for example, it may specify that the compensation is to be paid by instalments, and specify the date by which each instalment must be paid).

(4)   For the purpose of ascertaining the means of the parent or guardian, the court may, before specifying the amount of compensation, order him to provide the court, within such period as it may specify in the order, such a statement of his financial circumstances as the court may require.

(5)   A person who without reasonable excuse fails to comply with an order under subsection (4) above is guilty of an offence and is liable on summary conviction to a fine not exceeding level 3 on the standard scale.

(6)   If, in providing a statement of his financial circumstances pursuant to an order under subsection (4) above, a person—

      (a)   makes a statement which he knows to be false in a material particular;

      (b)   recklessly provides a statement which is false in a material particular; or

      (c)   knowingly fails to disclose any material fact,

he is liable on summary conviction to a fine not exceeding level 4 on the standard scale.

(7)   Proceedings in respect of an offence under subsection (6) above may, despite anything in section 127(1) of the 1980 Act (limitation of time), be commenced at any time within two years from the date of the commission of the offence or within six months of its first discovery by the local authority, whichever period expires earlier.

212

Serious Organised Crime and Police Act 2005 (c. 15)
Schedule 10 — Parental compensation orders
Part 1 — England and Wales

13C   Parental compensation orders: supplemental

(1)   Before deciding whether or not to make a parental compensation order in favour of any person, the magistrates' court shall take into account the views of that person about whether a parental compensation order should be made in his favour.

(2)   Before making a parental compensation order, the magistrates' court shall obtain and consider information about the child's family circumstances and the likely effect of the order on those circumstances.

(3)   Before making a parental compensation order, a magistrates' court shall explain to the parent or guardian of the child in ordinary language —
   (a)   the effect of the order and of the requirements proposed to be included in it;
   (b)   the consequences which may follow (under subsection (4)(b) below) as a result of failure to comply with any of those requirements;
   (c)   that the court has power (under subsection (4)(a) below) to review the order on the application either of the parent or guardian or of the local authority.

(4)   A magistrates' court which has made a parental compensation order may make an order under subsection (5) below if while the order is in force —
   (a)   it appears to the court, on the application of the local authority, or the parent or guardian subject to the order, that it is appropriate to make an order under subsection (5); or
   (b)   it is proved to the satisfaction of the court, on the application of the local authority, that the parent or guardian subject to it has failed to comply with any requirement included in the order.

(5)   An order under this subsection is an order discharging the parental compensation order or varying it —
   (a)   by cancelling any provision included in it; or
   (b)   by inserting in it (either in addition to or in substitution for any of its provisions) any provision that could have been included in the order if the court had then had power to make it and were exercising the power.

(6)   Where an application under subsection (4) above for the discharge of a parental compensation order is dismissed, no further application for its discharge shall be made under that subsection by any person except with the consent of the court which made the order.

(7)   References in this section to the magistrates' court which made a parental compensation order include any magistrates' court acting in the same local justice area as that court.

13D   Parental compensation orders: appeal

(1)   If a magistrates' court makes a parental compensation order, the parent or guardian may appeal against the making of the order, or against the amount of compensation specified in the order.

Serious Organised Crime and Police Act 2005 (c. 15)
Schedule 10 – Parental compensation orders
Part 1 – *England and Wales*

213

(2) The appeal lies to the Crown Court.

(3) On the appeal the Crown Court—

   (a) may make such orders as may be necessary to give effect to its determination of the appeal;

   (b) may also make such incidental or consequential orders as appear to it to be just.

(4) Any order of the Crown Court made on an appeal under this section (other than one directing that an application be re-heard by a magistrates' court) shall, for the purposes of section 13C above, be treated as if it were an order of the magistrates' court from which the appeal was brought and not an order of the Crown Court.

(5) A person in whose favour a parental compensation order is made shall not be entitled to receive any compensation under it until (disregarding any power of a court to grant leave to appeal out of time) there is no further possibility of an appeal on which the order could be varied or set aside.

13E Effect of parental compensation order on subsequent award of damages in civil proceedings

(1) This section has effect where—

   (a) a parental compensation order has been made in favour of any person in respect of any taking or loss of property or damage to it; and

   (b) a claim by him in civil proceedings for damages in respect of the taking, loss or damage is then to be determined.

(2) The damages in the civil proceedings shall be assessed without regard to the parental compensation order, but the claimant may recover only an amount equal to the aggregate of the following—

   (a) any amount by which they exceed the compensation; and

   (b) a sum equal to any portion of the compensation which he fails to recover.

(3) The claimant may not enforce the judgment, so far as it relates to such a sum as is mentioned in subsection (2)(b) above, without the permission of the court."

3 (1) Section 8 (parenting orders) is amended as follows.

   (2) In subsection (1), after paragraph (a) insert—
   "(aa) a parental compensation order is made in relation to a child's behaviour;".

   (3) In subsection (6)(a)—
   (a) after "paragraph (a)" insert ", (aa)",
   (b) after "child safety order," insert "parental compensation order,".

4 In section 18 (interpretation of Chapter 1), in subsection (1), after the definition of "local child curfew scheme" insert—
   ""parental compensation order" has the meaning given by section 13A(1) above;".

214

Serious Organised Crime and Police Act 2005 (c. 15)
Schedule 10 – Parental compensation orders
Part 1 – England and Wales

5   In section 114 (orders and regulations), in subsection (3), after "section" insert "13A(5),".

6   The amendments made by paragraph 2 of this Schedule do not apply in relation to any conduct which occurred before the coming into force of that paragraph.

PART 2

NORTHERN IRELAND

7   The Criminal Justice (Children) (Northern Ireland) Order 1998 (S.I. 1998/ 1504 (N.I. 9)) is amended as provided in paragraphs 8 and 9.

8   After Article 36 insert—

"36ZA Parental compensation orders

(1)   A magistrates' court may make an order under this Article (a "parental compensation order") if on the application of a person of a description specified for the purpose in an order made by the Secretary of State (referred to in this Article and in Articles 36ZB and 36ZC as the "applicant") the court is satisfied, on the civil standard of proof—

  (a)   that the condition mentioned in paragraph (2) is fulfilled with respect to a child under the age of 10; and

  (b)   that it would be desirable to make the order in the interests of preventing a repetition of the behaviour in question.

(2)   The condition is that the child has taken, or caused loss of or damage to, property in the course of—

  (a)   committing an act which, if he had been aged 10 or over, would have constituted an offence; or

  (b)   acting in a manner that caused or was likely to cause harassment, alarm or distress to one or more persons not of the same household as himself.

(3)   A parental compensation order is an order which requires any person specified in the order who is a parent or guardian of the child to pay compensation of an amount specified in the order to any person or persons specified in the order who is, or are, affected by the taking of the property or its loss or damage.

(4)   The amount of compensation specified may not exceed £5,000 in all.

(5)   The Secretary of State may by order amend paragraph (4) so as to substitute a different amount.

(6)   For the purposes of collection and enforcement, a parental compensation order is to be treated as if it were a sum adjudged to be paid on the conviction by the magistrates' court which made the order of the person or persons specified in the order as liable to pay the compensation.

(7)   An order under paragraph (1) or (5) is subject to annulment in pursuance of a resolution of either House of Parliament in the same manner as a statutory instrument; and, accordingly, section 5 of the Statutory Instruments Act 1946 (c. 36) applies to such an order.

Serious Organised Crime and Police Act 2005 (c. 15)
Schedule 10 — Parental compensation orders
Part 2 — Northern Ireland

215

36ZB Parental compensation orders: the compensation

(1) When specifying the amount of compensation for the purposes of Article 36ZA(3), the magistrates' court shall take into account—

    (a) the value of the property taken or damaged, or whose loss was caused, by the child;

    (b) any further loss which flowed from the taking of or damage to the property, or from its loss;

    (c) whether the child, or any parent or guardian of his, has already paid any compensation for the property (and if so, how much);

    (d) whether the child, or any parent or guardian of his, has already made any reparation (and if so, what it consisted of);

    (e) the means of those to be specified in the order as liable to pay the compensation, so far as the court can ascertain them;

    (f) whether there was any lack of care on the part of the person affected by the taking of the property or its loss or damage which made it easier for the child to take or damage the property or to cause its loss.

(2) If property taken is recovered before compensation is ordered to be paid in respect of it—

    (a) the court shall not order any such compensation to be payable in respect of it if it is not damaged;

    (b) if it is damaged, the damage shall be treated for the purposes of making a parental compensation order as having been caused by the child, regardless of how it was caused and who caused it.

(3) The court shall specify in the order how and by when the compensation is to be paid (for example, it may specify that the compensation is to be paid by instalments, and specify the date by which each instalment must be paid).

(4) For the purpose of ascertaining the means of the parent or guardian, the court may, before specifying the amount of compensation, order him to provide the court, within such period as it may specify in the order, such a statement of his financial circumstances as the court may require.

(5) A person who without reasonable excuse fails to comply with an order under paragraph (4) is guilty of an offence and is liable on summary conviction to a fine not exceeding level 3 on the standard scale.

(6) If, in providing a statement of his financial circumstances pursuant to an order under paragraph (4), a person—

    (a) makes a statement which he knows to be false in a material particular;

    (b) recklessly provides a statement which is false in a material particular; or

    (c) knowingly fails to disclose any material fact,

he is liable on summary conviction to a fine not exceeding level 4 on the standard scale.

216   *Serious Organised Crime and Police Act 2005 (c. 15)*
Schedule 10 — Parental compensation orders
Part 2 — Northern Ireland

(7) Proceedings in respect of an offence under paragraph (6) may, despite anything in Article 19 of the Magistrates' Courts (Northern Ireland) Order 1981 (limitation of time), be commenced at any time within two years from the date of the commission of the offence or within six months of its first discovery by the applicant, whichever period expires earlier.

(8) Paragraphs (1)(e) and (4) to (7) do not apply in the case of an order specifying an authority as liable to pay the compensation.

36ZC Parental compensation orders: supplemental

(1) Before deciding whether or not to make a parental compensation order in favour of any person, the magistrates' court shall take into account the views of that person about whether a parental compensation order should be made in his favour.

(2) Before making a parental compensation order, the magistrates' court shall obtain and consider information about the child's family circumstances and the likely effect of the order on those circumstances.

(3) Before making a parental compensation order, a magistrates' court shall explain to the parent or guardian of the child in ordinary language—

   (a) the effect of the order and of the requirements proposed to be included in it;

   (b) the consequences which may follow (under paragraph (4)(b)) as a result of failure to comply with any of those requirements;

   (c) that the court has power (under paragraph (4)(a)) to review the order on the application either of the parent or guardian or of the applicant.

(4) A magistrates' court which has made a parental compensation order may make an order under paragraph (5) if while the order is in force—

   (a) it appears to the court, on the application of the applicant, or the parent or guardian subject to the order, that it is appropriate to make an order under paragraph (5); or

   (b) it is proved to the satisfaction of the court, on the application of the applicant, that the parent or guardian subject to it has failed to comply with any requirement included in the order.

(5) An order under this paragraph is an order discharging the parental compensation order or varying it—

   (a) by cancelling any provision included in it; or

   (b) by inserting in it (either in addition to or in substitution for any of its provisions) any provision that could have been included in the order if the court had then had power to make it and were exercising the power.

(6) Where an application under paragraph (4) for the discharge of a parental compensation order is dismissed, no further application for its discharge shall be made under that paragraph by any person except with the consent of the court which made the order.

Serious Organised Crime and Police Act 2005 (c. 15)
Schedule 10 – Parental compensation orders
Part 2 – Northern Ireland

217

(7)   References in this Article to the magistrates' court which made a parental compensation order include any magistrates' court acting for the same county court division as that court.

36ZD Parental compensation orders: appeal

(1)   If a magistrates' court makes a parental compensation order, the parent or guardian may appeal against the making of the order, or against the amount of compensation specified in the order.

(2)   The appeal lies to the county court.

(3)   On the appeal the county court —
    (a)   may make such orders as may be necessary to give effect to its determination of the appeal;
    (b)   may also make such incidental or consequential orders as appear to it to be just.

(4)   Any order of the county court made on an appeal under this Article (other than one directing that an application be re-heard by a magistrates' court) shall, for the purposes of Article 36ZC, be treated as if it were an order of the magistrates' court from which the appeal was brought and not an order of the county court.

(5)   A person in whose favour a parental compensation order is made shall not be entitled to receive any compensation under it until (disregarding any power of a court to grant leave to appeal out of time) there is no further possibility of an appeal on which the order could be varied or set aside.

36ZE Effect of parental compensation order on subsequent award of damages in civil proceedings

(1)   This Article has effect where —
    (a)   a parental compensation order has been made in favour of any person in respect of any taking or loss of property or damage to it; and
    (b)   a claim by him in civil proceedings for damages in respect of the taking, loss or damage is then to be determined.

(2)   The damages in the civil proceedings shall be assessed without regard to the parental compensation order, but the claimant may recover only an amount equal to the aggregate of the following —
    (a)   any amount by which they exceed the compensation; and
    (b)   a sum equal to any portion of the compensation which he fails to recover.

(3)   The claimant may not enforce the judgment, so far as it relates to such a sum as is mentioned in paragraph (2)(b), without the leave of the court."

9   In Article 2 (interpretation), in paragraph (2), in the appropriate place insert —

""parental compensation order" has the meaning given by Article 36ZA(1);".

218

Serious Organised Crime and Police Act 2005 (c. 15)
Schedule 10 — Parental compensation orders
Part 2 — Northern Ireland

10   The amendments made by paragraph 8 of this Schedule do not apply in
          relation to any conduct which occurred before the coming into force of that
          paragraph.

SCHEDULE 11

Section 159

INVESTIGATIONS INTO CONDUCT OF POLICE OFFICERS: ACCELERATED PROCEDURE IN
SPECIAL CASES

1   Schedule 3 to the Police Reform Act 2002 (c. 30) is amended as follows.

2   In paragraph 20(1) —
          (a)   for "until" substitute "until —
                            (a)   the appropriate authority has certified the case as a
                                  special case under paragraph 20B(3) or 20E(3), or";
                                  and
          (b)   the words from "a report" to the end become paragraph (b).

3   After paragraph 20 insert —

          "Accelerated procedure in special cases

          20A (1) If, at any time before the completion of his investigation, a person
                    appointed or designated to investigate a complaint or recordable
                    conduct matter believes that the appropriate authority would, on
                    consideration of the matter, be likely to consider that the special
                    conditions are satisfied, he shall proceed in accordance with the
                    following provisions of this paragraph.

               (2) If the person was appointed under paragraph 16, he shall submit
                    to the appropriate authority —
                    (a)   a statement of his belief and the grounds for it; and
                    (b)   a written report on his investigation to that point;
                    and if he was appointed following a determination made by the
                    Commission under paragraph 15 he shall send a copy of the
                    statement and the report to the Commission.

               (3) If the person was appointed under paragraph 17 or 18 or
                    designated under paragraph 19, he shall submit to the appropriate
                    authority —
                    (a)   a statement of his belief and the grounds for it; and
                    (b)   a written report on his investigation to that point;
                    and shall send a copy of the statement and the report to the
                    Commission.

               (4) A person submitting a report under this paragraph shall not be
                    prevented by any obligation of secrecy imposed by any rule of law
                    or otherwise from including all such matters in his report as he
                    thinks fit.

               (5) A statement and report may be submitted under this paragraph
                    whether or not a previous statement and report have been
                    submitted; but a second or subsequent statement and report may
                    be submitted only if the person submitting them has grounds to

believe that the appropriate authority will reach a different determination under paragraph 20B(2) or 20E(2).

(6) After submitting a report under this paragraph, the person appointed or designated to investigate the complaint or recordable conduct matter shall continue his investigation to such extent as he considers appropriate.

(7) The special conditions are that—

  (a) the person whose conduct is the subject matter of the investigation may have committed an imprisonable offence and that person's conduct is of a serious nature;

  (b) there is sufficient evidence, in the form of written statements or other documents, to establish on the balance of probabilities that conduct justifying dismissal took place; and

  (c) it is in the public interest for the person whose conduct is the subject matter of the investigation to cease to be a member of a police force, or to be a special constable, without delay.

(8) In sub-paragraph (7)—

  (a) in paragraph (a), "imprisonable offence" means an offence which is punishable with imprisonment in the case of a person aged 21 or over; and

  (b) in paragraph (b), "conduct justifying dismissal" means conduct which is so serious that disciplinary proceedings brought in respect of it would be likely to result in a dismissal.

(9) In paragraphs 20B to 20H "special report" means a report submitted under this paragraph.

Investigations managed or carried out by Commission: action by appropriate authority

20B (1) This paragraph applies where —

  (a) a statement and special report on an investigation carried out under the management of the Commission, or

  (b) a statement and special report on an investigation carried out by a person designated by the Commission,

are submitted to the appropriate authority under paragraph 20A(3).

(2) The appropriate authority shall determine whether the special conditions are satisfied.

(3) If the appropriate authority determines that the special conditions are satisfied then, unless it considers that the circumstances are such as to make it inappropriate to do so, it shall—

  (a) certify the case as a special case for the purposes of Regulation 11 of the Police (Conduct) Regulations 2004 (S.I. 2004/645); and

  (b) subject to any request made under paragraph 20G(1), take such steps as are required by that Regulation in relation to a case so certified.

220   *Serious Organised Crime and Police Act 2005 (c. 15)*

Schedule 11 − Investigations into conduct of police officers: accelerated procedure in special cases

(4) The reference in sub-paragraph (3) to Regulation 11 includes a reference to any corresponding provision replacing that Regulation.

(5) If the appropriate authority determines that the special conditions are satisfied then it shall notify the Director of Public Prosecutions of its determination and send him a copy of the special report.

(6) The appropriate authority shall notify the Commission of a certification under sub-paragraph (3).

(7) If the appropriate authority determines—

 (a) that the special conditions are not satisfied, or

 (b) that, although those conditions are satisfied, the circumstances are such as to make it inappropriate at present to bring disciplinary proceedings,

it shall submit to the Commission a memorandum under this sub-paragraph.

(8) The memorandum required to be submitted under sub-paragraph (7) is one which—

 (a) notifies the Commission of its determination that those conditions are not satisfied or (as the case may be) that they are so satisfied but the circumstances are such as to make it inappropriate at present to bring disciplinary proceedings; and

 (b) (in either case) sets out its reasons for so determining.

(9) In this paragraph "special conditions" has the meaning given by paragraph 20A(7).

Investigations managed or carried out by Commission: action by Commission

20C (1) On receipt of a notification under paragraph 20B(6), the Commission shall give a notification—

 (a) in the case of a complaint, to the complainant and to every person entitled to be kept properly informed in relation to the complaint under section 21; and

 (b) in the case of a recordable conduct matter, to every person entitled to be kept properly informed in relation to that matter under that section.

(2) The notification required by sub-paragraph (1) is one setting out—

 (a) the findings of the special report;

 (b) the appropriate authority's determination under paragraph 20B(2); and

 (c) the action that the appropriate authority is required to take as a consequence of that determination.

(3) Subsections (5) to (7) of section 20 shall have effect in relation to the duties imposed on the Commission by sub-paragraph (1) as they have effect in relation to the duties imposed on the Commission by that section.

(4) Except so far as may be otherwise provided by regulations made by virtue of sub-paragraph (3), the Commission shall be entitled

(notwithstanding any obligation of secrecy imposed by any rule of law or otherwise) to discharge the duty to give a person mentioned in sub-paragraph (1) notification of the findings of the special report by sending that person a copy of that report.

20D (1) On receipt of a memorandum under paragraph 20B(7), the Commission shall —

    (a) consider the memorandum;

    (b) determine, in the light of that consideration, whether or not to make a recommendation under paragraph 20H; and

    (c) if it thinks fit to do so, make a recommendation under that paragraph.

(2) If the Commission determines not to make a recommendation under paragraph 20H, it shall notify the appropriate authority and the person appointed under paragraph 18 or designated under paragraph 19 of its determination.

Other investigations: action by appropriate authority

20E (1) This paragraph applies where —

    (a) a statement and a special report on an investigation carried out by an appropriate authority on its own behalf, or

    (b) a statement and a special report on an investigation carried out under the supervision of the Commission,

are submitted to the appropriate authority under paragraph 20A(2) or (3).

(2) The appropriate authority shall determine whether the special conditions are satisfied.

(3) If the appropriate authority determines that the special conditions are satisfied then, unless it considers that the circumstances are such as to make it inappropriate to do so, it shall —

    (a) certify the case as a special case for the purposes of Regulation 11 of the Police (Conduct) Regulations 2004 (S.I. 2004/645); and

    (b) subject to any request made under paragraph 20G(1), take such steps as are required by that Regulation in relation to a case so certified.

(4) The reference in sub-paragraph (3) to Regulation 11 includes a reference to any corresponding provision replacing that Regulation.

(5) If the appropriate authority determines that the special conditions are satisfied then it shall notify the Director of Public Prosecutions of its determination and send him a copy of the special report.

(6) Where the statement and report were required under paragraph 20A(2) to be copied to the Commission, the appropriate authority shall notify the Commission of a certification under sub-paragraph (3).

(7) If the appropriate authority determines —

    (a) that the special conditions are not satisfied, or

            (b)   that, although those conditions are satisfied, the circumstances are such as to make it inappropriate at present to bring disciplinary proceedings,

it shall notify the person appointed under paragraph 16 or 17 of its determination.

    (8) In this paragraph "special conditions" has the meaning given by paragraph 20A(7).

20F (1) If the appropriate authority certifies a case under paragraph 20E(3), it shall give a notification—

        (a)   in the case of a complaint, to the complainant and to every person entitled to be kept properly informed in relation to the complaint under section 21; and

        (b)   in the case of a recordable conduct matter, to every person entitled to be kept properly informed in relation to that matter under that section.

    (2) The notification required by sub-paragraph (1) is one setting out—

        (a)   the findings of the report;

        (b)   the authority's determination under paragraph 20E(2); and

        (c)   the action that the authority is required to take in consequence of that determination.

    (3) Subsections (5) to (7) of section 20 shall have effect in relation to the duties imposed on the appropriate authority by sub-paragraph (1) as they have effect in relation to the duties imposed on the appropriate authority by that section.

    (4) Except so far as may be otherwise provided by regulations made by virtue of sub-paragraph (3), the appropriate authority shall be entitled (notwithstanding any obligation of secrecy imposed by any rule of law or otherwise) to discharge the duty to give a person mentioned in sub-paragraph (1) notification of the findings of the special report by sending that person a copy of that report.

Special cases: Director of Public Prosecutions

20G (1) On receiving a copy of a special report under paragraph 20B(5) or 20E(5), the Director of Public Prosecutions may request the appropriate authority not to bring disciplinary proceedings without his prior agreement, if the Director considers that bringing such proceedings might prejudice any future criminal proceedings.

    (2) The Director of Public Prosecutions—

        (a)   shall notify the appropriate authority of any decision of his to take, or not to take, action in respect of the matters dealt with in a special report copied to him under paragraph 20B(5) or 20E(5); and

        (b)   where the special report was copied to him under paragraph 20B(5), shall send a copy of that notification to the Commission.

Serious Organised Crime and Police Act 2005 (c. 15)
Schedule 11 – Investigations into conduct of police officers: accelerated procedure in special cases

223

(3) It shall be the duty of the Commission to notify the persons mentioned in sub-paragraph (5) if criminal proceedings are brought against any person by the Director of Public Prosecutions in respect of any matters dealt with in a special report copied to him under paragraph 20B(5).

(4) It shall be the duty of the appropriate authority to notify the persons mentioned in sub-paragraph (5) if criminal proceedings are brought against any person by the Director of Public Prosecutions in respect of any matters dealt with in a special report copied to him under paragraph 20E(5).

(5) Those persons are—
  (a) in the case of a complaint, the complainant and every person entitled to be kept properly informed in relation to the complaint under section 21; and
  (b) in the case of a recordable conduct matter, every person entitled to be kept properly informed in relation to that matter under that section.

Special cases: recommendation or direction of Commission

20H (1) Where the appropriate authority has submitted, or is required to submit, a memorandum to the Commission under paragraph 20B(7), the Commission may make a recommendation to the appropriate authority that it should certify the case under paragraph 20B(3).

(2) If the Commission determines to make a recommendation under this paragraph, it shall give a notification—
  (a) in the case of a complaint, to the complainant and to every person entitled to be kept properly informed in relation to the complaint under section 21; and
  (b) in the case of a recordable conduct matter, to every person entitled to be kept properly informed in relation to that matter under that section.

(3) The notification required by sub-paragraph (2) is one setting out—
  (a) the findings of the special report; and
  (b) the Commission's recommendation under this paragraph.

(4) Subsections (5) to (7) of section 20 shall have effect in relation to the duties imposed on the Commission by sub-paragraph (2) as they have effect in relation to the duties imposed on the Commission by that section.

(5) Except so far as may be otherwise provided by regulations made by virtue of sub-paragraph (4), the Commission shall be entitled (notwithstanding any obligation of secrecy imposed by any rule of law or otherwise) to discharge the duty to give a person mentioned in sub-paragraph (2) notification of the findings of the special report by sending that person a copy of the report.

(6) It shall be the duty of the appropriate authority to notify the Commission whether it accepts the recommendation and (if it does) to certify the case and proceed accordingly.

(7) If, after the Commission has made a recommendation under this paragraph, the appropriate authority does not certify the case under paragraph 20B(3) —

    (a) the Commission may direct the appropriate authority so to certify it; and

    (b) it shall be the duty of the appropriate authority to comply with the direction and proceed accordingly.

(8) Where the Commission gives the appropriate authority a direction under this paragraph, it shall supply the appropriate authority with a statement of its reasons for doing so.

(9) The Commission may at any time withdraw a direction given under this paragraph.

(10) The appropriate authority shall keep the Commission informed of whatever action it takes in response to a recommendation or direction.

20I (1) Where —

    (a) the Commission makes a recommendation under paragraph 20H in the case of an investigation of a complaint, and

    (b) the appropriate authority notifies the Commission that the recommendation has been accepted,

the Commission shall notify the complainant and every person entitled to be kept properly informed in relation to the complaint under section 21 of that fact and of the steps that have been, or are to be, taken by the appropriate authority to give effect to it.

(2) Where in the case of an investigation of a complaint the appropriate authority —

    (a) notifies the Commission that it does not accept the recommendation made by the Commission under paragraph 20H, or

    (b) fails to certify the case under paragraph 20B(3) and to proceed accordingly,

it shall be the duty of the Commission to determine what (if any) further steps to take under paragraph 20H.

(3) It shall be the duty of the Commission to notify the complainant and every person entitled to be kept properly informed in relation to the complaint under section 21 —

    (a) of any determination under sub-paragraph (2) not to take further steps under paragraph 20H; and

    (b) where it determines under that sub-paragraph to take further steps under that paragraph, of the outcome of the taking of those steps."

4   In paragraph 25, after sub-paragraph (2) insert —

"(2A) In sub-paragraph (2) —

    (a) references to the findings of an investigation do not include a reference to findings on a report submitted under paragraph 20A; and

Serious Organised Crime and Police Act 2005 (c. 15)
Schedule 11 — Investigations into conduct of police officers: accelerated procedure in special cases

225

(b) references to the report of an investigation do not include a reference to a report submitted under that paragraph."

SCHEDULE 12   Section 160

INVESTIGATIONS OF DEATHS AND SERIOUS INJURIES DURING OR AFTER CONTACT WITH THE POLICE

1   The Police Reform Act 2002 (c. 30) has effect subject to the following amendments.

2   (1) Section 10(2) (general functions of the Commission) is amended as follows.

(2) After paragraph (b) insert—
"(ba) the recording of matters from which it appears that a person has died or suffered serious injury during, or following, contact with a person serving with the police;".

(3) In paragraph (c), after "paragraph (b)" insert "or (ba)".

3   In section 12 (matters to which Part 2 applies), after subsection (2) insert—

"(2A) In this Part "death or serious injury matter" (or "DSI matter" for short) means any circumstances (other than those which are or have been the subject of a complaint or which amount to a conduct matter)—
(a) in or in consequence of which a person has died or has sustained serious injury; and
(b) in relation to which the requirements of either subsection (2B) or subsection (2C) are satisfied.

(2B) The requirements of this subsection are that at the time of the death or serious injury the person—
(a) had been arrested by a person serving with the police and had not been released from that arrest; or
(b) was otherwise detained in the custody of a person serving with the police.

(2C) The requirements of this subsection are that—
(a) at or before the time of the death or serious injury the person had contact (of whatever kind, and whether direct or indirect) with a person serving with the police who was acting in the execution of his duties; and
(b) there is an indication that the contact may have caused (whether directly or indirectly) or contributed to the death or serious injury.

(2D) In subsection (2A) the reference to a person includes a person serving with the police, but in relation to such a person "contact" in subsection (2C) does not include contact that he has whilst acting in the execution of his duties."

4   In the following provisions, for "and conduct matters" substitute ", conduct matters and DSI matters"—
(a) the cross-heading preceding section 13;

    (b)   the heading for section 13 (handling of complaints and conduct matters); and

    (c)   that section itself.

5   (1)   Section 16(2) (assistance for which payment is required) is amended as follows.

    (2)   In paragraph (a), for the words from "an investigation relating to" to the end substitute—

        "(i)   an investigation relating to the conduct of a person who, at the time of the conduct, was a member of the other force, or

        (ii)   an investigation of a DSI matter in relation to which the relevant officer was, at the time of the death or serious injury, a member of the other force; and".

    (3)   In paragraph (b), for the words from "an investigation" to the end substitute—

        "(i)   an investigation relating to the conduct of a person who, at the time of the conduct, was not a member of that force, or

        (ii)   an investigation of a DSI matter in relation to which the relevant officer was, at the time of the death or serious injury, not a member of that force."

6   In section 18 (inspection of police premises on behalf of the Commission), in subsection (2)(a), after "conduct matters" insert "or DSI matters".

7   (1)   Section 21 (duty to provide information) is amended as follows.

    (2)   In subsection (1), for "or recordable conduct matter" substitute ", recordable conduct matter or DSI matter".

    (3)   In subsection (1)(a), after "subsection (2)" insert "or (2A)".

    (4)   In subsection (2), after "if" insert "(in the case of a complaint or recordable conduct matter)".

    (5)   After subsection (2) insert—

        "(2A)   A person falls within this subsection if (in the case of a DSI matter)—

           (a)   he is a relative of the person who has died;

           (b)   he is a relative of the person who has suffered serious injury and that person is incapable of making a complaint;

           (c)   he himself is the person who has suffered serious injury."

    (6)   In subsection (3)—

        (a)   after "subsection (2)" insert "or (2A)"; and

        (b)   for "or recordable conduct matter" (in both places) substitute ", recordable conduct matter or DSI matter".

    (7)   In subsection (5), for "or conduct matter" substitute ", conduct matter or DSI matter".

    (8)   In subsections (6) and (7), for "or recordable conduct matter" substitute ", recordable conduct matter or DSI matter".

Serious Organised Crime and Police Act 2005 (c. 15)
Schedule 12 — Investigations of deaths and serious injuries during or after contact with the police

227

(9) After subsection (9)(b) insert—

> "(ba) whether the Commission or the appropriate authority has made a determination under paragraph 21A of Schedule 3;".

(10) In subsection (9)(c), after "paragraph 22" insert "or 24A".

(11) In subsection (10), for "or recordable conduct matter" substitute ", recordable conduct matter or DSI matter".

8 (1) Section 22 (power of Commission to issue guidance) is amended as follows.

(2) In subsection (2)(b)(ii), after "recordable conduct matters" insert "or DSI matters".

(3) In subsection (5)—

    (a) in paragraph (a), after "recordable conduct matters" insert "or DSI matters";

    (b) in paragraphs (b) and (d)(ii), after "recordable conduct matter" insert "or DSI matter"; and

    (c) in paragraph (e)(i), for "or conduct matter" substitute ", conduct matter or DSI matter".

9 (1) Section 23(2) (regulations) is amended as follows.

(2) In paragraph (b), after "recordable conduct matters" insert "and DSI matters".

(3) For paragraph (h) substitute—

> "(h) for combining into a single investigation the investigation of any complaint, conduct matter or DSI matter with the investigation or investigations of any one or more, or any combination, of the following—
>
> > (i) complaints (whether or not relating to the same conduct),
> >
> > (ii) conduct matters, or
> >
> > (iii) DSI matters,
>
> and for splitting a single investigation into two or more separate investigations;".

(4) In paragraph (j), for "or conduct matter" substitute ", conduct matter or DSI matter".

(5) In paragraph (n)(ii), after "recordable conduct matters" insert "or DSI matters".

10 (1) Section 29 (interpretation) is amended as follows.

(2) In subsection (1)—

    (a) for the definition of "the appropriate authority" substitute—

> ""the appropriate authority"—
>
> > (a) in relation to a person serving with the police or in relation to any complaint, conduct matter or investigation relating to the conduct of such a person, means—
> >
> > > (i) if that person is a senior officer, the police authority for the area of the

228

Serious Organised Crime and Police Act 2005 (c. 15)
Schedule 12 — Investigations of deaths and serious injuries during or after contact with the police

                              police force of which he is a member; and

    (ii)   if he is not a senior officer, the chief officer under whose direction and control he is; and

  (b)   in relation to a death or serious injury matter, means—

    (i)   if the relevant officer is a senior officer, the police authority for the area of the police force of which he is a member; and

    (ii)   if he is not a senior officer, the chief officer under whose direction and control he is;"; and

  (b)   after the definition of "conduct matter" insert—

      ""death or serious injury matter" and "DSI matter" have the meaning given by section 12;".

(3)   After subsection (1) insert—

  "(1A)   In this Part "the relevant officer", in relation to a DSI matter, means the person serving with the police (within the meaning of section 12(7))—

    (a)   who arrested the person who has died or suffered serious injury,

    (b)   in whose custody that person was at the time of the death or serious injury, or

    (c)   with whom that person had the contact in question;

    and where there is more than one such person it means, subject to subsection (1B), the one who so dealt with him last before the death or serious injury occurred.

  (1B)   Where it cannot be determined which of two or more persons serving with the police dealt with a person last before a death or serious injury occurred, the relevant officer is the most senior of them."

11   Schedule 3 (handling of complaints and conduct matters) is amended as set out in the following paragraphs.

12   After paragraph 14 insert—

"PART 2A

HANDLING OF DEATH AND SERIOUS INJURY (DSI) MATTERS

Duty to record DSI matters

14A (1)   Where a DSI matter comes to the attention of the police authority or chief officer who is the appropriate authority in relation to that matter, it shall be the duty of the appropriate authority to record that matter.

    (2)   If it appears to the Commission—

Serious Organised Crime and Police Act 2005 (c. 15)
Schedule 12 — Investigations of deaths and serious injuries during or after contact with the police

229

(a)   that any matter that has come to its attention is a DSI matter, but

(b)   that that matter has not been recorded by the appropriate authority,

the Commission may direct the appropriate authority to record that matter; and it shall be the duty of that authority to comply with the direction.

Duty to preserve evidence relating to DSI matters

14B (1) Where—

(a)   a DSI matter comes to the attention of a police authority, and

(b)   the relevant officer in relation to that matter is the chief officer of the force maintained by that authority,

it shall be the duty of that authority to secure that all such steps as are appropriate for the purposes of Part 2 of this Act are taken, both initially and from time to time after that, for obtaining and preserving evidence relating to that matter.

(2) Where—

(a)   a chief officer becomes aware of a DSI matter, and

(b)   the relevant officer in relation to that matter is a person under his direction and control,

it shall be his duty to take all such steps as appear to him to be appropriate for the purposes of Part 2 of this Act for obtaining and preserving evidence relating to that matter.

(3) The chief officer's duty under sub-paragraph (2) must be performed as soon as practicable after he becomes aware of the matter in question.

(4) After that, he shall be under a duty, until he is satisfied that it is no longer necessary to do so, to continue to take the steps from time to time appearing to him to be appropriate for the purposes of Part 2 of this Act for obtaining and preserving evidence relating to the matter.

(5) It shall be the duty of a police authority to comply with all such directions as may be given to it by the Commission in relation to the performance of any duty imposed on it by virtue of sub-paragraph (1).

(6) It shall be the duty of the chief officer to take all such specific steps for obtaining or preserving evidence relating to any DSI matter as he may be directed to take for the purposes of this paragraph by the police authority maintaining his force or by the Commission.

Reference of DSI matters to the Commission

14C (1) It shall be the duty of the appropriate authority to refer a DSI matter to the Commission.

(2) The appropriate authority must do so within such period as may be provided for by regulations made by the Secretary of State.

230

Serious Organised Crime and Police Act 2005 (c. 15)
Schedule 12 – Investigations of deaths and serious injuries during or after contact with the police

(3) A matter that has already been referred to the Commission under this paragraph on a previous occasion shall not be required to be referred again under this paragraph unless the Commission so directs.

Duties of Commission on references under paragraph 14C

14D (1) It shall be the duty of the Commission, in the case of every DSI matter referred to it by a police authority or a chief officer, to determine whether or not it is necessary for the matter to be investigated.

(2) Where the Commission determines under this paragraph that it is not necessary for a DSI matter to be investigated, it may if it thinks fit refer the matter back to the appropriate authority to be dealt with by that authority in such manner (if any) as that authority may determine."

13   In paragraph 15(1)(a) and (8) (power of the Commission to determine the form of an investigation), for "or recordable conduct matter" substitute ", recordable conduct matter or DSI matter".

14   (1) Paragraph 16 (investigations by the appropriate authority on its own behalf) is amended as follows.

(2) In sub-paragraph (1), for "or recordable conduct matter" substitute ", recordable conduct matter or DSI matter".

(3) In sub-paragraph (2)(a), after "recordable conduct matter" insert "or under paragraph 14D(2) in relation to any DSI matter".

(4) In sub-paragraph (3), after "(4)" insert "or (5)".

(5) In sub-paragraph (4), for "matter" substitute "conduct matter".

(6) After sub-paragraph (4) add—

"(5) The person appointed under this paragraph to investigate any DSI matter—
    (a) in relation to which the relevant officer is a chief officer, must not be a person under that chief officer's direction and control;
    (b) in relation to which the relevant officer is the Commissioner of Police of the Metropolis or the Deputy Commissioner of Police of the Metropolis, must be the person nominated by the Secretary of State for appointment under this paragraph."

15   (1) Paragraph 17 (investigations supervised by the Commission) is amended as follows.

(2) In sub-paragraph (1), for "or recordable conduct matter" substitute ", recordable conduct matter or DSI matter".

(3) In sub-paragraph (6), for "matter" substitute "conduct matter".

Serious Organised Crime and Police Act 2005 (c. 15)
Schedule 12 – Investigations of deaths and serious injuries during or after contact with the police

231

(4) After sub-paragraph (6) insert—

"(6A) The person appointed under this paragraph to investigate any DSI matter—

    (a) in relation to which the relevant officer is a chief officer, must not be a person under that chief officer's direction and control;

    (b) in relation to which the relevant officer is the Commissioner of Police of the Metropolis or the Deputy Commissioner of Police of the Metropolis, must be the person nominated by the Secretary of State for appointment under this paragraph."

16 (1) Paragraph 18 (investigations managed by the Commission) is amended as follows.

(2) In sub-paragraph (1), for "or recordable conduct matter" substitute ", recordable conduct matter or DSI matter".

(3) In sub-paragraph (2), for "(6)" substitute "(6A)".

17 (1) Paragraph 19 (investigations by the Commission itself) is amended as follows.

(2) In sub-paragraph (1), for "or recordable conduct matter" substitute ", recordable conduct matter or DSI matter".

(3) After sub-paragraph (3) insert—

"(3A) The person designated under sub-paragraph (2) to be the person to take charge of an investigation of a DSI matter in relation to which the relevant officer is the Commissioner of Police of the Metropolis or the Deputy Commissioner of Police of the Metropolis must be the person nominated by the Secretary of State to be so designated under that sub-paragraph."

18 In paragraph 20(1) (restrictions on proceedings pending the conclusion of an investigation), after "22" insert "or 24A".

19 In paragraph 21(4) (power of the Commission to discontinue an investigation), for "or recordable conduct matter" substitute ", recordable conduct matter or DSI matter".

20 After paragraph 21 insert—

"Procedure where conduct matter is revealed during investigation of DSI matter

21A (1) If during the course of an investigation of a DSI matter it appears to a person appointed under paragraph 18 or designated under paragraph 19 that there is an indication that a person serving with the police ("the person whose conduct is in question") may have—

    (a) committed a criminal offence, or

    (b) behaved in a manner which would justify the bringing of disciplinary proceedings,

he shall make a submission to that effect to the Commission.

(2) If, after considering a submission under sub-paragraph (1), the Commission determines that there is such an indication, it shall—

> (a)   notify the appropriate authority in relation to the DSI matter and (if different) the appropriate authority in relation to the person whose conduct is in question of its determination; and
>
> (b)   send to it (or each of them) a copy of the submission under sub-paragraph (1).
>
> (3) If during the course of an investigation of a DSI matter it appears to a person appointed under paragraph 16 or 17 that there is an indication that a person serving with the police ("the person whose conduct is in question") may have—
>
> > (a)   committed a criminal offence, or
> >
> > (b)   behaved in a manner which would justify the bringing of disciplinary proceedings,
>
> he shall make a submission to that effect to the appropriate authority in relation to the DSI matter.
>
> (4) If, after considering a submission under sub-paragraph (3), the appropriate authority determines that there is such an indication, it shall—
>
> > (a)   if it is not the appropriate authority in relation to the person whose conduct is in question, notify that other authority of its determination and send to that authority a copy of the submission under sub-paragraph (3); and
> >
> > (b)   notify the Commission of its determination and send to it a copy of the submission under sub-paragraph (3).
>
> (5) Where the appropriate authority in relation to the person whose conduct is in question—
>
> > (a)   is notified of a determination by the Commission under sub-paragraph (2),
> >
> > (b)   (in a case where it is also the appropriate authority in relation to the DSI matter) makes a determination under sub-paragraph (4), or
> >
> > (c)   (in a case where it is not the appropriate authority in relation to the DSI matter) is notified by that other authority of a determination by it under sub-paragraph (4),
>
> it shall record the matter under paragraph 11 as a conduct matter (and the other provisions of this Schedule shall apply in relation to that matter accordingly)."

21   For paragraph 22 (final reports on investigations) substitute—

"Final reports on investigations: complaints, conduct matters and certain DSI matters

> 22 (1) This paragraph applies on the completion of an investigation of—
>
> > (a)   a complaint,
> >
> > (b)   a conduct matter, or
> >
> > (c)   a DSI matter in respect of which the Commission or the appropriate authority has made a determination under paragraph 21A(2) or (4).
>
> (2) A person appointed under paragraph 16 shall submit a report on his investigation to the appropriate authority.

    (3) A person appointed under paragraph 17 or 18 shall—

      (a) submit a report on his investigation to the Commission; and

      (b) send a copy of that report to the appropriate authority.

    (4) In relation to a DSI matter in respect of which a determination has been made under paragraph 21A(2) or (4), the references in sub-paragraphs (2) and (3) of this paragraph to the appropriate authority are references to—

      (a) the appropriate authority in relation to the DSI matter; and

      (b) (where different) the appropriate authority in relation to the person whose conduct is in question.

    (5) A person designated under paragraph 19 as the person in charge of an investigation by the Commission itself shall submit a report on it to the Commission.

    (6) A person submitting a report under this paragraph shall not be prevented by any obligation of secrecy imposed by any rule of law or otherwise from including all such matters in his report as he thinks fit."

22 (1) In the heading preceding paragraph 23, after "investigation report" insert "under paragraph 22".

    (2) In paragraph 23(1)—

      (a) in paragraph (a), for "(2)" substitute "(3)"; and

      (b) in paragraph (b), for "(3)" substitute "(5)".

    (3) After paragraph 23(12) insert—

    "(13) In relation to a DSI matter in respect of which a determination has been made under paragraph 21A(2) or (4), the references in this paragraph to the appropriate authority are references to the appropriate authority in relation to the person whose conduct is in question."

23 (1) In the heading preceding paragraph 24, after "investigation report" insert "under paragraph 22".

    (2) In paragraph 24(1)—

      (a) in paragraph (a), for "22(1)" substitute "22(2)"; and

      (b) in paragraph (b), for "22(2)" substitute "22(3)".

    (3) After paragraph 24(10) insert—

    "(11) In relation to a DSI matter in respect of which a determination has been made under paragraph 21A(2) or (4), the references in this paragraph to the appropriate authority are references to the appropriate authority in relation to the person whose conduct is in question."

24 After paragraph 24 insert—

"Final reports on investigations: other DSI matters

24A (1) This paragraph applies on the completion of an investigation of a DSI matter in respect of which neither the Commission nor the appropriate authority has made a determination under paragraph 21A(2) or (4).

(2) A person appointed under paragraph 16, 17 or 18 or designated under paragraph 19 shall —

 (a) submit a report on the investigation to the Commission; and

 (b) send a copy of that report to the appropriate authority.

(3) A person submitting a report under this paragraph shall not be prevented by any obligation of secrecy imposed by any rule of law or otherwise from including all such matters in his report as he thinks fit.

(4) On receipt of the report, the Commission shall determine whether the report indicates that a person serving with the police may have —

 (a) committed a criminal offence, or

 (b) behaved in a manner which would justify the bringing of disciplinary proceedings.

Action by the Commission in response to an investigation report under paragraph 24A

24B (1) If the Commission determines under paragraph 24A(4) that the report indicates that a person serving with the police may have —

 (a) committed a criminal offence, or

 (b) behaved in a manner which would justify the bringing of disciplinary proceedings,

it shall notify the appropriate authority in relation to the person whose conduct is in question of its determination and, if it appears that that authority has not already been sent a copy of the report, send a copy of the report to that authority.

(2) Where the appropriate authority in relation to the person whose conduct is in question is notified of a determination by the Commission under sub-paragraph (1), it shall record the matter under paragraph 11 as a conduct matter (and the other provisions of this Schedule shall apply in relation to that matter accordingly).

24C (1) If the Commission determines under paragraph 24A(4) that there is no indication in the report that a person serving with the police may have —

 (a) committed a criminal offence, or

 (b) behaved in a manner which would justify the bringing of disciplinary proceedings,

it shall make such recommendations or give such advice under section 10(1)(e) (if any) as it considers necessary or desirable.

(2) Sub-paragraph (1) does not affect any power of the Commission to make recommendations or give advice under section 10(1)(e) in other cases (whether arising under this Schedule or otherwise)."

Serious Organised Crime and Police Act 2005 (c. 15)   235
Schedule 13 – Abolition of Royal Parks Constabulary: supplementary
Part 1 – Transfers to Metropolitan Police Authority

SCHEDULE 13   Section 161

ABOLITION OF ROYAL PARKS CONSTABULARY: SUPPLEMENTARY

PART 1

TRANSFERS TO METROPOLITAN POLICE AUTHORITY

Interpretation

1   In this Part of this Schedule —

"the Authority" means the Metropolitan Police Authority, and

"transfer scheme" means a scheme made by the Secretary of State under this Schedule.

Establishment of eligibility for transfer

2   The Secretary of State may by regulations impose requirements in relation to persons serving as park constables with the Royal Parks Constabulary for the purpose of establishing whether they are eligible —

(a)   to be employed by the Authority, or

(b)   to serve as a members of the police force for the metropolitan police district.

3   (1)   The Secretary of State may terminate the Crown employment of any person who fails to comply with or satisfy any requirement imposed in relation to him by regulations made under paragraph 2.

    (2)   A person whose Crown employment is terminated under sub-paragraph (1) is not to be treated (whether for the purposes of any enactment or otherwise) as being dismissed by virtue of that termination.

Relevant persons

4   (1)   A transfer scheme may provide for any relevant person to become an employee of the Authority on the appointed day.

    (2)   The scheme may make provision —

(a)   for the termination of the relevant person's Crown employment on the appointed day,

(b)   as to the terms and conditions which are to have effect as the terms and conditions of the relevant person's contract of employment with the Authority,

(c)   transferring to the Authority the rights, powers, duties and liabilities of the employer under or in connection with the relevant person's Crown employment,

(d)   for things done before the appointed day by or in relation to the employer in respect of the relevant person or his Crown employment to be treated from that day as having been done by or in relation to the Authority,

(e)   for the period during which the relevant person has been in Crown employment to count as a period of employment with the Authority (and for the operation of the transfer scheme not to be treated as having interrupted the continuity of that employment), and

236

Serious Organised Crime and Police Act 2005 (c. 15)
Schedule 13 — Abolition of Royal Parks Constabulary: supplementary
Part 1 — Transfers to Metropolitan Police Authority

(f)   for the termination of the Crown employment of a relevant person who would otherwise be transferred by the scheme but who has informed the Secretary of State that he does not wish to be so transferred.

(3)   The scheme may provide for a person who would be treated (whether by an enactment or otherwise) as being dismissed by the operation of the scheme not to be so treated.

5   (1)   A transfer scheme may provide for the appointment as a member of the police force for the metropolitan police district of any relevant person who becomes an employee of the Authority by virtue of the scheme.

(2)   The appointment does not take effect until the person has been attested as a constable for the metropolitan police district in accordance with section 29 of the Police Act 1996 (c. 16).

(3)   On being so attested his contract of employment with the Authority is terminated by virtue of this sub-paragraph.

(4)   He is not to be treated (whether for the purposes of any enactment or otherwise) as being dismissed by virtue of the operation of sub-paragraph (3).

Property, rights and liabilities, etc.

6   (1)   The transfer scheme may provide for the transfer of property, rights and liabilities of the Secretary of State to the Authority on the appointed day.

(2)   The scheme may include provision for anything (including any legal proceedings) which relates to anything transferred by virtue of sub-paragraph (1) to be continued from the appointed day by or in relation to the Authority.

Consultation

7   Before making a transfer scheme which contains any provision relating to persons serving as park constables with the Royal Parks Constabulary the Secretary of State must consult such bodies appearing to represent the interests of those persons as he considers appropriate.

Termination of employment

8   The Secretary of State may by regulations make provision as to the consequences of the termination of a person's Crown employment under paragraph 3(1) or by a transfer scheme (including provision removing any entitlement to compensation which might otherwise arise in such circumstances).

PART 2

AMENDMENTS

Royal Parks (Trading) Act 2000 (c. 13)

9   In section 4 of the Royal Parks (Trading) Act 2000 (seizure of property) after

Serious Organised Crime and Police Act 2005 (c. 15)
Schedule 13 — Abolition of Royal Parks Constabulary: supplementary
Part 2 — Amendments

237

subsection (3) add —

"(4) In the application of this section to a specified park —
  (a) the reference in subsection (1) to a park constable has effect as a reference to a constable, and
  (b) subsections (2) and (3) do not apply.

(5) In subsection (4) "specified park" has the same meaning as in section 162 of the Serious Organised Crime and Police Act 2005."

Regulation of Investigatory Powers Act 2000 (c. 23)

10   In Schedule 1 to the Regulation of Investigatory Powers Act 2000 (relevant authorities) omit paragraph 27D and the cross-heading before it.

Police Reform Act 2002 (c. 30)

11   The Police Reform Act 2002 has effect subject to the following amendments.

12 (1) Section 82 (police nationality requirements) is amended as follows.

(2) In subsection (1) —
  (a) at the end of paragraph (e) insert "or", and
  (b) omit paragraph (f).

(3) In subsection (3)(e) for "the Civil Nuclear Constabulary or the Royal Parks Constabulary" substitute "or the Civil Nuclear Constabulary".

(4) Omit subsection (5).

13 (1) Schedule 4 (powers exercisable by police civilians) is amended as follows.

(2) In paragraph 2(6) after paragraph (aa) insert —
  "(ab) an offence committed in a specified park which by virtue of section 2 of the Parks Regulation (Amendment) Act 1926 is an offence against the Parks Regulation Act 1872; or".

(3) After paragraph 7C insert —

"Park Trading offences

7D (1) This paragraph applies if —
  (a) a designation applies it to any person ("the CSO"), and
  (b) the CSO has under paragraph 2(3) required another person ("P") to wait with him for the arrival of a constable.

(2) If the CSO reasonably suspects that P has committed a park trading offence, the CSO may take possession of anything of a non-perishable nature which —
  (a) P has in his possession or under his control, and
  (b) the CSO reasonably believes to have been used in the commission of the offence.

(3) The CSO may retain possession of the thing in question for a period not exceeding 30 minutes unless P makes an election under paragraph 2(4), in which case the CSO may retain possession of

238

Serious Organised Crime and Police Act 2005 (c. 15)
Schedule 13 — Abolition of Royal Parks Constabulary: supplementary
Part 2 — Amendments

the thing in question until he is able to transfer control of it to a constable.

(4) In this paragraph "park trading offence" means an offence committed in a specified park which is a park trading offence for the purposes of the Royal Parks (Trading) Act 2000."

(4) In paragraph 36 after sub-paragraph (3) insert—

"(3A) In this Schedule "specified park" has the same meaning as in section 162 of the Serious Organised Crime and Police Act 2005."

SCHEDULE 14

Section 163

Amendments of Part 5 of Police Act 1997

1 Part 5 of the Police Act 1997 (c. 50) (certificates of criminal records etc.) is amended as follows.

2 In section 114(3) for "Section 113(3) to (5)" substitute "Sections 113A(3) to (6) and 113C to 113F".

3 In section 116—
   (a) in the application to Scotland of subsection (2)(b) for "to which subsection (3) or (4) of section 115 applies" substitute "of such description as may be prescribed";
   (b) in subsection (3) for "Section 115(6) to (10)" substitute "Sections 113B(3) to (11) and 113C to 113F".

4 In section 119—
   (a) in subsection (1A) for "section 113(3A) or (3C) or (3EA) or (3EC)" substitute "section 113C(3) or 113D(3)";
   (b) in subsection (2) for "115" substitute "113B".

5 In section 119A(2) for the words from "under" to "adults)" substitute "in a list mentioned in section 113C(3) or 113D(3)".

6 In section 120—
   (a) in subsection (3)(b) for "113 or 115" substitute "113A or 113B";
   (b) in subsection (5)(b) for "113 or 115" substitute "113A or 113B";
   (c) in subsection (7) for "113" substitute "113A".

7 In section 120ZA(4)(b) for "113 or 115" substitute "113A or 113B".

8 In section 120A (as inserted by section 134(1) of the Criminal Justice and Police Act 2001 (c. 16))—
   (a) in subsection (3)(b) for "section 113(3A) or (3C) or (3EA) or (3EC)" substitute "section 113C(3) or 113D(3)";
   (b) in subsection (5) for "113" substitute "113A".

9 In section 120A (as inserted by section 70 of the Criminal Justice (Scotland) Act 2003 (asp 7))—
   (a) in subsection (3)(a) for "113" substitute "113A";
   (b) in subsection (3)(b) for "113(3C)" substitute "113C(3) or 113D(3)";

(c)   after subsection (6) (as inserted by section 165(2) of this Act) insert—

> "(7)   In the case of such a body the reference in subsection (5) to a police authority must be construed as a reference to such body as is prescribed."

10   In section 121 for "under section 114(2), 115(4) or (10), 116(2), 122(1) or (2) or 125" substitute "in relation to the making of regulations or orders".

11   In section 122(3) and (4)(b) for "113 or 115" substitute "113A or 113B".

12   In section 124—
    (a)   in subsections (1), (2), (3), (4) and (6) for "113 or 115" substitute "113A or 113B";
    (b)   in subsection (5) for "115(8)" substitute "113B(5)";
    (c)   in subsection (6)(e) for "113" substitute "113A".

13   In section 124B—
    (a)   in subsection (1) for "113" substitute "113A";
    (b)   in subsection (3) for "113(5)" substitute "113A(6)".

14   In section 125, at the end add—

> "(6)   If the power mentioned in subsection (1) is exercised by the Scottish Ministers, the reference in subsection (3) to each House of Parliament must be construed as a reference to the Scottish Parliament."

SCHEDULE 15   Section 171

PRIVATE SECURITY INDUSTRY ACT 2001: SCOTTISH EXTENT

1   The Private Security Industry Act 2001 (c. 12) is amended as follows.

2   In section 2 (directions etc. by the Secretary of State)—
    (a)   in subsection (2), the existing words "shall consult the Authority" become paragraph (a) and after that paragraph add "and
      (b)   where any of those directions relates wholly or mainly to the exercise of the Authority's activities in or as regards Scotland, shall obtain the consent of the Scottish Ministers."; and
    (b)   in subsection (3), the existing words "the Secretary of State with such information about its activities as he may request" become paragraph (a) and after that paragraph add "and
      (b)   the Scottish Ministers with such information about its activities in or as regards Scotland as they may request."

3   After section 2 insert—

"2A   Authority to be treated as cross-border public authority etc. for certain purposes

For the purposes of—

    (a)   section 5(5B) of the Parliamentary Commissioner Act 1967 (restriction on investigatory powers of Parliamentary Commissioner for Administration);

    (b)   section 23(2)(b) of the Scotland Act 1998 (power of Scottish Parliament to require persons outside Scotland to give evidence or produce documents);

    (c)   section 70(6) of that Act of 1998 (accounts prepared by cross-border authorities);

    (d)   section 91(3)(d) of that Act of 1998 (provision for investigation of certain complaints); and

    (e)   section 7(5) of the Scottish Public Services Ombudsman Act 2002 (restriction on investigatory powers of ombudsman),

the Authority is to be treated as a cross-border public authority within the meaning of that Act of 1998."

4   In section 3 (conduct prohibited without a licence), after subsection (3) insert—

"(3A)   In the application of this Act to Scotland—

    (a)   the reference in subsection (3) to the Secretary of State must be construed as a reference to the Scottish Ministers; but

    (b)   before making any order under subsection (3) the Scottish Ministers are to consult the Secretary of State."

5   In section 7 (licensing criteria), after subsection (5) insert—

"(5A)   Before giving approval under subsection (5), the Secretary of State shall consult the Scottish Ministers."

6   In section 11 (appeals in licensing matters)—

    (a)   in subsection (1), after "court" insert "(in Scotland, to the sheriff)";

    (b)   in subsection (4), the existing words from "a magistrates'" to "Crown Court" become paragraph (a) and after that paragraph insert "or

        (b)   the sheriff makes a decision on an appeal under that subsection, an appeal to the Sheriff Principal,"; and

    (c)   in subsection (6)(d), the existing words from "the appropriate" to the end become sub-paragraph (i) and after that sub-paragraph add "or

        "(ii)   the sheriff or the Sheriff Principal may direct pending an appeal from a determination made on an appeal to the sheriff."

7   In section 13 (licensing at local authority level), at the end add—

"(8)   This section does not apply to Scotland."

8   In section 15(1) (duty to secure arrangements are in force for granting certain approvals), at the end of paragraph (a) add "or in Scotland".

9   In section 18 (appeals relating to approvals)—

    (a)   in subsection (1), after "court" insert "(in Scotland, to the sheriff)";

    (b)   in subsection (4), the existing words from "a magistrates'" to "Crown Court" become paragraph (a) and after that paragraph insert "or

        (b)   the sheriff makes a decision on an appeal under that subsection, an appeal to the Sheriff Principal,"; and

    (c)   in subsection (5)(d), the existing words from "the appropriate" to the end become sub-paragraph (i) and after that sub-paragraph add "or

          (ii)   the sheriff or the Sheriff Principal may direct pending an appeal from a determination made on an appeal to the sheriff."

10   In section 23 (criminal liability of directors etc.), the existing words become subsection (1) and after that subsection add —

    "(2)   Where an offence under any provision of this Act is committed by a Scottish partnership and is proved to have been committed with the consent or connivance of, or to be attributable to any neglect on the part of —

        (a)   a partner; or

        (b)   any person who was purporting to be a partner,

    he (as well as the partnership) shall be guilty of that offence and liable to be proceeded against and punished accordingly."

11   In section 24 (consultation with Security Industry Authority before making orders or regulations etc.) —

    (a)   after subsection (1) insert —

      "(1A)   But in Scotland "prescribed" in paragraph 8(3)(d) of Schedule 2 to this Act includes prescribed by regulations made by the Scottish Ministers.";

    (b)   in subsection (2), after "Secretary of State" insert "or the Scottish Ministers";

    (c)   in subsection (3), after paragraph (b) insert "or

        (c)   an order or regulations made by the Scottish Ministers,";

    (d)   after subsection (3) insert —

      "(3A)   A statutory instrument containing an order or regulations made by the Scottish Ministers, other than an order under section 26(2), shall be subject to annulment in pursuance of a resolution of the Scottish Parliament.";

    (e)   in subsection (4), after "consult" insert "the Scottish Ministers (except where the order is made by virtue of section 3(2)(j)) and"; and

    (f)   in subsection (5)(b), at the end add "(or where the order is, or regulations are, made by the Scottish Ministers, as the Scottish Ministers think fit)".

12   In section 26 (short title, commencement and extent) —

    (a)   after subsection (2) insert —

      "(2A)   In the application of this Act to Scotland —

        (a)   the reference in subsection (2) to the Secretary of State must be construed as a reference to the Scottish Ministers; but

        (b)   before making any order under subsection (2) the Scottish Ministers are to consult the Secretary of State."; and

    (b)   in subsection (4), after "Wales" insert "and to Scotland".

13   In Schedule 1 (the Security Industry Authority) —

(a)   in paragraph 1 (membership and chairman), at the end add —

      "(4) Before appointing the chairman, the Secretary of State shall consult the Scottish Ministers.";

(b)   in paragraph 3 (removal from office), the existing words become sub-paragraph (1) and after that sub-paragraph insert —

      "(2) Before removing a person from office as chairman of the Authority, the Secretary of State shall consult the Scottish Ministers.";

(c)   in paragraph 6 (staff etc.), after sub-paragraph (2) insert —

      "(2A) Before giving consent under sub-paragraph (2), the Secretary of State shall consult the Scottish Ministers.";

(d)   in paragraph 14 (money), after sub-paragraph (1) insert —

      "(1A) The Scottish Ministers may make payments to the Authority out of the Scottish Consolidated Fund in relation to the exercise by the Authority of its functions in or as regards Scotland.";

(e)   in paragraph 16 (accounts) —

    (i)   in sub-paragraph (3), after second "State" insert ", to the Scottish Ministers"; and

    (ii) after sub-paragraph (3) insert —

      "(3A) The Scottish Ministers shall present documents received by them under sub-paragraph (3) to the Scottish Parliament."; and

(f)   in paragraph 17 (annual report) —

    (i)   in sub-paragraph (1), after "State" insert "and to the Scottish Ministers"; and

    (ii) at the end add —

      "(3) The Scottish Ministers shall lay a copy of each such report before the Scottish Parliament."

14   In Schedule 2 (activities liable to control under the Private Security Industry Act 2001 (c. 12)) —

(a)   in paragraph 3 (immobilisation of vehicles), at the end add —

      "(4) This paragraph does not apply to any activities carried out in Scotland.";

(b)   in paragraph 4 (private investigations), after sub-paragraph (4) insert —

      "(4A) This paragraph does not apply to any activities of a person who is an advocate or solicitor in Scotland in the provision of legal services —

        (a) by him;

        (b) by any firm of which he is a partner or by which he is employed;

        (c) by any body corporate of which he is a director or member or by which he is employed.";

Serious Organised Crime and Police Act 2005 (c. 15)
Schedule 15 – Private Security Industry Act 2001: Scottish extent

243

(c)   after paragraph 4 insert—

"Taking precognitions

4A   (1)   This paragraph applies (subject to sub-paragraph (2)) to the taking, other than on behalf of the Crown, of a precognition for the purposes of, or in anticipation of—
  (a)   criminal or civil proceedings in Scotland; or
  (b)   proceedings on an application under section 65(7) or (9) of the Children (Scotland) Act 1995.

(2)   This paragraph does not apply to any activities of a person who is an advocate or solicitor in Scotland.";

(d)   in paragraph 8(2) (door supervisors etc. for public houses, clubs and comparable venues) after paragraph (e) add—

  "(f)   any premises specified in a public house licence (within the meaning of the Licensing (Scotland) Act 1976) which is for the time being in force;

  (g)   any premises specified in an hotel licence (within the meaning of that Act) which is for the time being in force;

  (h)   any premises specified in an entertainment licence (within the meaning of that Act) which is for the time being in force if they comprise a dance hall;

  (i)   any premises comprised in a place to which an occasional licence granted under section 33(1) of that Act (occasional licence for premises other than licensed premises or clubs) to the holder of a public house licence or hotel licence extends;

  (j)   any premises comprised in a place to which an occasional permission granted under section 34(1) of that Act (occasional permission for sale of alcohol in the course of catering for events arising from or related to the activities of a voluntary organisation) extends;

  (k)   any premises comprised in a place or class of place for the time being specified by resolution under section 9(5)(b) of the Civic Government (Scotland) Act 1982 (resolution specifying place or class of place falling to be licensed if to be used as place of public entertainment);

  (l)   any premises comprised in a place where an activity for the time being designated under section 44(1) of that Act (additional activities for which a licence is required) is carried on provided that, in the case of an activity designated under paragraph (a) of that section, the requisite resolution under section 9 of that Act has been obtained;"; and

(e)   after paragraph 9 add —

"Taking precognitions

> 10   This paragraph applies to any activities which are activities of a security operative by virtue of paragraph 4A of this Schedule."

SCHEDULE 16   Section 174

REMAINING MINOR AND CONSEQUENTIAL AMENDMENTS (SEARCH WARRANTS)

Incitement to Disaffection Act 1934 (c. 56)

1   In section 2 of the Incitement to Disaffection Act 1934 (which makes provision about search warrants), in subsection (2), for "one month" substitute "three months".

Public Order Act 1936 (1 Edw. 8 & 1 Geo. 6 c. 6)

2   In section 2 of the Public Order Act 1936 (prohibition of quasi-military organisations), in subsection (5), for "one month" substitute "three months".

Wireless Telegraphy Act 1949 (c. 54)

3   In section 15 of the Wireless Telegraphy Act 1949 (entry and search of premises), in subsection (1), for "one month" substitute "three months".

Licensing Act 1964 (c. 26)

4   Until their repeal by the Licensing Act 2003 (c. 17), the following provisions of the Licensing Act 1964 have effect as if for "one month" there were substituted "three months" —

> section 54 (search warrants relating to clubs),
> section 85(1) (search warrants relating to parties organised for gain),
> section 187(1) (search warrants relating to sale of alcohol).

Biological Weapons Act 1974 (c. 6)

5   In section 4 of the Biological Weapons Act 1974 (powers to search etc.), in subsection (1)(a), for "one month" substitute "three months".

Copyright, Designs and Patents Act 1988 (c. 48)

6   (1) The Copyright, Designs and Patents Act 1988 is amended as follows.

       (2) In section 109 (search warrants), in subsection (3)(b), for "28 days" substitute "three months".

       (3) In section 200 (search warrants), in subsection (3)(b), for "28 days" substitute "three months".

       (4) In section 297B (search warrants), in subsection (3)(b), for "28 days" substitute "three months".

Serious Organised Crime and Police Act 2005 (c. 15)
Schedule 16 — Remaining minor and consequential amendments (search warrants)

245

Computer Misuse Act 1990 (c. 18)

7   In section 14 of the Computer Misuse Act 1990 (search warrants), in subsection (3)(b), for "twenty-eight days" substitute "three months".

Trade Marks Act 1994 (c. 26)

8   In section 92A of the Trade Marks Act 1994 (search warrants), in subsection (3)(b), for "28 days" substitute "three months".

SCHEDULE 17   Section 174

REPEALS AND REVOCATIONS

PART 1

REPEALS COMING INTO FORCE ON ROYAL ASSENT

Short title and chapter	*Extent of repeal*
Police Reform Act 2002 (c. 30)	Section 95. In Schedule 8, the reference to section 5 of the Police (Health and Safety) Act 1997 (c. 42).

PART 2

OTHER REPEALS AND REVOCATIONS

Short title and chapter or title and number	*Extent of repeal or revocation*
Unlawful Drilling Act 1819 (60 Geo. 3 & 1 Geo. 4 c. 1)	In section 2, the words ", or for any other person acting in their aid or assistance,".
Vagrancy Act 1824 (c. 83)	Section 6.
Railway Regulation Act 1842 (c. 55)	Section 17.
Companies Clauses Consolidation Act 1845 (c. 16)	In section 156, the words ", and all persons called by him to his assistance,".
Railways Clauses Consolidation Act 1845 (c. 20)	Sections 104 and 154.
Licensing Act 1872 (c. 94)	In section 12, the words "may be apprehended, and".
Public Stores Act 1875 (c. 25)	Section 12(1).
London County Council (General Powers) Act 1894 (c. ccxii)	In section 7, the words "and any person called to the assistance of such constable or person authorised".
London County Council (General Powers) Act 1900 (c. cclxviii)	In section 27, the words "and any person called to the assistance of such constable or officer".
Licensing Act 1902 (c. 28)	In section 1, the words "apprehended and".

246

Serious Organised Crime and Police Act 2005 (c. 15)
Schedule 17 — Repeals and revocations
Part 2 — Other repeals and revocations

Short title and chapter or title and number	*Extent of repeal or revocation*
Licensing Act 1902 (c. 28) — *cont.*	In section 2(1), the words "may be apprehended, and".
Protection of Animals Act 1911 (c. 27)	Section 12(1).
Official Secrets Act 1911 (c. 28)	Section 6.
Public Order Act 1936 (1 Edw. 8 & 1 Geo. 6 c. 6)	Section 7(3).
Army Act 1955 (3 & 4 Eliz. 2 c. 18)	Section 83BC(2)(k).
Air Force Act 1955 (3 & 4 Eliz. 2 c. 19)	Section 83BC(2)(k).
Naval Discipline Act 1957 (c. 53)	Section 52IJ(2)(k).
Public Records Act 1958 (c. 51)	In Schedule 1, in Part 2 of the Table at the end of paragraph 3, the entries relating to the Service Authorities for the National Crime Squad and the National Criminal Intelligence Service.
Street Offences Act 1959 (c. 57)	Section 1(3).
Trustee Investments Act 1961 (c. 62)	In section 11(4), in paragraph (a), the words ", the Service Authority for the National Crime Squad", and paragraph (e). In Part 2 of Schedule 1, paragraph 9(da).
Parliamentary Commissioner Act 1967 (c. 13)	In Schedule 2, the entries relating to the Service Authorities for the National Crime Squad and the National Criminal Intelligence Service.
Police (Scotland) Act 1967 (c. 77)	In section 33, in subsections (3) and (4), the words "and the National Criminal Intelligence Service". Section 38A(1)(ba). In section 41(4)(a), the words "or by a member of the National Criminal Intelligence Service or of the National Crime Squad".
Criminal Justice Act 1967 (c. 80)	In section 91(1), the words "may be arrested without warrant by any person and".
Leasehold Reform Act 1967 (c. 88)	Section 28(5)(bc).
Ministry of Housing and Local Government Provisional Order Confirmation (Greater London Parks and Open Spaces) Act 1967 (c. xxix)	In Article 19 of the Order set out in the Schedule, the words "and any person called to the assistance of such constable or officer".
Theft Act 1968 (c. 60)	Section 25(4).
Port of London Act 1968 (c. xxxii)	In section 2, the definition of "arrestable offence". Section 170.

Serious Organised Crime and Police Act 2005 (c. 15)
Schedule 17 — Repeals and revocations
Part 2 — Other repeals and revocations

247

Short title and chapter or title and number	*Extent of repeal or revocation*
Employment Agencies Act 1973 (c. 35)	In section 13(7)(f), the words ", the Service Authority for the National Criminal Intelligence Service, the Service Authority for the National Crime Squad".
House of Commons Disqualification Act 1975 (c. 24)	Section 1(1)(da). In Schedule 1, in Part 2, the entries relating to the Service Authorities for the National Crime Squad and the National Criminal Intelligence Service.
Northern Ireland Assembly Disqualification Act 1975 (c. 25)	Section 1(1)(da). In Schedule 1, in Part 2, the entries relating to the Service Authorities for the National Crime Squad and the National Criminal Intelligence Service.
Sex Discrimination Act 1975 (c. 65)	In section 17(7), in the definition of "chief officer of police", paragraph (aa), in the definition of "police authority", paragraph (aa) and, in the definition of "police fund" the words from ", in relation to" (in the second place where they occur) to "the Police Act 1997".
Police Pensions Act 1976 (c. 35)	In section 11(5), in paragraph (a) of the definition of "central service", "(ca), (cb),".
Race Relations Act 1976 (c. 74)	In section 76B, subsection (1) and, in subsection (2), the word "also". In Schedule 1A, in Part 1, paragraphs 59 and 60 and, in Part 3, the entry relating to the Director General of the National Crime Squad.
Criminal Law Act 1977 (c. 45)	Section 6(6). Section 7(6). Section 8(4). Section 9(7). In section 10(5), the words "A constable in uniform,".
Theft Act 1978 (c. 31)	Section 3(4).
Health and Safety at Work (Northern Ireland) Order 1978 (S.I. 1978/1039 (N.I. 9))	In Article 47A(2), sub-paragraph (b).
Animal Health Act 1981 (c. 22)	Section 61(1). Section 62(1).
Local Government (Miscellaneous Provisions) Act 1982 (c. 30)	In Schedule 3, paragraph 24.
Aviation Security Act 1982 (c. 36)	Section 28(3).
Stock Transfer Act 1982 (c. 41)	In Schedule 1, in paragraph 7(1), paragraph (bb) and the word "or" before it.
Police and Criminal Evidence Act 1984 (c. 60)	Section 5(1A).

248

Serious Organised Crime and Police Act 2005 (c. 15)
Schedule 17 — Repeals and revocations
Part 2 — Other repeals and revocations

Short title and chapter or title and number	Extent of repeal or revocation
Police and Criminal Evidence Act 1984 (c. 60) — *cont.*	In section 15(2)(a)(i), the word "and" at the end. Section 25. Section 55(14A). In section 66(1)(a)(i), the word "or" at the end. Section 116. In section 118(1), the definition of "arrestable offence". In Schedule 1, in paragraph 14(a), the words "to which the application relates". Schedule 1A. In Schedule 2, the entries relating to the Military Lands Act 1892 (c. 43), the Protection of Animals Act 1911 (c. 27), the Public Order Act 1936 (1 Edw. 8 & 1 Geo. 6 c. 6), the Street Offences Act 1959 (c. 57), the Criminal Law Act 1977 (c. 45) and the Animal Health Act 1981 (c. 22). Schedule 5. In Schedule 6, paragraph 17.
Prosecution of Offences Act 1985 (c. 23)	In section 3(3), in the definition of "police force", the words ", the National Crime Squad".
Sporting Events (Control of Alcohol etc.) Act 1985 (c. 57)	In section 7(2), the words ", and may arrest such a person".
Public Order Act 1986 (c. 64)	Section 3(6). Section 4(3). Section 4A(4). Section 5(4) and (5). Section 12(7). Section 13(10). Section 14(7). Section 14B(4). Section 14C(4). Section 18(3).
Ministry of Defence Police Act 1987 (c. 4)	In section 2B(3), in the definitions of "chief officer" and "relevant force", paragraphs (c) and (d).
Criminal Justice Act 1988 (c. 33)	Section 140(1)(a) and (b). In Schedule 15, paragraphs 98 and 102.
Road Traffic Act 1988 (c. 52)	Section 4(6) to (8). In section 124(2), the definitions of "chief officer of police", "police authority" and "police force". Section 144(2)(ba). Section 163(4).
Road Traffic (Consequential Provisions) Act 1988 (c. 54)	In Schedule 3, paragraph 27(5).
Football Spectators Act 1989 (c. 37)	Section 2(4).
Aviation and Maritime Security Act 1990 (c. 31)	In section 22(4)(b), sub-paragraph (iii) and the word "or" before it. In Schedule 3, paragraph 8.

Serious Organised Crime and Police Act 2005 (c. 15)
Schedule 17 — Repeals and revocations
Part 2 — Other repeals and revocations

249

Short title and chapter or title and number	Extent of repeal or revocation
Football (Offences) Act 1991 (c. 19)	Section 5(1).
Road Traffic Act 1991 (c. 40)	In Schedule 4, paragraph 39.
Local Government Finance Act 1992 (c. 14)	In section 43(7)(b), ", (5A)".
Transport and Works Act 1992 (c. 42)	Section 30(1) and (3). Section 40.
Trade Union and Labour Relations (Consolidation) Act 1992 (c. 52)	Section 241(3).
Tribunals and Inquiries Act 1992 (c. 53)	In section 7(2), after "36A", "(a) or (b)". In Schedule 1, in paragraph 36A, "(a)" and sub-paragraph (b).
Criminal Justice and Public Order Act 1994 (c. 33)	Section 61(5). Section 62B(4). Section 63(8). Section 65(5). Section 68(4). Section 69(5). Section 76(7). Section 85(1), (2) and (3). Section 155. Section 166(4). Section 167(7). In Schedule 10, paragraph 59.
Drug Trafficking Act 1994 (c. 37)	In Schedule 1, paragraph 9 and, in paragraph 25, the words "section 9(6) of" and the words after "1990".
Criminal Appeal Act 1995 (c. 35)	In section 22(2), in paragraph (a), the words ", the National Crime Squad", paragraph (b)(ii) and paragraphs (d) and (e).
Criminal Procedure (Consequential Provisions) (Scotland) Act 1995 (c. 40)	In Schedule 4, paragraph 76(2).
Disability Discrimination Act 1995 (c. 50)	In the section 64A inserted by the Disability Discrimination Act 1995 (Amendment) Regulations 2003 (S.I. 2003/1673), in subsection (7), in the definitions of "chief officer of police", "police authority" and "police fund", paragraph (b).
Reserve Forces Act 1996 (c. 14)	In Schedule 2, paragraph 2(1).
Police Act 1996 (c. 16)	Section 23(8). Section 24(5). In section 54(2), the words "the National Criminal Intelligence Service and the National Crime Squad". Section 55(7). Section 59(8). Section 60(2A).

250   *Serious Organised Crime and Police Act 2005 (c. 15)*
Schedule 17 – Repeals and revocations
Part 2 – Other repeals and revocations

Short title and chapter or title and number	*Extent of repeal or revocation*
Police Act 1996 (c. 16) – *cont.*	Section 61(1)(aa) and (ba). In section 62, subsection (1)(aa) and (ab), the subsection (1A) inserted by paragraph 82(2) of Schedule 9 to the Police Act 1997, and subsections (1B) and (1C). In section 63, subsections (1A) and (1B). In section 64, subsections (4A) and (4B). In section 88(5)(b), the words "or section 23 of the Police Act 1997". In section 89(4)(a), the words "or by a member of the National Criminal Intelligence Service or of the National Crime Squad". Section 97(1)(ca) and (cb). In section 98, in subsections (2) and (3), the words "or the Director General of the National Crime Squad" and "or the National Crime Squad", subsection (3A), in subsection (4) the words "or the National Crime Squad" and "or the Director General of the National Crime Squad", in subsection (5) the words "or the National Crime Squad" (in both places) and "or the Director General of the National Crime Squad" and subsection (6A).
Employment Rights Act 1996 (c. 18)	Section 50(2)(ca).
Offensive Weapons Act 1996 (c. 26)	Section 1(1).
Public Order (Amendment) Act 1996 (c. 59)	The whole Act.
Juries (Northern Ireland) Order 1996 (S.I. 1996/1141 (N.I. 6))	In Schedule 2, the entry relating to members of the National Criminal Intelligence Service, members of the Service Authority for the National Criminal Intelligence Service and persons employed by the Authority.
Employment Rights (Northern Ireland) Order 1996 (S.I. 1996/1919 (N.I. 16))	Article 67KA(3)(b). Article 72A(2)(b). Article 169A(2)(b).
Confiscation of Alcohol (Young Persons) Act 1997 (c. 33)	Section 1(5).
Police (Health and Safety) Act 1997 (c. 42)	In section 5(3), in the definition of "relevant authority" paragraphs (c) and (d), in the definition of "relevant fund" paragraphs (b) and (c) and, in the definition of "responsible officer", paragraph (b).
Police Act 1997 (c. 50)	Sections 1 to 87. Sections 89 and 90. In section 93(6), paragraphs (d) and (e). In section 94, in subsection (1) paragraph (c) and the word "or" before it and subsections (3) and (4)(c).

Serious Organised Crime and Police Act 2005 (c. 15)
Schedule 17 — Repeals and revocations
Part 2 — Other repeals and revocations

251

Short title and chapter or title and number	Extent of repeal or revocation
Police Act 1997 (c. 50) — *cont.*	In section 111, in subsection (1), paragraphs (c) and (d), in subsection (2), paragraphs (d) and (e) and, in subsection (3), paragraphs (c) and (d).
	Section 113.
	Section 115.
	In section 125 as it applies to Scotland, subsection (3) and, in subsection (4), the words "to which subsection (3) does not apply".
	In section 137(2), paragraphs (b) and (c).
	Schedules 1 to 2A.
	In Schedule 9, paragraphs 1, 4 to 6, 11, 14(b), 15, 16, 20, 26, 29(2), 30(2), 31, 44, 46 to 48, 54, 58 to 62, 69, 70, 71(2)(a), (c), (d) and (3), 73, 74, 76, 77, 79 to 84, 86(3) and (4), 87, 88 and 92.
Police (Health and Safety) (Northern Ireland) Order 1997 (S.I. 1997/1774 (N.I. 6))	In Article 7(3), in the definition of "the relevant authority", sub-paragraph (b), in the definition of "the relevant fund", sub-paragraph (a) and, in the definition of "the responsible officer", sub-paragraph (b).
Police (Northern Ireland) Act 1998 (c. 32)	Section 27(1)(b).
	In section 42, in subsection (1) ", (3)", and subsection (7).
	In Schedule 4, paragraph 22.
Crime and Disorder Act 1998 (c. 37)	In section 1C, subsections (6) to (8).
	Section 27(1).
	Section 31(2) and (3).
	Section 113.
Protection of Children Act 1999 (c. 14)	Section 8.
Terrorism Act 2000 (c. 11)	In Schedule 15, paragraph 5(11).
Care Standards Act 2000 (c. 14)	Section 90.
	Section 102.
	Section 104.
	In Schedule 4, paragraph 25.
Regulation of Investigatory Powers Act 2000 (c. 23)	In section 33, in subsection (1) the words ", the National Criminal Intelligence Service or the National Crime Squad" and ", Service or Squad", in subsection (3) the words ", the National Criminal Intelligence Service or the National Crime Squad" and (in both places) ", Service or Squad" and, in subsection (6), in paragraph (e) the words "and also of the National Criminal Intelligence Service" and paragraph (f).
	In section 34, subsections (5) and (6)(c).
	In section 45(6), paragraphs (d) and (e).
	In section 56(1), in the definition of "chief officer of police", paragraphs (j) and (k)
	Section 75(6)(b).

252
Serious Organised Crime and Police Act 2005 (c. 15)
Schedule 17 — Repeals and revocations
Part 2 — Other repeals and revocations

Short title and chapter or title and number	*Extent of repeal or revocation*
Regulation of Investigatory Powers Act 2000 (c. 23) —*cont.*	In section 76A(11)(c) the words "the National Crime Squad or". In Schedule 1, paragraph 27D and the cross-heading before it. In Schedule 4, paragraph 8(4)(c) and (5).
Football (Disorder) Act 2000 (c. 25)	Section 2. In Schedule 2, paragraph 2.
Police (Northern Ireland) Act 2000 (c. 32)	In Schedule 6, in paragraph 20, sub-paragraphs (4) to (7).
Freedom of Information Act 2000 (c. 36)	In section 23(3), the word "and" at the end of paragraph (k). In Schedule 1, in Part 6, the entries relating to the National Crime Squad and the Service Authority for the National Crime Squad.
Criminal Justice and Court Services Act 2000 (c. 43)	In Schedule 7, paragraph 77.
Health and Social Care Act 2001 (c. 15)	Section 19.
Criminal Justice and Police Act 2001 (c. 16)	Section 42(8). Section 47(3). In section 104, subsection (3), in subsection (4) paragraph (c) and the word "and" before it, and subsection (8). In section 107, subsections (1)(c) and (4). Sections 108 to 121. Section 138(6)(d). In Schedule 4, paragraph 7(3)(b). Schedule 5. In Schedule 6, paragraphs 1 to 21, 55, 56, 60, 61 and 77.
Anti-terrorism, Crime and Security Act 2001 (c. 24)	Section 39(8).
Regulation of Care (Scotland) Act 2001 (asp 8)	In Schedule 3, paragraph 21.
International Development Act 2002 (c. 1)	In Schedule 3, paragraphs 3(3), 11(3) and 12(3).
National Health Service Reform and Health Care Professions Act 2002 (c. 17)	In Schedule 2, paragraph 64.
Proceeds of Crime Act 2002 (c. 29)	In section 313(1), paragraphs (c) and (d). In section 330, subsection (5)(b), and, in subsection (9)(b), the words after "employment". Section 331(5)(b). In section 332(1) and (3), "337 or". Section 332(5)(b). In section 337(5)(b), the words after "employment".

Serious Organised Crime and Police Act 2005 (c. 15)
Schedule 17 — Repeals and revocations
Part 2 — Other repeals and revocations

253

Short title and chapter or title and number	Extent of repeal or revocation
Proceeds of Crime Act 2002 (c. 29) — *cont.*	In section 338, subsection (1)(b) (except the word "and" at the end) and, in subsection (5)(b), the words after "employment". Section 339(5) and (6). In section 447(3)(a), the word "or" at the end. In Schedule 11, paragraphs 3(3), 14(4), 30(3) and (4) and 34(3) and (4).
Police Reform Act 2002 (c. 30)	Section 8. In section 9(3)(e) the words "is or". In section 10, in subsection (1), at the end of paragraph (e) the word "and", in paragraph (f) the words "the National Criminal Intelligence Service, the National Crime Squad and", in subsection (3), paragraph (a) and, in paragraph (d), the words "the National Criminal Intelligence Service, the National Crime Squad or" and, in subsection (7), the word "or" at the end of paragraph (a). In section 15(6), the words from "or, as the case may be" to the end of the subsection. Section 25. In section 38, subsection (3), in subsection (4) the words "or a Director General" and, in subsection (7), the words "or of a Service Authority". Section 42(4) and (8). In section 45, in subsection (1) the words "and by Directors General", in subsection (3) paragraphs (a), (b), (d) and (e) and, in subsection (5), the words "or a Director General". In section 47(1), the definitions of "Director General" and "Service Authority". Section 48. Section 49(1). In section 82, subsection (1)(c) and (f), in subsection (2), paragraph (c) and the word "or" before it, subsection (3)(d) and subsection (5). Sections 85 to 91. Section 93. In section 102, in subsection (2), paragraphs (c) and (d) and, in subsection (5), paragraphs (b) and (c). In section 103, subsections (2) and (3) and, in subsection (6), the words ", the NCIS service fund or the NCS service fund,". Section 108(7)(e). Schedule 1. In Schedule 4, paragraph 2(5)(a) and (7), and in paragraph 36(1), paragraph (b) and the word "and" before it.

254

Serious Organised Crime and Police Act 2005 (c. 15)
Schedule 17 — Repeals and revocations
Part 2 — Other repeals and revocations

Short title and chapter or title and number	Extent of repeal or revocation
Police Reform Act 2002 (c. 30) — cont.	In Schedule 5, in paragraph 1(2)(aa), the words "except in respect of an offence under section 12 of the Licensing Act 1872 or section 91 of the Criminal Justice Act 1967". Schedule 6. In Schedule 7, paragraphs 16, 17, 19(2) and (3), 21 and 22(2).
Education Act 2002 (c. 32)	Part 2 of Schedule 12. In Schedule 13, paragraphs 7 and 8. In Schedule 21, paragraphs 72 and 73.
Adoption and Children Act 2002 (c. 38)	Section 135. In Schedule 3, paragraph 93.
Licensing Act 2003 (c. 17)	In Schedule 6, paragraphs 93 and 116.
Aviation (Offences) Act 2003 (c. 19)	Section 1(1).
Communications Act 2003 (c. 21)	Section 181(1).
Crime (International Co-operation) Act 2003 (c. 32)	In section 17(3), the words "the Police and Criminal Evidence Act 1984 (c. 60) or (as the case may be)". Section 85.
Anti-social Behaviour Act 2003 (c. 38)	Section 4(5). Section 23(5). Section 32(3). Section 37(3).
Courts Act 2003 (c. 39)	In Schedule 8, paragraphs 12 and 281(2).
Sexual Offences Act 2003 (c. 42)	In Schedule 6, paragraph 28(3) and (4).
Criminal Justice Act 2003 (c. 44)	Section 3. In Schedule 35, paragraphs 3 and 4.
Protection of Children (Scotland) Act 2003 (asp 5)	Section 12.
Criminal Justice (Scotland) Act 2003 (asp 7)	Section 70(3).
Protection of Children and Vulnerable Adults (Northern Ireland) Order 2003 (S.I. 2003/417 (N.I. 4))	Article 17(4) to (6). Article 47(3) to (5).
Energy Act 2004 (c. 20)	In section 59(3), in the definition of "chief officer", paragraphs (c) and (d) and, in the definition of "relevant force", paragraphs (c) and (d). In Schedule 14, paragraph 11(b).
Domestic Violence, Crime and Victims Act 2004 (c. 28)	Section 10(1). In Schedule 10, paragraph 24.
Hunting Act 2004 (c. 37)	Section 7.

Serious Organised Crime and Police Act 2005 (c. 15)
Schedule 17 — Repeals and revocations
Part 2 — Other repeals and revocations

255

Short title and chapter or title and number	Extent of repeal or revocation
Prevention of Terrorism Act 2005 (c. 2)	Section 9(9).
Serious Organised Crime and Police Act 2005 (c. 15)	Section 112(6) and (7). Section 126(2) and (3). Section 130(1). Section 136(5).

Printed in the UK by The Stationery Office Limited
under the authority and superintendence of Carol Tullo, Controller of
Her Majesty's Stationery Office and Queen's Printer of Acts of Parliament

4/2005   305686   19585